The Debate over Vietnam

THE AMERICAN MOMENT
Stanley I. Kutler, Series Editor

The Twentieth-Century American City
Jon C. Teaford

American Workers, American Unions, 1920–1985
Robert H. Zieger

A House Divided: Sectionalism and Civil War, 1848–1865
Richard H. Sewell

Liberty under Law: The Supreme Court in American Life
William M. Wiecek

Winning Is the Only Thing; Sports in America since 1945
Randy Roberts and James Olson

America's Half-Century: United States Foreign Policy in the Cold War
Thomas J. McCormick

American Anticommunism: Combating the Enemy Within, 1830–1970
Michael J. Heale

The Culture of the Cold War
Stephen J. Whitfield

America's Welfare State
Edward D. Berkowitz

The Debate over Vietnam
David W. Levy

THE DEBATE

OVER VIETNAM

David W. Levy

The Johns Hopkins University Press
Baltimore and London

© 1991 The Johns Hopkins University Press
All rights reserved. Published 1991
Printed in the United States of America on acid-free paper

Second printing, paperback, 1993

The Johns Hopkins University Press
2715 North Charles Street
Baltimore, Maryland 21218-4319
The Johns Hopkins Press Ltd., London

Library of Congress Cataloging-in-Publication Data

Levy, David W., 1937–
The debate over Vietnam / David W. Levy.
    p.   cm. — (The American moment)
Includes bibliographical references and index.
ISBN 0-8018-4148-8. — ISBN 0-8018-4149-6 (pbk.)
1. Vietnamese Conflict, 1961–1975—United States.   2. United
States—Politics and government—1945– . I. Title. II. Series.
DS558.L47   1991
959.704′3373—dc20   90-49525

A catalog record for this book is available from the British Library.

To the memory of
PAUL R. DAVID
(1907–1984),
scientist, scholar, teacher,
and for a third of a century, the fearless conscience
of the place where he was.

Socrates: And what sort of difference creates enmity and anger? Suppose, for example, that you and I, my good friend, differ about a number; do differences of this sort make us enemies and set us at variance with one another? Do we not go at once to arithmetic, and put an end to them by a sum?

Euthyphro: True.

Socrates: Or suppose that we differ about magnitudes, do we not quickly end the difference by measuring?

Euthyphro: Very true.

Socrates: And we end a controversy about heavy and light by resorting to a weighing machine?

Euthyphro: To be sure.

Socrates: But what differences are there which cannot be thus decided, and which therefore make us angry and set us at enmity with one another? I dare say the answer does not occur to you at the moment, and therefore I will suggest that these enmities arise when the matters of difference are the just and unjust, good and evil, honourable and dishonourable. Are not these the points about which men differ, and about which when we are unable satisfactorily to decide our differences, you and I and all of us quarrel, when we do quarrel?

Euthyphro: Yes, Socrates, the nature of the differences about which we quarrel is such as you describe.

Plato, *Euthyphro*

Contents

Editor's Foreword

A democratic nation's capacity to sustain war "is maintained only by a distinct view of what one is fighting for," Alexis de Tocqueville wrote in *Democracy in America*. War has its just causes, but what is just, good, and honorable has divided societies since Socrates, and views rarely are distinct. No nation is immune from such conflicts, as even the Soviet government learned when it attempted to impose its will in Afghanistan in the 1980s. Throughout American history, beginning with the War for Independence, and almost without exception, we have fought our wars with significant division and dissent. The controversy over the Vietnam War, of course, is most vivid in memory, because of its closeness in time and because of its wide-ranging ramifications. The war at home in those "stormy and passionate days" not only aroused debate and violence over the war abroad but reflected deep political fissures over the nature and goals of the society.

The domestic political conflict over the Vietnam War—America's longest war, incidentally—reverberates a generation later. We often hear of a "Vietnam Syndrome," a term applied by supporters of that war and other military adventures, and designed implicitly to discredit those who criticized the war effort. Equally, opponents of the Vietnam War have invoked the "lessons" of Vietnam as an injunction against subsequent interventions. We are destined, it seems, to have political opportunists invoke history tailored for a particular political agenda. Similarly, for several generations, we have been subjected to the "Munich Analogy," instructing us that aggression must be thwarted and that negotiation with aggressors is *ipso facto* appeasement. And so, in the name of "Munich," we intervene in civil wars (contrary to the pointed warnings of Abraham Lincoln, who prevented foreign powers from involvement in our own civil war) and proclaim the virtues of maintaining democratic governments, even when those governments are dictatorships or monarchies. All this, of course, is an ironic twist to the ideals of a nation founded in a revolt against tyranny.

In this engaging, often profound, essay, David Levy measures the agonizing debate over Vietnam that so fractured American society. For many Americans, the war was a great "noble cause," as Ronald Reagan later said, while for others, the American involvement contradicted the principled ideals of American foreign policy. Obviously, it was a moment, as Levy observes, "when the most basic faiths, the most dreadful fears, the most profound hopes of the nation were spoken, considered, and judged." In his essay, Levy offers us another opportunity to hear that debate, and now, perhaps, to judge for ourselves its relevance to this nation's ongoing conflicts between its avowed ideals and the yearnings for a world order responsive to our will and needs.

Stanley I. Kutler
THE UNIVERSITY OF WISCONSIN

Preface

I.

In the pages that follow I propose to explore the momentous discussion that raged in America over the war in Vietnam. My intention is to examine the fundamental assumptions that were at work in this discussion, the bedrock values that contested with one another and that stand clearly revealed in the stress of debate. I will also attempt to explain the difficult dilemmas that this episode forced upon entire groups of American citizens as well as upon millions of individual men and women. And I will recount the way in which these contentions were brought before the public, until, at last, the whole nation was absorbed in weighing the wisdom, the necessity, and the morality of the war.

There is little point in trying to compare this debate to other crucial discussions that have punctuated and illuminated American history. But surely it is worth observing that in many respects the controversy over Vietnam resembled other moments of intense national self-examination. Like the historic issues of independence and a proper form of government, of slavery in the western territories and the nature of the Union, like the large questions surrounding industrialization or the acquisition of an overseas empire or participation in previous wars, the debate over Vietnam was clearly a moment of critical and traumatic self-scrutiny for the American people. Like those other debates, this one too gave rise both to glib sloganeering and to thoughtful, even brilliant, analysis. Like those others, this one too conveyed the sense that highly important matters were being pondered and that deeply held values were at stake. And when we remember the vast numbers of people who were engaged, the fevered quality of their discussion, the amount of public print and media attention devoted to it, the rising and falling of political leaders on account of the stands they took, it is very hard to escape the conclusion that the debate over American participation in the Vietnam war was one of those times when the most basic faiths, the most dreadful fears, the most profound hopes of the nation were spoken, considered, and judged.

I want to make it perfectly explicit that my purpose here is to understand and to explain, not to pass judgment. My intention is to avoid recrimination, to suppress the temptation to fix blame, to tell each side's views as fairly and persuasively as possible. This purpose rests on two assumptions, and it seems best to make them explicit too, for it is likely that some readers will wish to quarrel with one or both of them. The first is that this sort of balance is possible, that enough time has passed since those stormy and passionate days, enough distance traveled, to enable us to look backward in a way less hypnotized by the compulsions, the orthodoxies, and fighting slogans of those years. The second assumption is that this kind of approach has merit. While recognizing that perfect objectivity is an unattainable dream, I believe enough time has elapsed to permit the attempt to understand without recrimination. I also believe that there is considerable value in trying to do so. Indeed, it seems to me that the history that aims at enlarging understanding and increasing tolerance, that causes us to reconsider both the beliefs we love and those we hate, is the liveliest and most exciting history of all.

Finally, I wish to enter one more disclaimer. I have excused myself from the task of trying to measure the "sincerity" of those who entered this debate. It was fashionable at the time to attempt to discredit various arguments by suggesting that they were invented to mask private interests. Thus young men who opposed the Vietnam war were sometimes accused of taking that position only because they were afraid of being drafted; and generals, heads of corporations, or workers in defense plants were sometimes accused of supporting the war only because they hoped to further their careers or line their pockets. Innermost motives are not usually accessible to historians. I have assumed that men and women can generally find ways to harmonize their interests and their beliefs without being hypocrites and that, with few exceptions, people believe what they say. In any case, whether they were tainted by unworthy motives or not, the ideas put forth in this, as in any debate, made their way in the world of the undecided largely on the basis of their plausibility.

In the interests of clarity I wish to state the central contention baldly at the start. The debate over Vietnam occurred when a carefully constructed ideology, a set of ideas that had guided and justified American foreign policy for more than a generation, began to fragment. The story of how that ideology was originally woven together, how it came under unbearable stress during the Vietnam war and eventually tore apart, and how the American people responded to this crisis in thought and action is the subject of this book.

II.

Over the long centuries many men and women have tried to apply certain moral principles to the bloody and brutal business of warfare, and a vast literature has emerged that attempts to distinguish between "just" and "unjust" wars. Part of that literature is concerned with the proper and improper ways of fighting a war once it has started. Questions of proportion are raised: what sort of a provocation or threat by an enemy must be present, for example, to morally justify slaying all the male inhabitants of a city-state and selling the women and children into slavery? Also raised are questions about the propriety or impropriety of particular weapons and tactics: is it morally forbidden, in every case, to spread smallpox among the enemy or starve civilians, to torture prisoners or bomb cities, to practice terror and assassination or employ nuclear weapons? That this ancient aspect of the discussion had its echo in the debate over Vietnam—as some Americans pointed with horror to the ways in which the North Vietnamese and the Vietcong conducted the war, while others expressed a similar outrage at the conduct of South Vietnamese and American troops—is clear enough.

Most writing about just and unjust war, however, deals not with the means of carrying on the fighting, but with the prior question of whether and when it is morally permissible to engage in a war in the first place. That there has been substantial disagreement, from authority to authority and from culture to culture, will not be surprising. Except for strict pacifists, however, commentators have generally agreed that certain circumstances warrant a resort to the slaughter and destruction of war. These circumstances traditionally fall into two categories. Defensive wars—fought to repel an invader or to protect, in other ways, the safety, the territory, or the welfare of the nation—have almost always been regarded as morally justifiable. But wars of self-defense are not the only ones that philosophers have thought proper. Even if no defensive motive could be offered, theorists have often justified wars when, it was alleged, they were embarked upon for a noble purpose or (what is usually the same thing) to defeat an evil one. The conquest of the Canaanites by the Israelites seemed sufficiently sanctioned by the cruelty and impiety of the enemy, and no plausible claim of self-defense was registered (or required) on behalf of either the holy warriors of Islam as they swept across Asia and

North Africa during the sixth and seventh centuries or the Crusaders as they battled against the heathen during the twelfth and thirteenth.

The idea that armed violence could be just, even without a defensive purpose, provided that it was undertaken on behalf of the good and against the evil, has a long and honorable lineage. Traces of it may be found in both the Old and the New Testaments, in Aristotle, Cicero, Augustine, and many others. By the thirteenth century the doctrine had been given definitive expression by Thomas Aquinas: "In order for a war to be just . . . ," he insisted, "a just cause is required, namely that those who are attacked should be attacked because they deserve it on account of some fault." Among other requirements, St. Thomas argued "that the belligerents should have a rightful intention, so that they intend the advancement of good, or the avoidance of evil." After Aquinas the doctrine of the just war was secularized a bit, made the province of international law and philosophy as well as of theology, but the content of the doctrine was largely fixed. War was deemed morally allowable if it was undertaken in self-defense, or if it was embarked upon in order to oppose some evil or accomplish some good.

The first thing to notice about the American debate over Vietnam is how largely it was carried out—whether consciously or not—in these traditional terms, revolving around the very old questions of the just and the unjust war.

III.

Some readers will surely feel that there is something terribly naive, almost otherworldly, in all this agonizing about the justice or injustice of wars. They probably suspect that throughout history wars were started by powerful individuals who were not much swayed by abstract considerations of right and wrong, but who very often led their nations into war for highly questionable motives and then invented pious claims about the "morality" of their adventuring in order to mask their private ambitions.

No doubt there have been times when an absolute monarch could hire the mercenaries and wage the war without being convinced of the justice of the cause and without having to persuade ordinary people of its righteousness. But it has been a very long time since any powerful individual (or any class of them) has known the luxury of undertaking wars without obtaining some measure of popular support. To whatever extent a war involved social dislocations, the disruption of economic life, the large-scale regimentation of the population, the expenditure of taxes that had to be replenished and increased—to that extent at least, those who embarked upon such a war had to win the approval, however grudging, of significant portions of the citizenry. For whatever reason, therefore, almost every belligerent has felt compelled to recognize the distinction between just and unjust wars and to insist that this or that special belligerency was fully sanctioned by religion, morality, and law.

With the advent of modern democracy, the necessity to win public approval was very much accentuated. Most immediately, political leaders who advocated, voted for, and conducted wars now had to submit their actions to the electorate, and they could be quite certain that there would be no shortage of articulate rivals ready with some pointed questions. Democratic wars, moreover, have tended to employ huge armies composed of ordinary young men, often reluctantly drafted for the purpose. These young men, their parents, relatives, and friends had to be given reasons for the risks, reasons for the interruption of lives and careers, reasons for the expenditure of blood and treasure. Under such circumstances of public accountability and mass participation, the justification of wars took on a distinct political and military importance as well as a theological and moral one. The persuasiveness of the reasons given for fighting a war affected the population's willingness to pursue it and thereby influenced the actual prospects for military success.

Finally, as Alexis de Tocqueville observed in the 1830s, democracies are not particularly easy to convince. In democracies, he suggested, "the spirit of military glory" is weakened because ambitious men can pursue so many other paths to advancement. "I think it may be admitted as a general and constant rule," he predicted, "that among civilized nations the warlike passions will become more rare and less intense in proportion as social conditions are more equal." Wars in a democracy may begin in enthusiasm ("the first efforts are made by passion alone"), but Tocqueville was certain that "perseverance is maintained only by a distinct view of what one is fighting for." Whether or not Tocqueville was correct in every particular, in at least one way he was entirely accurate as far as the United States has been concerned. For good or ill, when asked to put aside peaceful pursuits, take up arms, and go off to war, very sizable numbers of Americans have always been extremely hard to persuade.

Even in the case of the legendary struggle for independence, many hung back. Perhaps eighty thousand Americans fled the country during the Revolution. Opponents of that war were an absolute majority in some states and offered stubborn pockets of resistance in others. States refused to contribute their shares of men and money and proved reluctant to permit their young men to fight in other people's states. During the War of 1812 New Englanders were so unpersuaded of the propriety of the conflict that they voted against it in Congress, carried on more trade with the British enemy than with their own countrymen, and, by the time of the notorious Hartford Convention of 1814, were seriously considering leaving the Union. The Mexican War was seen throughout the North as a misguided attempt to increase the territory where slavery could thrive; the Whig party condemned it, and the Massachusetts legislature branded it an unconstitutional war of conquest, repugnant to honest men. Two decades later the Civil War also provoked the opposition of many Americans, North and South. Southerners—whether outright opponents of secession or states rights advocates who resented the wartime authority of their new government—organized determined resistance to the war and to Jefferson Davis. Meanwhile northerners—whether pacifists, southern sympathizers, opponents of Negro emancipation, draft resisters, or Peace Democrats—obstructed conscription, demanded peaceful settlement of the conflict, and organized resistance to Lincoln. Thousands of them were arrested because of their opposition to the war.

The war against Spain lasted only ten weeks and was generally supported by the American people, but its aftermaths, the acquisition of an overseas empire and the suppression by military force of a Philippine insurrection, aroused a furor of anti-imperialist activity. Many citizens bitterly opposed using American power to subjugate and police native peoples. Resistance to World War I was also extremely extensive. Numerous German, Irish, and Jewish Americans, as well as many socialists, pacifists, and progressives, clamored against it. Widespread isolationist sentiment, especially in the Middle West, refused to be convinced of the justice or the necessity of the war; an armed anti-draft revolt exploded in Oklahoma. So threatening to the prosecution of the war was this opposition that both vigilante groups and the government believed it proper to take extreme steps—harsh persecution and intimidation of the "lukewarm," the suspension of some basic civil liberties, imprisonments, and the denial of the mails to critics of government policy.

Of all American wars, World War II commanded the most universal, unreserved, and sustained popular approval. Indeed, as will be seen, the memory of that enthusiasm, together with the erroneous popular belief that World War II was somehow typical of the country's behavior in wartime, helped to color the response to those who, only twenty years later, opposed the war in Vietnam. In the meantime, it is worth keeping in mind that the absence of unity with regard to Vietnam was far more typical of the hesitant democratic response to other American war efforts than it was unique.

IV.

I have accumulated numerous debts in writing this book, and it is a great pleasure to be able to acknowledge some of them here. A Humanities Fellowship from the Rockefeller Foundation was extremely helpful during the formative stages of the project. Likewise, a summer Humanities Fellowship from the Southwestern Bell Company made possible the completion of the last chapters. To both of these organizations I am deeply grateful. I hope that they will feel that the final result is, at least in some measure, worthy of their generosity and confidence.

A number of friends have read this manuscript and, in every case, I have profited from their comments. For their especially incisive suggestions I wish to thank Daniel Bjork, Russell Buhite, Bob Flexner, Paul Glad, William T. Hagan, Penny Hopkins, Drew Kershen, Richard Levy, Andy Magid, Robert Shalhope, Kenneth Taylor, and Melvin Urofsky. This would be a much poorer book without the benefit of the conscientious and skillful attention given to it by each of them. Stanley Kutler, editor of the American Moment series, has been as patient, efficient, and wise as anyone had a right to hope; and Henry Tom, senior editor of the Johns Hopkins University Press, has offered nothing but encouragement, sensitivity, and sound advice. J. Kent Calder gave the manuscript a most beneficial and thorough final reading.

My wife Lynne has excused me from a thousand duties, selflessly assuming them herself despite her own demanding professional obligations. I have, while writing this book, been guilty of many sins of omission as far as she has been concerned, but I would like to think that neither a lack of awareness nor an absence of gratitude for what she has done on my behalf are among them. Beth and Benjamin have, as always, been unfailing sources of support and joy.

The Debate over Vietnam

1: THE CONSENSUS

How Americans Reached Some General Agreements about

Their Foreign Policy

I.

During the 1930s international relations grew suddenly acrimonious, and the world quickly became a very dangerous place. Tensions that seemed to have eased after the end of World War I (as if that enormous effort had exhausted people and nations), re-emerged now, a dozen years later, full-blown, terrifying, and uglier than ever. By the middle of the decade books, newspapers, and magazines were giving unprecedented attention to the international situation; countless commentators, politicians, and overnight experts attempted to explain and assess the threatening climate abroad. Even those Americans normally indifferent to events beyond the borders of their own country began to wonder and worry about foreign affairs.

By the end of 1935 Americans had many good reasons to worry. Some concerns were simply fresh chapters in a long continuing story: Should the United States cooperate with the League of Nations? Should America join the World Court? What, if anything, could be done to collect the war debts owed to the American people by foreigners? Some of the policy issues commanding public attention were rather new: Would the rash of recent commercial treaties (eight of them in 1935) revive international trade in the wake of the depression? Would President Roosevelt's new "good neighbor policy" toward Latin America dangerously limit America's capacity to intervene directly in the affairs of the hemisphere? What precisely was implied by the recent recognition of the Soviet Union, and what forms of cooperation were now possible with the Bolshevist regime of Joseph Stalin? Both the old questions and the new ones were troubling enough; most Americans who were disturbed by international affairs, how-

ever, were especially bothered by the attitudes and activities of three
nations that seemed to have gone strangely mad.

In September 1931 a group of Japanese officers, acting without the
approval of the civilian government in Tokyo, manufactured an incident in Manchuria and then proceeded to conquer and occupy that
entire Chinese province. This bold aggression violated several international agreements and provided an alarming indication of the
growing strength of nationalistic and militaristic elements within the
Japanese army and society. The Chinese were helpless to defend
themselves; the western nations, including the United States, were
preoccupied by their own economic problems and unwilling to go to
war to save Manchuria; and the League of Nations quickly proved
itself impotent. Between 1931 and the end of 1935, therefore, the
Japanese were able to consolidate their gains and to continue their
shocking behavior: in January 1932 they bombarded the Chinese port
city of Shanghai; two months later they set up a puppet state in Manchuria; and in February 1933 they strode out of the League and took
over Jehol province in northern China. In 1934 and 1935 Tokyo announced plans for a political and economic hegemony over East Asia,
accelerated the economic penetration of the northern provinces of
China (even of territories south of the Great Wall itself), and began
excluding foreign commercial interests from areas under Japanese
control. As 1935 came to an end the Imperial army was massed pro-
vocatively along the border of Inner Mongolia. Played out, as it was,
against the backdrop of a long-standing American commitment to
the territorial integrity of China and to an "open door" in Chinese
commercial life, the drama of Japanese aggression was particularly
disturbing.

Meanwhile, more than six thousand miles from Tokyo, the auda-
cious Italian dictator, Benito Mussolini, was stirring his people by appeals that were remarkably similar to those being employed by the
Japanese militarists. Coming into power in October 1922, Mussolini
and his Fascists devoted themselves, at first, to organizing the Italian
economy and solidifying their own position. They pursued both of
these objectives ruthlessly and with considerable brutality, until Mussolini ruled over a one-party state, stripped of the basic freedoms of
speech and press. Increasingly, after the economic collapse of the
early 1930s, however, the Italian dictator shifted his attention to foreign expansion. His grandiloquent vision of a restored and glorious
new Roman Empire was designed, in part, to distract Italians from
domestic troubles. But Mussolini also sensed that other nations were
so absorbed by their own economic crises that the time was ripe for
grabbing some territory. Nor were international agreements going to

stand in the way. "Words are very fine things," he said in 1930, "but rifles, machine-guns, warships, airplanes, and cannon are still finer things." His exaltation of naked force, his undisguised ambition for Italian expansion, his personal assumption, in 1932, of the duties of foreign minister, his expansion of the navy—these actions were scarcely calculated to relax those who watched foreign affairs. In 1935 all of Mussolini's pugnacious posturing and fist-thumping spilled over in a concrete act of unadulterated aggression: in the first week of October, his army invaded Ethiopia, a tribal East African nation, poorly armed and quite unable to defend its territory.

Most ominous of all, of course, was what was happening in Germany. Adolf Hitler assumed power in January 1933 and proceeded speedily to uproot whatever remained of the hopeful Weimar experiment in democratic government. Even those Americans who had watched Mussolini with disbelief were stunned by the savagery of Hitler's domestic repression. Opposition parties and labor unions were outlawed; freedom of speech, of the press, of the academy, of religion, and of association were ruthlessly destroyed. By assassination, by intimidation, by Nazi law, Hitler fashioned a brutal despotism equal, in its cruelty, to any in the history of the world. He combined that despotism, moreover, with a fanatical racism of the most virulent and unrestrained sort, and non-Aryans, especially Jews, found themselves stripped of their citizenship and subjected to pernicious and degrading legal disabilities. The Nazis also surpassed the Italians in their willingness to upset international tranquillity. Hitler had risen on a program of extreme nationalism and on demands for German expansion, promising to recover lost colonies, to redress the wrongs perpetrated by the Treaty of Versailles, and to unite Europe's Germans in one large, powerful, proud German empire. Ten months after taking over, he withdrew Germany from the Disarmament Conference and the League, and in March 1935 he announced that his country would no longer be bound by the Versailles provisions limiting the size of the armed forces. Hitler planned to conscript an army of a half million men (five times the number permitted by the treaty) and to enlarge greatly his navy and air force.

Is it any wonder, then, that by the end of 1935 the air was filled with foreboding, with talk of "gathering storm clouds" and "rough seas ahead"? President Roosevelt, at his news conference of November 6, admitted that international affairs were "not encouraging." Everyone knew that the president was absorbed by working his ambitious domestic program of 1935 through Congress and that the start of the reelection campaign was only a few months away. Nevertheless, the president told the reporters that he was "spending such an awful lot of time on the foreign situation. It is a good deal more worry to me personally than the domestic situation." The anonymous, year-end editorial in the *New Republic* summed up the anxieties of many Americans: "Christmas this year finds the world drawing perceptibly nearer that outbreak of a major war which all mankind dreads and yet seems helpless to prevent. Conflict is raging in Ethiopia; . . . Germany is rearming to the extreme limit of her speed and capacity; Japan continues her relentless and menacing advance in Asia; and lesser points of friction exist in a dozen places. . . . Such, in 1935, is the anniversary of the birth of the Prince of Peace."

No doubt many Americans chose to ignore the storm warnings, and many others hoped and believed that the clouds would soon dissipate and permit smooth sailing to resume. But as international events continued to unfold during the second half of the decade, fewer and fewer reasonable men and women could maintain that sort of equanimity. The skies grew darker as one catastrophic event followed another with bewildering rapidity. In 1936 Japan continued its drive in northern China; Italy completed the conquest of Ethiopia; and Germany reoccupied the Rhineland and concluded pacts with both Italy and Japan. In 1937 Japan launched a full scale war against China, while both Germany and Italy sent thousands of "volunteers" to aid the Fascists in the Spanish Civil War. In 1938 Japan proclaimed "a new order" for East Asia, and Hitler annexed Austria, declared it to be a state of the German Reich, and rode triumphantly into Vienna. The international conference at Munich, in September, demonstrated the democracies' radical lack of will and became, thereby, a powerful and permanent symbol of craven appeasement; the agreement reached there cleared the way for the Nazis' advance into western Czechoslovakia. In 1939 the Germans completed the takeover of Czechoslovakia, invaded Poland, and inaugurated World War II. Mussolini chose the moment to seize the independent state of Albania. Americans watched in horror and disbelief as the German army took only ten weeks in the spring of 1940 to conquer Norway, Denmark, the Netherlands, Belgium, and France.

In the face of this mounting pressure, increasing numbers of citizens came to the immensely significant conclusion, during the last years of the 1930s, that the United States could no longer afford the luxury of indifference. The world was on fire, and it was not particularly moral or wise to turn away, to pretend not to hear the alarms. Some of the hardiest of these Americans undertook to prepare the nation for the difficult tests that lay ahead. They formed organizations and read books. They lobbied politicians and editors and argued with their neighbors. Some of them made speeches and wrote articles.

They tried, in whatever ways they could, to influence the public policy of their government. These activists attempted, in short, nothing less than the reeducation of the American people regarding the nature of the outside world and the dangers and responsibilities that faced the country in an age of barbarism.

II.

Their work was cut out for them. Those who labored for a more active interest and energetic involvement in world affairs had set themselves against a tradition of isolationism that was one of the nation's most tenacious beliefs. From the earliest days of the republic, wisdom in foreign policy had consisted of having as little as possible to do with other nations. For generations Americans had been guided by the solemn warning of President Washington's Farewell Address. Strive for good relations with all peoples, Washington had counseled in 1796, but remember that "the great rule of conduct for us in regard to foreign nations is, in extending our commercial relations to have with them as little *political* connection as possible. . . . Why, by interweaving our destiny with that of any part of Europe, entangle our peace and prosperity in the toils of European ambition, rivalship, interest, humor, or caprice?" Insofar as ordinary Americans professed any *positive* program of foreign policy, that program was summed up, almost thirty years after Washington's address, by the Monroe Doctrine: American abstension from the affairs of Europe must be reciprocated by European abstension from the affairs of the Western Hemisphere.

Throughout the nineteenth century the American people remained, in general, true to this faith. Except for times when territorial ambitions brought the nation face to face with some European power, the standard attitudes of most Americans were that their country was separated from the senseless and petty quarrels of the rest of the world and that this was a very good thing. It has often been pointed out that the United States was able to enjoy this policy of isolation because of a set of entirely fortuitous circumstances. The country was protected by two huge oceans; its abundant resources made it self-sufficient, and Americans had little need to comb the world searching desperately for their simple necessities; the European powers obligingly absorbed themselves with their own balance of power and could not spare North America much attention, much less make it into the object of any concerted action; and for most of the century American interests and those of the British coincided, thereby bestowing upon the young nation the effective (and free) protection of the greatest navy in the world. In any case, the firmly established purpose of American foreign relations was to remain unencumbered. "The foreign policy of the United States is eminently expectant," wrote Tocqueville; "it consists more in abstaining than in acting."

At the end of the nineteenth century and the start of the twentieth, the United States seemed to depart significantly from this isolationist tradition. First, under the Republican leadership of William McKinley and Theodore Roosevelt, the country embarked upon a war to free Cuba from Spain, acquiring in the process a far-flung overseas empire of its own, the responsibilities of administering and policing it, and a need to assert American interests in places as remote as Panama and China. Second, under the Democratic leadership of Woodrow Wilson, the nation entered the very sort of European war that President Washington had warned against. Before that war was finished in 1918 the United States had sent more than a million young men across the ocean to fight the Germans. The adventure in Cuba, with its unforeseen consequences and heavy new responsibilities, was so-bering enough] ("The jocund youth of our people now passes away never to return," observed the imperialist, Captain Alfred Thayer Mahan, as he surveyed America in 1898. "The cares and anxieties of manhood's years henceforth are ours.") But the adventure in Europe was positively traumatic.

Everything about the American participation in World War I was calculated to breed disappointment. The fighting itself—the tanks, the airplanes, the poison gas, the ghastly trenches that were alter-nately dreary and horrifying, the incredible slaughter of human life—was much more brutal and costly than anyone could have pre-dicted. The announced aims of the war (to inaugurate an era of world peace, to bring about a world in which democracy and freedom might thrive), expressed so loftily by President Wilson, proved quite im-possible to achieve. The ugly outpouring of domestic violence, the persecution of citizens of particular ethnic backgrounds, the damage done to traditional civil liberties both by overeager private citizens and the federal government, the choking off of hopeful progressive reform in the name of a strident nationalism—all combined to make the experience a bitter and unhappy one. Above all, the results of the war, as embodied both in the Treaty of Versailles and in the shat-tered and profoundly frightening condition of the world, made the whole thing appear to millions of Americans as an absurd and tragic mistake.

The reaction was inevitable, and it took various forms; but for the formulation of foreign policy, the chief consequence was a fairly gen-eral return to the normal slogans of isolationism. Countless Americans—even many who had enthusiastically supported the war—became convinced that active involvement in the affairs of foreigners was scarcely worth the price and that Washington's Farewell Address and the Monroe Doctrine had spoken eternal truths that would be perilous to ignore in the future. Under the impulse of this mood, the foreign policy of the United States in the 1920s was devoted to a series of rather narrow objectives. Most Americans wanted other nations to pay their debts, of course, and the nation was as aggressive as ever in pursuing its commercial interests around the globe. The central thrust of American diplomacy, however, was to avoid the kind of involvement that had led to such disaster. The architects of American foreign policy, therefore, actively pursued international disarmament. They favored arbitration and conciliation treaties that might reduce the possibilities of international conflict. In 1928 they even went so far as to engineer a worldwide agreement, one that seems ridiculous and naive in retrospect, to "outlaw" war forever as an instrument of national policy. But whenever any proposal arose that smacked of deepening American entanglement (joining the League of Nations, participating in the deliberations of the World Court, rebuilding, even modestly, the army or navy), it was opposed and denounced with fierce, decisive resistance.

The initial effect of the growing world crisis of the 1930s was to redouble the efforts of isolationists. Each new episode of international outlawry seemed to confirm the old wisdom of minding one's own business. The main responses to Japanese aggression, therefore, were piously to deplore it, resolutely to refuse to "recognize" it, and carefully to refrain from doing anything that might conceivably be interpreted as warlike. By mid-decade historians were competing with politicians to prove that in 1917 the country had been delivered into the European war by its own bankers and munitions-makers, who were ready to sacrifice American boys in order to protect their loans or drive up the demand for the implements of death. Ordinary Americans were convinced that the nation had been much too willing to risk all in order to protect the "rights" of the handful who insisted on climbing aboard belligerent vessels in time of war. These errors of judgment and policy were to be avoided in the future, and Congress set out to make certain that the country would not again be so reckless. Beginning in 1935, therefore, a series of neutrality acts were proposed, and not even the wishes of the most popular president of the twentieth century could forestall their passage. The new laws, resolutely refusing to discriminate between aggressors and nonaggressors, drastically restricted loans, trade in munitions and other strategic material, and passenger travel. This time the American people were willing to surrender even the traditional neutral rights in a desperate attempt to stay out of trouble.

It was against this background of alert and determined isolationism that those who advocated a more active foreign policy had to labor. They could not, of course, have foreseen it, but the appeals they made to the American people, the tone they set and the arguments they offered, continued to exert a profound influence on the public discussion of foreign relations long after the crisis of the late 1930s. For a full generation afterwards, the terms of the debate were fixed. It is impossible to understand the fervor of the Vietnam discussion without understanding the work of these Americans who set out to prepare their fellow citizens for the immediate dangers they saw looming ahead.

III.

Proponents of a more energetic foreign policy before World War II relied on two principal arguments. The first of these arguments was that the United States had now acquired certain vital interests in the world, interests that had become essential to the safety of the nation. These interests were legitimate, reasonable, and peaceful ones; they were presently being threatened by the policies of the dictators and militarists of Europe and Asia; and the national security required that Americans stand ready, if necessary, to protect themselves. Perhaps it might be possible to defend these lawful claims by measures short of war: by taking a firmer stand against aggression, by cooperating with other countries through the League of Nations or otherwise, by providing friends with support and material, by being willing to apply economic sanctions against international outlaws, by arming. But it was entirely possible that American security could not be insured adequately by such measures, and in that case a resolute and realistic people must be prepared to fight, to counter force with force and to rely upon its own military strength to keep it safe rather than trusting to noble rhetoric or simplistic isolationist slogans.

Definitions of national security interests have never been very precise, and diversity of opinion was certainly present among the activists of the late 1930s. On several points, however, they generally agreed. Naturally, no attack on the mainland of the United States could possibly be tolerated—even the stubbornest isolationists agreed to that. The country, moreover, had shouldered responsibility for the security of overseas possessions from the Philippines to Puerto Rico, from Alaska and Hawaii to the Panama Canal; any aggression that touched those places had also to be reckoned as an attack on vital security interests. In addition, America had been asserting, since the administration of James Monroe, a crucial strategic interest throughout the Western Hemisphere, and the completion of the Panama Canal had done nothing to diminish the importance of Latin America to national security.

Besides these territorial claims, Americans also insisted that the preservation of commercial rights was essential to the country's basic economic health. Moreover, national security now depended upon access to certain strategic materials available only from outside the United States. (Thus Professor Robert B. Hall, a University of Michigan economic geographer, warned in April 1940 that the reliance on the Pacific trade was "so vital and complete that our very existence as a great industrial power, and perhaps even as an independent state, is threatened if the sources should be cut off.") These strategic and nonstrategic commercial requirements, in turn, strongly implied a commitment to protecting the freedom of the seas in general and certain trade routes in particular. Finally, these activists pointed out that in the past the relatively even balance of power among the nations of Europe and Asia had permitted America to preserve these vital security interests—and to preserve them at minimal cost. Some Americans argued, therefore, that the nation had a huge stake in maintaining that balance of power.

Now, the foreign policy activists tirelessly argued, the United States was facing determined and highly dangerous aggressors. They had overturned the balances of power in both Europe and Asia. By the summer of 1940 they had trampled the sovereignty of the Chinese, the Ethiopians, the Spaniards, the Austrians, the Czechs, the Albanians, the Norwegians, the Poles, the Danes, the Belgians, and the French. Clearly there were loose in the world men whose ambitions knew no boundaries. And if the isolationists thought that America could remain untouched by this menace, could ignore it and stay snug between its two oceans, then they were being naïve and irresponsible.

The second general argument offered by proponents of greater involvement in world affairs was equally direct and easy for the American people to understand. In the conflict presently agitating the world, they argued, there could be very little dispute over who were the evil-doers. Not only were the dictators menacing America's security, they were also ruthless, brutal, and immoral men. One sign of their evil was the way they treated their own people: the destruction of basic liberties, the wholesale persecution of minorities and dissenters, the assassination or imprisonment of political rivals, the unscrupulous use of domestic propaganda, and the merciless onslaught upon any vestige of freedom of thought, any trace of the democratic process, any surviving habits of human independence. "We have buried the putrid corpse of liberty," Mussolini boasted. Another sign of the immorality of these power-crazed madmen was their behavior in world affairs. To them, international agreements meant nothing. Hitler flaunted his violations of Versailles and solemnly signed non-aggression pacts with Poland and the Soviet Union prior to invading them. The Japanese had never declared war on China but pursued that adventure with what seemed like special brutality. To Americans, the dictators and militarists seemed like wolves: greedily, ferociously ranging the earth looking for the easiest prey.

And it was not only their overt behavior at home and abroad that marked them as frightening men bent on doing evil. It was the things for which they stood, the things they preached and in which they apparently believed. They were constantly exalting force and scorning restraint. They were continually praising the military virtues—iron discipline, obedience to the will of the leader, absolute loyalty to the purposes of the nation. They laughed at representative government and at the democratic process. They seemed eager to transform free individuals into slaves of the state. These beliefs they inculcated in young children and enforced with uncompromising insistence upon learned university professors. In short, they demonstrated and openly expressed their utter contempt for the most cherished values of western civilization: honesty, reason, liberty, fairness, peace.

Henry L. Stimson was very far from being an alarmist. He had been secretary of war under William Howard Taft, governor of the Philippines under Calvin Coolidge, and secretary of state under Herbert Hoover. He was a leading Republican statesman, well respected for his many qualities; Franklin Roosevelt would appoint him secretary of war despite his political affiliations and advanced age. In March 1939 Stimson wrote a long letter to the *New York Times*, summarizing his view of the international situation. "There is a flood of reaction and violence overrunning the world today," he observed. The Fascist governments ("by which term I mean the three nations united by the so-called Berlin-Rome-Tokyo axis") must not be confused with previous autocracies that coexisted peacefully with free countries. This time, he warned, it was different, rendered different both by the immediate danger to American security and by the frankly immoral nature of this particular threat. This time the assault on both the basic rules of international behavior and the basic traditions of decency represented nothing less than "a complete reversal of the whole trend of European civilization." The Fascist threat was "a radical attempt to reverse entirely the long evolution out of which our democracies of Europe and America have grown, and . . . probably the most serious attack on their underlying principles which those principles have ever met." Stimson put forward the standard question: "Shall we bury our heads in the sands of isolationism and timidly await the time when our security shall be lessened and perhaps destroyed by the growing success of lawlessness around us?"

Henry Stimson's letter was typical of the growing anxiety among thoughtful and moderate Americans during the late 1930s. It was typical, in the first place, because it struck the two notes that everyone else arguing for greater international involvement also struck. They all insisted that this country was called to action both by the need to protect our legitimate interests in a hostile and dangerous world and by the need to defend the ethical principles of western civilization from a class of barbaric and immoral men. But Stimson's letter was typical in a second way as well: he and the others scrambled these two arguments together until the two propositions were almost inextricably joined, combined so intimately, so unconsciously, that it was hard to see that the blend was, in fact, composed of two ingredients. Indeed, only by means of the historian's trick of retrospective analysis are we able to see that *two* presumably separable arguments had been interwoven.

No one was more adept at combining these two appeals than the president of the United States. He had been increasingly concerned about foreign affairs (more concerned than he ever expected or wanted to be) since 1935. Throughout his first term, however, Franklin Roosevelt was content to speak the language of the isolationists. Whether he did so out of genuine personal conviction or out of a shrewd political realism that had gauged the temper of the American people is a matter of dispute among historians, but by the fall of 1937 world affairs had grown so precarious that the president decided to comment on the international situation in considerably stronger words. According to the historian Robert A. Divine, the so-called Quarantine Speech, delivered in Chicago on October 5, marked "the beginning of Roosevelt's long campaign to wean his fellow countrymen away from the extreme isolationism of the mid-thirties."

In that speech Roosevelt interwove the two arguments with consummate skill. He began with the moral indictment. "The present reign of terror and international lawlessness," he noted, "began a few years ago."

> It began through unjustified interference in the internal affairs of other nations or the invasion of alien territory in violation of treaties; and has

now reached a stage where the very foundations of civilization are seriously threatened. The landmarks and traditions which have marked
the progress of civilization toward a condition of law, order and justice
are being wiped away.

Without a declaration of war and without warning or justification of
any kind, civilians, including vast numbers of women and children, are
being ruthlessly murdered with bombs from the air. In times of so-
called peace, ships are being attacked and sunk by submarines without
cause or notice. Nations are fomenting and taking sides in civil warfare
in nations that have never done them any harm. . . .

Innocent peoples, innocent nations, are being cruelly sacrificed to a
greed for power and supremacy which is devoid of all sense of justice
and humane considerations.

And one sentence later he intoned the second argument, the one
about the safety of the United States: "If those things come to pass in
other parts of the world, let no one imagine that America will escape,
that America may expect mercy, that this Western Hemisphere will
not be attacked and that it will continue tranquilly and peacefully to
carry on the ethics and the arts of civilization." Then quickly back to
the appeal to moral decency as the president urged peace-loving peoples to "work together for the triumph of law and moral principles in
order that peace, justice and confidence may prevail in the world. . . .
There must be recognition of the fact that national morality is as vital
as private morality."

For the next four years—in press conferences and speeches
around the nation, in formal addresses to the Congress and radio
chats to the American people—Roosevelt hammered away at these
themes. Six weeks before American entry into World War II, for example, the president made a speech in which he announced that two
secret Nazi documents had come into his possession. The first was a
"map made in Germany by Hitler's government—by the planners of
the new world order." The map showed Latin America, but instead
of the fourteen countries presently there, explained the president,
"the geographical experts of Berlin have ruthlessly . . . divided South
America into five vassal states, bringing the whole continent under
their domination. And they have also so arranged it that the territory
of one of these new puppet states includes the Republic of Panama
and our great life line—the Panama Canal. . . . This map, my friends,
makes clear the Nazi design not only against South America but
against the United States as well." If the first secret document shed
light on the threat to America's security, the second showed just how
depraved this enemy was. It was "a plan to abolish all existing reli-

gions." The Nazis planned to confiscate church property, to forbid use of the cross and other religious symbols, and to silence the clergy or throw them into concentration camps. The picture was not a pretty one: "In the place of the churches of our civilization, there is to be set up an International Nazi Church. . . . And in the place of the Bible, the words of *Mein Kampf* will be imposed and enforced as Holy Writ. And in the place of the cross of Christ will be put two symbols—the swastika and the naked sword."

Thus had it come about that those Americans advocating a more active involvement in foreign affairs, advocating, eventually, direct intervention in the European conflict, fell into the vocabulary of "the just war." From the president of the United States on down, thousands of Americans tried desperately, before December 1941, to alert a lethargic nation to the possibility that war might come. That they employed arguments Thomas Aquinas would have found congenial was, for the most part, unconscious and coincidental. They set about to ready the nation for a mortal struggle, and they slipped quite naturally into the vocabulary that people had always used to justify their excursions into combat. A war was "just" when it was fought to defend oneself, and it was "just" when it was fought to protect the good and oppose the evil.

Their case was aided immeasureably by the conduct of the enemy. The Japanese, the Italians, and the Germans offered every day new evidence of ambition and barbarity. In the end, their work rendered the claims plausible. They really *did* seem to constitute a direct threat to American security and to American interests; they really *did* seem to embody the traits and espouse the principles that civilized men had always associated with diabolical evil. And the fact that World War II, when it actually came, could be so convincingly vindicated on *both* scores, resulted in its being the most popular war, the least opposed, least resisted war in American history. A democratic people, with a long history of being reluctant to put aside peaceful pursuits (as Tocqueville had prophesied), fought *this* war with an almost joyful resolve and with unprecedented patriotism and community solidarity.

Whether or not the words of the president and others had actually persuaded most Americans of the necessity for foreign involvement before December 7, 1941, can never be known, but the events of that morning and of the days immediately following effectively ended the discussion. Whatever the state of public opinion when the war started, the wartime pressure was so great and the message was repeated so incessantly and so urgently over the next four years that a substantial number of Americans would be ready, by 1945, to abandon the traditional isolationist position. The planet did, in fact, harbor enemies

who posed grave dangers to America's safety and who boldly espoused horrifying principles. In October of that year the Gallup Poll
reported that better than seven out of ten Americans believed that
the country should take an active role in world affairs. So thoroughly
had the isolationists been discredited that most Americans were convinced (in contrast to the public mood following World War I) that
the time when the nation could ignore the rest of the world was gone,
probably forever, that from now on the United States would have to
be involved. Both its national interest and its commitment to democracy, freedom, and morality demanded it.

IV.

Many of those Americans who, despite everything, still yearned for a
return to the happier days of isolationism, had that dream shattered
by the quick emergence of the Cold War so hard upon the heels of
World War II. Even before the cessation of the fighting, tensions between the United States and the Soviet Union had begun to surface.
In general they were kept muted by the necessity of defeating the
Fascists, but once that task had been completed the two former allies
found increasingly that their marriage had been one of convenience
and that the reasons for it were now largely gone. Each country easily
compiled a growing list of complaints against the other, and by the
end of 1947 these grievances developed into full-fledged suspicion
and genuine hostility. Each side came to see the other as engaged in
a vast conspiracy against its own interests, and each viewed the other
as the repository of a dangerous and immoral philosophy. As American and Soviet interests and ideologies rubbed up against each other
in the late 1940s, the isolationist wish came to be regarded as little
more than an unattainable vision of a world that was no longer possible for Americans, an exercise in nostalgia.

The American view of the Soviet Union is well known. The devotion to Marxism, the diatribes against capitalism, the often repeated
desire to foment Communist revolutions in other countries had made
that nation the object of American suspicion long before the coming
of World War II. Now that the war was over Russia was the second
most powerful country in the world—battle hardened, with an immense army and an awesome industrial potential. The danger it
posed was no longer merely ideological, but geopolitical as well.
American writers, political leaders, and opinion makers lost no time
in applying to Stalin and the Communists the very same traits that
had characterized the fallen Hitler and his Nazis. Stalin was no less

totalitarian than the Fascists; he was no less ambitious to conquer the world; no less devious in his international dealings; no less brutal to his own enslaved population; no less the bitter foe of freedom, democracy, and religion. In a remarkably short time millions of Americans were persuaded—by countless books and articles, by hundreds of political speeches, by movies and comedians and editors and ministers and radio broadcasters—that, once again, their country stood face to face with a ruthless aggressor, one who imperiled American interests and assaulted the basic values of western civilization. In September 1945 Gallup found that only 30 percent of the American people thought the Russians could not be trusted; five years later he discovered that 70 percent believed that Russia was trying "to rule the world."

The Cold War manifested itself to Americans as a series of events, crises, and confrontations that pitted their power and will against Russia's. Every few months some pressing and annoying fresh problem arose. Although these episodes raised differing questions and required differing responses, taken together they constituted a single, lengthy national discussion, and in general they were correctly perceived by the American people as being variations on a common theme, chapters in a continuing story. Should the country join the United Nations? Should America push forward its economic interests in Iran at the expense of the Russians? Should the United States share atomic secrets with the Soviets or develop its nuclear capability as rapidly and independently as possible? What should be its response to the Russian blockade of Berlin? Should America come to the aid of the Greeks and the Turks? Was the Marshall Plan for massive financial aid to war-devastated Europe a proper expenditure of American tax dollars? Did joining the North Atlantic Treaty Organization mean turning away from President Washington's sage advice about entangling alliances? Should American blood be spent to defend South Koreans? How could Soviet advances in the "third world" be countered? How far should the United States go to overthrow Castro or to keep Soviet missiles out of Cuba?

There is no need to consider each of these matters in detail; a couple of instances will be sufficient to draw the necessary generalizations. Secretary of State George C. Marshall proposed his program for financial assistance to war-ravaged Europe in a brief commencement address at Harvard University on June 5, 1947. By March 1948, both houses of Congress had overwhelmingly approved the plan, and by the time it ended in 1952 the people of the United States had sent $13 billion to the suffering peoples of Europe. Even if one takes into account that many of these dollars returned to America in trade, the Marshall Plan was an extraordinary policy for Americans to have embarked upon, one that no observer of traditional attitudes could have reasonably predicted ten or fifteen years before. How was it possible that the American people were persuaded of the wisdom of the proposal?

The Marshall Plan was justified to the public in two ways. The people of Europe were facing terrible difficulties. The war had broken down the normal mechanisms of economic life, and the dislocations were pervasive and heart-rending. The poverty, the disease, the lack of shelter and clothing were truly desperate. Surely the duty of an affluent and humane nation in the face of such suffering was clear; the most fundamental moral obligations to others required Americans to feed the starving, care for the sick, clothe the naked. "Our policy is directed not against any country or doctrine," Secretary Marshall told the Harvard graduates, "but against hunger, poverty, desperation, and chaos." At the same time, it was always observed, Americans would be foolish not to recognize that communism thrives on want, confusion, and popular discontent. The surest way to combat the fearful spread of Soviet influence in western Europe was to build healthy and prosperous societies there, societies that could resist the seductive promises of the Kremlin and retain their faith in freedom. Thus the Marshall Plan made its claims upon the citizens of the United States by appealing both to certain moral principles and to fears about national security in a world of Russian expansionism.

Once again, these two arguments were interwoven so intimately, so naturally, and so persistently that it would have been difficult at the time to have noticed that two essentially different appeals were being directed at the public. Virtually every advocate of Secretary Marshall's proposal touched upon both of these themes, often in the same breath. In his famous and widely publicized Senate speech advocating passage, the "old isolationist," Arthur H. Vandenberg, a leading Republican, spoke of the people of Europe: "They are struggling against great and ominous odds, to regain their feet. They must not be allowed to fall. The world—America emphatically included—needs them as both producers and consumers. Peace needs their healthy restoration to the continuing defense of those ideals by which free men live. This vast friendly segment of the earth must not collapse. The iron curtain must not come to the rims of the Atlantic either by aggression or default." The arguments used to explain why the Marshall Plan was wise foreign policy are typical of the whole series of justifications for the numerous programs of humanitarian aid—from Point Four to the Peace Corps, from the Alliance for Progress in Latin

America to similar efforts in Asia and Africa—during the two decades after World War II.

Similarly the arguments used to defend military aid to South Korea are typical of justifications for using military force or for entering into military alliances to contain Communist expansionism during the Cold War. President Truman ordered troops into action in June 1950, shortly after the Russian puppet-state of North Korea launched a full scale surprise attack across the thirty-eighth parallel. The fighting lasted for more than three years; it cost thirty-three thousand American lives and $20 billion. In this case too, American involvement was urged for what was by now the usual two reasons. Clearly, it was not right for one country to launch a sneak attack on a peaceful and unsuspecting neighbor or to attempt to supplant a free and democratic state with Communist tyranny. "The attack upon Korea makes it plain beyond all doubt," President Truman announced, "that communism has passed beyond the use of subversion to conquer independent nations and will now use armed invasion and war. . . . A return to the rule of force in international affairs would have far-reaching effects. The United States will continue to uphold the rule of law." Writing in the *New York Times* a month after the invasion, John Foster Dulles made a similar point: "What happened in Korea proves that the Bolshevik Communist leaders are contemptuous of the moral principles and aspirations which drew the people of the world together to form the United Nations."

Truman's bold response to the North Korean attack, however, was not motivated solely by his outrage at its immorality. He later recalled the thoughts that coursed through his mind as he flew back to Washington to rally the nation.

> I had time to think aboard the plane. In my generation, this was not the first occasion when the strong had attacked the weak. I recalled some earlier instances: Manchuria, Ethiopia, Austria. I remembered how each time that the democracies failed to act it had encouraged the aggressors to keep going ahead. Communism was acting in Korea just as Hitler, Mussolini, and the Japanese had acted ten, fifteen, and twenty years earlier. I felt certain that if South Korea was allowed to fall Communist leaders would be emboldened to override nations closer to our own shores. . . . If this was allowed to go unchallenged it would mean a third world war, just as similar incidents had brought on the second world war.

American self-interest required prompt and resolute action to contain the Communist threat. Thus the intervention in Korea was justified by the same combination of appeals as the Marshall Plan: a combination so jumbled and interwoven in practice as to obscure the double-sided nature of the call.

One other legacy of the period 1935 to 1965 deserves to be mentioned briefly. During these years the presidency came to exercise an almost unquestioned ascendancy in the formulation of foreign policy (just as it did, to only a slightly lesser degree, in the control of domestic affairs). The president's role in international relations, of course, had always been important, but by mid-century it was dominant, virtually unrivaled by any other institution in American society. In part, no doubt, the shabby performance of the Congress in the late 1930s provided a powerful demonstration of that body's unfitness for the task of managing international relations. But the transfer of authority to the White House was more directly attributable to the changed nature of the world. Emergencies require prompt, energetic, unified action, the nation responding with a single will. This sort of efficiency is the specialty of the president, and to whatever extent world affairs presented themselves to Americans after 1935 as a series of crises, to that extent the hand of the president was strengthened and that of the Congress correspondingly weakened. Congress itself generally acceded in this evolution.

In any case, by 1960 political scientists and historians, constitutional lawyers and political philosophers found themselves in remarkable agreement on this point. In the realm of foreign affairs, they repeated over and over again, the president had to be accorded the utmost respect, his judgments given the benefit of every doubt. He alone was elected by all the people and could arrive at a comprehensive national policy, unswayed by the narrow interests of a particular state or district. He, after all, was the commander-in-chief of the armed forces and capable of efficient and decisive responses to international emergencies. He was also the head of the immense diplomatic apparatus and, unlike any other individual in the nation, able to negotiate convincingly with other foreign leaders. The president, moreover, had access to secret sources of intelligence and could base decisions on up-to-the-minute information. Presidents after Franklin Roosevelt were more than ready to shoulder this awesome responsibility and grew accustomed to analyzing foreign developments and conducting international relations with a minimum of "interference" from the Congress, the press, or the public. Arthur Schlesinger, Jr., who has chronicled the rise of "the imperial presidency," has written that "by the early 1970s the American President had become on issues of war and peace the most absolute monarch (with the possible exception of Mao Tse-tung of China) among the great powers of the world."

This immense authority translated itself into the ability to make pronouncements regarding both aspects of the ideology of the nation's foreign policy. The president of the United States could never completely define, for all Americans, the precise nature of international morality and immorality. A few stubborn dissenters (motivated by ethnic loyalties, economic philosophies, or standards of ethical behavior) would always be willing to challenge the moral judgments of the presidents. Neverytheless, the chief executive could exert a tremendous influence over how the public evaluated the moral standing of other nations. What he said (or simply declined to say)—about the behavior of Russia, Germany, Japan, or Italy; about Spain, South Africa, Libya, or Israel; about North or South Korea, Iran, Chile, Cuba, India, or England—went a long way toward determining the attitudes of the American people as to who was "good" and who was "evil" on the world scene. And if the president's power to define international morality and immorality was enormous, his power to define the national interest, to lay out the defensive perimeters of the United States, to declare when and how the country's safety was threatened was virtually unassailable. His pronouncements on matters of the security of the United States were almost like royal decrees. Those who would challenge the president in either realm (as the opponents of the war in Vietnam were about to discover) would be facing a severe uphill struggle to win over public opinion.

V.

Thus the three decades after 1935 saw the fashioning of an extremely powerful justification for greater American involvement in the affairs of the world. On the one hand, that justification consisted of an appeal to fulfill clear moral duties whenever such basic principles as justice, freedom, and democracy were under attack by unscrupulous men and nations. Americans were called by their most cherished ideals not merely to defend those sacred principles, but also to stand, in this troubled and distracted world, for decency, for charity and the protection of the weak. On the other hand, American participation in the world was required, the public was told, by a set of reasonable and peaceful interests that had to be vigilantly guarded. These interests were far-flung and complex, but they were also vital to the national security.

Whether these arguments were directed against the Fascists or the

Communists, the American people found them, on the whole, plausible, and for the quarter century following Pearl Harbor American leaders had the satisfaction of operating a foreign policy to which the vast majority of the American people could subscribe wholeheartedly. (It is not necessary to believe that the foreign policy they chose to implement was the very best and wisest that can be imagined. It is only necessary to understand that, because of the persuasiveness of its claims and purposes, most Americans, most of the time, were willing to give their assent.)

In retrospect, it is, perhaps, a little surprising that nobody paused to point out that Americans were subscribing to this foreign policy for different reasons, that they had come to their position of general support out of quite different concerns. Some were led by their deep attachment to certain ideals, beliefs, and principles; others, by their profound commitment to the necessity to keep their country safe. And in retrospect, it is, perhaps, a little surprising that nobody wondered very much about what would happen to the general consensus if these two articles of faith ever appeared to separate, to conflict, to lead in different directions.

The debate over Vietnam occurred when this venerable blend of ideas seemed, to large numbers of Americans, to divide into its component parts, the parts each drawing the nation toward differing courses of action.

2: THE CONTEST

How Americans Got Involved in a Land War in Asia

I.

Vietnam is a long way from the United States, and Americans during the late 1950s probably knew very little about the place. Sporadic attention was accorded to Vietnamese affairs in the summer of 1954, when the dramatic defeat of the French and American participation in the Geneva Conference captured some public notice. But once that brief flurry of interest subsided, most Americans gladly forgot about Vietnam, content to relegate it to the general obscurity reserved for faraway places that it was no longer necessary for them to worry about. *The Readers' Guide to Periodical Literature* indexes more than a hundred of the most popular magazines in the United States; it therefore gives historians some sense of what Americans were interested in at any particular moment. For 1960 the *Readers' Guide* lists only fifteen entries for Vietnam, nine of them brief mentions in one of the weekly news magazines. (In contrast, the same year saw twice as many articles about the execution of a California kidnapper named Caryl Chessman and the *Readers' Guide* could direct the curious to nine dozen articles about the new compact cars Detroit was producing.)

Thus when John F. Kennedy took his oath of office in January 1961 and warned Americans that some sacrifices might be required of them in the years ahead, one suspects that few of them could have located Vietnam on a map of the world. Fewer still could have said anything intelligible about the Vietnamese political situation. And the idea that Vietnam might have possessed a rich and ancient history or a complex and variegated culture was probably confined to a few academics, some area-experts in the State Department, and a handful of well-read citizens scattered through the country. But a nation's culture and history (like an individual's) propel its courses of action and go a

long way toward accounting for its political behavior. As events un-
folded, Americans would have cause to regret their earlier ignorance
and indifference.

Indochina is a large peninsula jutting southward from the Chinese
mainland, situated, as its name implies, between India and China. It
consists of a part of Malaysia and the separate countries of Burma,
Thailand, Cambodia, Laos, and Vietnam.* Vietnam is the S-shaped
nation that occupies the entire eastern edge of Indochina. It contains
127,000 square miles (roughly the size of New Mexico) and runs
about a thousand miles from north to south (approximately the distance from the southern boundary of California to the northern
boundary of Oregon). Vietnam's geography is dominated by two
large river systems: the Red River in the north and the Mekong in the
south. Both possess fertile deltas, ideal for the cultivation of rice and
other crops. Along the east coast a low-lying plain connects the two
deltas. The great majority of Vietnamese live in the delta regions or
in the narrow connecting plain. The western two-thirds of the country is covered by dense forests and rugged, sometimes strikingly beautiful mountain landscapes. Vietnam is not a poor nation. It can produce more than enough food, mostly rice and fish, for itself, and it
contains significant mineral deposits, mostly in the north.

For more than two thousand years a distinct Vietnamese ethnic
and linguistic group has occupied this territory. This group originally
settled in the rich northern delta, driving the indigenous peoples—
a welter of racially and culturally diverse tribes—into the western
mountains where their descendants still live in primitive and scattered enclaves. Despite a spirited resistance the Vietnamese were con-
quered by the Chinese about a hundred years before the birth of
Christ. During the next thousand years they bore a curious relation
to their Chinese overlords. On the one hand, they welcomed and absorbed numerous Chinese innovations. These included not only the
agricultural and engineering techniques that radically improved their
physical existence, but also advances in law, education, political administration, religion, and literary and artistic culture. On the other
hand, the Vietnamese steadfastly resented Chinese domination, stubbornly refusing to become citizens of a Chinese province.

A strong tradition of resistance to imperial claims therefore
evolved. This resistance, located at first among jealous Chinese administrators and Vietnamese feudal lords, spread over the years to
intellectuals, bureaucrats, and then to the peasantry at large. The

---

*A great many authorities, however, restrict their use of the word *Indochina* to denote
only the former French colonies: Laos, Cambodia, and Vietnam.

long period of Chinese rule, consequently, was characterized by reluctant accommodation to superior force and punctuated, whenever opportunity offered, by vigorous armed rebellion. By the time the Chinese were finally cast out in the year 939, therefore, the Vietnamese had earned a particular kind of history—one that glorified unity, armed resistance, and political independence and that extolled as national heroes men and women who resolutely opposed, often at the cost of their lives, the domination of foreigners.

The thousand years of Chinese rule were followed by nine centuries of independence. These years were marked by constant armed struggle, both internal and external. The Vietnamese repulsed no fewer than five Chinese invasions, and when a sixth succeeded in 1407, they mounted a massive resistance that lasted twenty years and eventually drove the old enemy back north. The Vietnamese quickly turned their attention southward and, by the end of the fifteenth century, had virtually destroyed the neighboring Champa, a thousand-year-old kingdom that had been founded by Indian sailors; they also made systematic incursions into the territory claimed by Cambodia, until, by the mid-eighteenth century, they controlled all of the lands that comprise present-day Vietnam. If these military ventures were not enough, the nation was also torn by periodic civil wars between powerful competing families. The country was divided, north and south, twice, the second division lasting for a century and a half. But at about the same time that the thirteen American colonies were struggling to create a new nation in the Western Hemisphere, the Vietnamese also launched a strenuous revolution that ended in 1802 with the establishment of a single nation under a single emperor.

The first European contact with Vietnam was by Portuguese traders, who arrived in 1535. They established commercial outposts along the coast and monopolized the region's trade for a hundred years. As Portuguese maritime power began to decline, the Dutch, starting in 1636, began the process of replacing them. In 1672 the English entered the contest, and eight years later, the French. It was not commerce, however, that led to the eventual subjugation of Vietnam; once the various native factions made peace, thereby reducing the need for the war material that Europe supplied, trade declined rapidly. It was, rather, religion that provided the pretext for taking over the country. Roman Catholic missionary activity among the Vietnamese had been a feature of the western presence from the start, but by 1700 the evangelical work was under the supervision of the French. Until the early nineteenth century Christianity was thought relatively harmless and was good naturedly tolerated by the Vietnamese. For a variety of political, economic, theological, and nationalistic reasons, however, the Vietnamese government came to regard the missionaries as dangerous subversives. Following a campaign of expulsion and persecution, including some brutal executions of missionaries, the French navy steamed to the rescue. The hostilities began on April 15, 1847. "Within seventy minutes," writes the historian Joseph Buttinger, "French guns had taken a hundred times more lives than all the Vietnamese governments in two centuries of missionary persecution." The French undertook in earnest the project of conquering Vietnam in 1858; they completed it by 1883.

The concern for persecuted priests was genuine enough, but it also served as a cover for the standard set of imperialist motives. France wanted Vietnam for its raw materials, as a market for the surplus products of French manufacturers, as a naval and military base for further territorial and economic expansion in Asia, and as a proof of French greatness in an age when European nations registered their greatness by acquiring colonial empires. These ambitions could not be realized without pacifying the native population, and for the rest of the nineteenth century the French waged a bloody campaign of conquest and repression. The triumph of western military technology was probably inevitable, but barbarous excesses were committed by both sides, bequeathing a legacy of bitter animosity that would plague the victors for the whole of their colonial career. Once French rule had fastened itself, the usual imperialist patterns emerged. On the one hand, the conquerors introduced improvements in education, health care, agriculture, transportation, and industrial productivity. On the other hand, there was the normal, sordid story of exploitation and abuse: the uprooting of traditional Vietnamese culture, the imposition of the French language, heavy taxation, the dislocation of agricultural and economic life in the interest of foreigners, the abolition of basic freedoms, and the degrading demotion of the Vietnamese to second-class citizenship in their own country. Nothing was surer than that there would be vigorous resistance to this latest attempt by outsiders to reduce the Vietnamese people to the status of subjects in someone else's empire.

There was never a time when French rule was not challenged by Vietnamese nationalists preaching one form or another of patriotic resistance to foreign domination. Some favored reforming the colonial system in collaboration with the French; others pursued their nationalist goals by emphasizing education or religion or armed revolt. Throughout the first decades of the twentieth century, native politics was characterized by a lively competition between nationalist groups and by conflict, demonstrations, opposition newspapers and literature, and secret and open efforts to throw off the yoke of the oppressors. By the mid-1930s the Communists had achieved a clear ascendancy among those advocating Vietnamese independence. Several factors enabled them to overcome their rivals. The failure of the collaborationists to get concessions from the French, for example, made the frankly revolutionary Communists more credible. The climate of police surveillance favored the secret, highly disciplined, and entirely unscrupulous tactics of the Communists as well. Their message of human equality, of hatred for wealthy landlords and businessmen (both French and Vietnamese), of the necessity for the radical redistribution of wealth and land, combined with their insistence upon absolute independence—all served to attract thousands of Vietnamese from all walks of life into their ranks. The abortive revolt of a rival group, brutally crushed by the French, opened an opportunity for seizing leadership. Certainly another factor in the Communists' success was the leadership of Ho Chi Minh, a brilliant organizer, effective and tireless in the pursuit of Vietnamese nationhood. After an absence of thirty years, Ho Chi Minh returned to his native land in 1940 to take up the struggle in person.

The years of World War II witnessed stunning changes in Vietnamese politics. The Nazis rolled over France in June 1940, and the proud people who had controlled Vietnam for so long suddenly discovered that even Europeans could be rudely ordered about by foreign-speaking administrators. The Japanese, seeing their chance, issued an ultimatum to the helpless French governor-general of Indochina in the same week as the fall of Paris. For most of the war the Japanese wielded ultimate political and economic authority in Vietnam, but they permitted the French to continue the day-to-day administration of the country. Vietnamese nationalists of various persuasions gathered in May 1941 and pledged themselves to struggle against France and Japan alike. Under Communist leadership, these nationalists formed a militant new organization called the Vietminh. The secretary-general of the Vietminh was Ho Chi Minh himself, and he immediately set out to raise a guerrilla army that trained in the mountains and soon numbered ten thousand men.

Events in Vietnam moved with bewildering rapidity as the global conflict came to a conclusion. With France liberated by the Allies, the Japanese in Vietnam ended the cooperative enterprise on March 9, 1945, by launching a surprise attack on their French partners and disarming them. Next they declared Vietnam to be an independent country under the young figurehead emperor Bao Dai, who was as willing to cooperate with the Japanese as he had been with the French. The Vietminh turned their attention to Japanese targets and stepped up their activities against what seemed to be the last remaining obstacle to nationhood. (During the spring and summer of 1945, therefore, the Vietminh and the United States government were engaged in the same enterprise, and there were several instances of friendly cooperation in the mutual effort to defeat the Japanese.) In any case, the Japanese arrangement could last only so long as Japanese power was present to back it up. Within ten days of Japan's surrender to the United States, the Vietminh had complete control in the north and effective control in the south. Ho Chi Minh declared his country to be independent. He became its president, and Bao Dai abdicated.

Unfortunately, those Vietnamese who celebrated the end of French rule celebrated prematurely. In the south the British army arrived in late September 1945 to accept the Japanese surrender. They made no attempt to disguise their intention to hand the territory back to the French as soon as possible. In a month the French were back in force; the Vietminh had fled to the countryside; and the long guerrilla war began anew. In the north two things were different. In the first place, the Vietminh were better established there; in the second, the Chinese disarmed the Japanese, and they were not immediately willing to return authority to France, at least not without getting some concessions. The concessions were not long in coming, however, and the Chinese agreed to withdraw in favor of the French in February 1946. Ho went to Paris hoping to negotiate for Vietnamese independence, but the talks quickly deadlocked to no purpose. In November the French shelled the part of Haiphong controlled by the Vietminh, killing thousands of Vietnamese civilians, and by the end of 1946 the bloody war was under way in deadly seriousness.

That war soon settled into patterns that would become agonizingly familiar to Americans two decades later. The French army controlled the cities and the larger towns; the guerrillas owned the countryside and the night. Under the direction of their brilliant tactician, General Vo Nguyen Giap, they struck in small, highly mobile units, did their pin-prick damage, and melted back into the jungles. The triumph of Mao Tse-tung, who ended the Chinese civil war in 1949 by driving Chiang Kai-shek off the mainland, placed a friendly Communist government at the northern border of Vietnam. Soon the Vietminh were getting modern weapons and the advice of experts on matters of guerrilla warfare. Now Giap's men began appearing in larger units, attacking in overwhelming numbers at some French outpost and quickly disappearing. The French were largely powerless against this strategy. For a while they tried erecting strings of watchtowers along the major roads, but soldiers displayed an understandable reluctance to man those deathtraps after dark. Occasionally, the French would move out into the country in force and secure a region, but as soon as they moved on the guerrillas reasserted their authority. In desperation Paris even undertook a political experiment, reinstating Emperor Bao Dai and hinting about eventual "dominion status" for Vietnam. But the Communist leadership was adamant for independence, and few of the other nationalists would have anything to do with the French overtures. Year by year the Vietminh enlarged the territory under their control; year by year they gained credibility with the peasantry; and their blows grew bolder and harder. The climax (and for the French, the bitter and irreversible ending) came in the spring of 1954, when General Giap surrounded eleven thousand French soldiers at Dienbienphu and, after eight weeks of terrible pounding, forced their humiliating surrender.

Ironically, the French had sought the battle at Dienbienphu. They did so thinking that a victory would strengthen their hand for an international conference on Korea and Indochina already scheduled for Geneva. As luck would have it, the French loss of Dienbienphu came only twenty-four hours before the Geneva Conference turned to the Indochina question. It was clear to all that the French were finished militarily and politically in the region, that what was needed was a way for them to extricate themselves with some modicum of dignity, and that the principal job at Geneva would be to construct as orderly and reasonable a settlement as possible under the circumstances. Participants in the Geneva Conference were the four parties that had called for the meeting, France, Great Britain, the Soviet Union, and the United States; also present were China, Cambodia, and Laos; and representing elements within Vietnam itself were spokesmen for Bao Dai's government and for the Vietminh. Because of a complex set of individual motives, both domestic and international, each of the participants had a serious interest in arriving at some workable settlement.

The discussions lasted from May 8 to July 21 and resulted in two agreements. The first was a cease-fire between the Vietminh and the French. It established a "provisional military demarcation line" at the seventeenth parallel. France agreed to regroup its forces to the south, and the Vietminh, to the north of that line within ten months. Also during that time civilians who wished to relocate to either zone would be "permitted and helped" to do so. It was clearly understood by the agreement that the seventeenth parallel was not to become a permanent boundary between two separate nations, but that the two zones would be unified into a single country by a free nationwide election; thus Article 14 discussed the administration of the two zones "pending the general elections which will bring about the unification of Vietnam. . . ." The cease-fire agreement also prohibited either zone from introducing new weapons or military personnel, permitting the establishment of a military base by a foreign nation, or entering into any military alliance. The second agreement was the famous Final Declaration of the conference. It "took note" of the provisions of the first agreement and fixed the elections for two years hence, July 1956, emphasizing particularly "that the military demarcation line is provisional and should not in any way be interpreted as constituting a political or territorial boundary."

The emperor's government in the south refused to give assent to the Geneva Accords. At the time, those observers inclined to look on the brighter side pointed out that the refusal did not matter very much; the emperor's government, after all, governed practically no one and could not be expected to endorse an election that would demonstrate its radical lack of support among the Vietnamese people. Those observers who were not inclined to look on the brighter side warned against placing too much faith in the arrangement that had been imposed upon the Vietnamese by the major powers at Geneva. They solemnly and, as it turned out, accurately forecast trouble ahead.

II.

One old tale has assumed legendary significance in many histories of twentieth-century Vietnam. In January 1919 Ho Chi Minh was in his late twenties and living in Paris. Born a peasant, he had left home in 1911 as a cabin boy and struggled to survive in the French capital as a dishwasher, a snow-sweeper, a photographer. He was already well known among fellow Vietnamese as a passionate advocate of independence for his country. World War I had ended in November 1918, and now the victors were coming to Paris to fashion the peace. One of them was Woodrow Wilson, the American statesman famous for his devotion to international justice and the self-determination of peoples. Ho, with two friends, drafted a quite modest eight-point program for Vietnam: amnesty for political prisoners, representation in the French parliament, freedom of speech and the press in his country, and other rights. The Peace Conference paid not the slightest attention, and President Wilson, whose words had filled with hope oppressed people all over the world, never even granted an audience. The episode is said to have convinced Ho Chi Minh and others that hat-in-hand requests for liberal reform were doomed to fail, that only revolutionary struggle could succeed.

That the rejection at Paris turned Ho Chi Minh decisively toward armed revolution may be doubted; he had, after all, associated with radical and revolutionary groups ever since his arrival in Paris. Nevertheless, the story accurately reveals much about the official American attitude toward European imperialism. For most of the twentieth century American leaders had solemnly denounced colonialism—especially the sort that employed direct political administration of subject territories—and just as solemnly refused to do very much about it. Particularly in the cases of France and Great Britain, the maintenance of good relations with the imperial powers always seemed somehow more urgent than insisting upon national independence for their colonies. This tension between noble expressions of sympathy and the exigencies of practical international politics has often lent an ambiguous character to American policy, and from time to time educated colonial leaders have been bitterly angered by what seemed to them hypocrisy and untrustworthiness.

The American government gave no direct and specific attention to Vietnam until World War II. President Roosevelt harbored the standard sentiments. In a memorandum to Secretary of State Hull, dated January 24, 1944, he reported telling the British ambassador "quite frankly" that he had, "for over a year, expressed the opinion that Indo-China should not go back to France but that it should be administered by an international trusteeship. France has had the country—thirty million inhabitants for nearly one hundred years, and the people are worse off than they were at the beginning. . . . Each case must, of course, stand on its own feet, but the case of Indo-China is perfectly clear. France has milked it for one hundred years. The people of Indo-China are entitled to something better than that." Yet despite his apparently genuine wish for some kind of international administration leading to independence, Roosevelt was finally willing to bow to firm resistance on the part of the French and the British (who, with one eye fixed nervously on their own possessions, had no desire to encourage the practice of breaking up empires).

Roosevelt's successor, President Harry Truman, also urged ultimate independence for the countries of Indochina and also was careful not to press the French too hard about it. In 1947 and 1948 American policy-makers generally agreed that the main arena for resisting Communist expansion was war-torn Europe. Since France would have to play an important part in European defense, there was no point in irritating Paris about dismantling its Asian empire. The fateful decision actually to contribute to the French effort in Vietnam was made in the early weeks of 1950, and it was undoubtedly made under the heavy compulsions of the Cold War. The Russians detonated an atomic bomb in September 1949; the Chinese Communists completed their conquest of the mainland by December; Senator Joseph McCarthy launched his ferocious attack against "softness" toward communism in the Truman administration in February 1950; and by mid-summer American fighting men were engaged in full-scale war in Korea.

The rising intensity of anticommunism in American society caused innumerable changes in policy and attitude. None was more important for the future than the magical conversion—in the view of average citizens and powerful officials alike—of the French purpose in Vietnam. From arrogant and greedy imperialists who had milked Vietnam for a century, they were suddenly transformed into courageous opponents of the spread of communism in Asia. To the many Americans who supported Truman's decisive action with respect to Greece and Turkey and praised the Marshall Plan, who regarded the Berlin airlift and the intervention in Korea as demonstrations of heroic firmness, it seemed only natural that the United States should lend a hand in Vietnam. The aid that began in 1950 with a mere $10 million grew so phenomenally that by the time of Dienbienphu, in 1954, it totalled $1.063 billion. At the end, almost eighty cents of every dollar being spent to fight the Vietminh was coming from the United States.

By the time President Eisenhower came to power in January 1953, most observers could see that the French cause in Vietnam was faltering in spite of America's lavish financial aid. The Republican administration was forced, therefore, to consider the Vietnam problem with far more seriousness than had theretofore been required. Four of its decisions, made under the pressure of fast-moving events, were especially difficult. The first matter to decide was whether to give direct military assistance to the French. Various proposals to do so arose after January 1954, and the question became particularly urgent in April, as General Giap's tactics at Dienbienphu grew clearer and more ominous. Admiral Arthur Radford, chair of the Joint Chiefs of Staff, proposed that the United States bomb and strafe the hills around the beleaguered French garrison. Other advisers, however, doubted that such an action could reverse the disastrous course of the war and warned the president that it would lead inevitably to deeper involvement in an Asian land war the United States could not win. Congressional leaders, when consulted, vehemently insisted that there be "no more Koreas" and that no congressional support could be expected without cooperation from Britain and genuine French concessions in the direction of eventual independence. In view of these obstacles to committing American power, Eisenhower unequivocally refused to do so.

The next problem facing American policy-makers was what to do about the Geneva Conference. From the beginning both President Eisenhower and Secretary of State John Foster Dulles had been lukewarm about such a meeting, fearing that war-weary France would seize the chance to throw in the towel and turn over Vietnam to the Communists. Unable to prevent the conference without appearing to be enemies of peace, they determined to downplay it. Secretary Dulles stayed in Geneva only a week before turning things over to Undersecretary Walter Bedell Smith, and the United States was as much an observer as a full participant. When the work of the conference was completed and the Final Declaration brought before the delegates, only America and the Bao Dai regime refused to register their oral assent. "My government is not prepared to join in a Declaration," Smith announced, but wished instead to make a unilateral declaration that it would "refrain from the threat or the use of force" to disturb the Geneva Accords and that "it would view any renewal of the aggression in violation of the aforesaid Agreements with grave concern and as seriously threatening international peace and security." Smith also repeated the view that the American government favored free and fair elections. Finally, he stated, "the United States reiterates its traditional position that peoples are entitled to determine their own future and that it will not join in an arrangement which would hinder this."

Meanwhile, the Eisenhower administration had been grappling with a third problem, namely, who should head the anti-Communist government in southern Vietnam. Ngo Dinh Diem, chosen by Bao Dai as his prime minister in June 1954 (while the Geneva Conference was meeting), was settled upon as the most likely available leader to oppose Ho Chi Minh. Diem labored under certain disadvantages: he had left Vietnam in August 1950 and had thus played no part in the glorious struggle against the French, living in America for most of that period; he had few political allies and was hesitant to trust anyone except members of his own powerful family; he was aloof and distant, a man with no popular following and neither inclined nor equipped to acquire one; and he was a devout Catholic in a Vietnam that was less than 15 percent Catholic. But Diem had sound credentials as a nationalist and impeccable ones as an anti-Communist. During his years in the United States, moreover, he had cultivated friendships with a number of important Americans. By mid-1955 he was clearly Washington's man in Saigon. As the French withdrew, American aid was channeled through Diem, and it was made perfectly plain to his rivals that the continuation of aid would depend on Diem's remaining in power. For better or worse, America was going to gamble on the ability of Diem to establish his authority, make the necessary reforms, and win over the nationalists to his banner. In October 1955 Diem staged a referendum in which, his supporters claimed, 98 percent of the people voted to oust the emperor. He promptly declared himself president of the new Republic of Vietnam.

Finally, the United States had to decide what attitude to take toward the Vietnamese elections that had been promised for July 1956. President Diem stubbornly refused to participate in any negotiations leading to the holding of such elections, arguing that, with a Communist regime in the north, no exercise in democracy could possibly take place and that there was no point even in discussing the matter. Of course, the prospect of those elections (together with pressure from both China and the Soviet Union) had persuaded the reluctant Vietminh to stop the fighting while they were so clearly ahead. Convinced that Ho Chi Minh, the hero of the struggle against imperialism, would easily triumph in any free expression of Vietnamese public opinion, the Communists had even agreed to evacuate temporarily the sizable portions of central Vietnam, south of the seventeenth parallel, that their forces indisputably controlled. That the refusal to hold elections, the refusal even to discuss the possibility, would inevitably lead to a resumption of hostilities was well understood by all parties. Nevertheless, the Eisenhower administration not only acquiesced in Diem's decision in this matter, but positively encouraged it.

Both Saigon and Washington were hoping that the south could strengthen and unify itself sufficiently to resist any military response that might come from the Communists. American experts probably expected a full-scale invasion from the north, like the one the Communists had launched in Korea only a few years before. Instead, the war, when it came, took the form of widespread guerrilla actions directed against the government of the south. These actions were led by Vietminh agents who had never moved north, by indigenous Communists, and by large numbers of non-Communist opponents of the regime who objected on religious or political grounds to the increasingly severe dictatorship of the Diem family. The Saigon government lumped all of its opponents together and gave them the contemptuous name "Vietcong," Vietnamese Communists. By 1960 the guerrilla warfare in the south was being pursued without restraint. It was a particularly brutal struggle, fought at the village level and throughout the countryside. The Saigon government employed such unsavory tactics as uprooting village democracy by replacing elected local officals with Diem's appointees, undercover police spying and midnight arrests, harsh punitive raids on villages and hamlets, the destruction of political and civil liberties, and the wide use of concentration camps for opponents. The Vietcong, meanwhile, practiced ambush, subversion, merciless political assassination, extortion, and terrorism. Beginning in the summer of 1959, well-trained troops from the north began to infiltrate into the south; perhaps as many as ten thousand joined forces with the Vietcong in 1961 alone.

President Eisenhower thus passed on to his successor a Vietnam situation even more dangerous and complex than the one he had inherited, and President Kennedy was required, during his short administration, to face constantly the choice between getting out completely or getting in more deeply. Furthermore, public indifference to Vietnam was starting to dissipate, thereby rendering the domestic political implications of the problem more acute. In contrast to the fifteen articles of 1960, the *Readers' Guide* listed almost two hundred fifty during the last twelve months of Kennedy's life. The president regularly dispatched envoys and fact-finding missions and began to weigh, with increasing concern, their reports and advice.

III.

Many of those advocating deeper involvement in Vietnam—whether arguing from inside or outside of the administration—had come to maturity during the debates over national policy on the eve of World War II. For them the "lessons" of that experience were formative and very deeply ingrained. Those who had chosen to enter public service during the 1940s and 1950s, and who were now responsible for formulating America's foreign policies, had spent their apprenticeships grappling with the struggles of the Cold War. It will not be surprising, therefore, that the case for intervention in Vietnam was made on precisely the same grounds that had been so persuasive since the mid-1930s. Despite the rising interest in Vietnam and the steady multiplication of voices addressing the issues, the call to be firm in Southeast Asia had a decidedly familiar ring to it. In the final analysis, the message rested inevitably on the same two contentions as always: the need to defend the national security and the need to vindicate American ideals by combating the forces of evil. That those points developed naturally out of the foreign policy debates of the preceding generation, out of what had already become a sort of American tradition in discussions of international affairs, was no doubt entirely predictable.

On October 2, 1963, seven weeks before his death, President Kennedy issued a "statement of United States policy" with regard to Vietnam. Two trusted advisers, Secretary of Defense Robert S. McNamara and General Maxwell D. Taylor, chair of the Joint Chiefs of Staff, had returned early that morning from a week-long survey of the situation, and after hearing their report the president was ready to announce his conclusions to the country. The first sentence of the first point of the statement is notable for its stark and unequivocal declaration: "1. The security of South Viet-Nam is a major interest of the United States as other free nations." This position—that the fate of Vietnam had serious implications for the safety and well-being of America and the free world and that the nation therefore had a legitimate interest in the outcome of the struggle—was the first general line of argument by those urging American involvement. It was destined to become one of the most often repeated justifications of those, both inside and outside of government, who thought that American participation in the war was necessary. But when such a pronouncement came directly from the White House (and this notion had already been given ample expression by both Truman and Eisenhower), it came clothed in a special authority and was accorded all the deference due to the one official who, for a quarter century, enjoyed virtually unchallenged responsibility for defining the requirements of American security.

As we have seen in connection with the coming of World War II, appeals to national security are not always models of exactitude. It is almost as if the term was somehow self-explanatory, acting as a kind of linguistic shorthand for a set of facts that were thought to be generally understood by everyone. In this case, those who argued that our security was at risk in Vietnam usually justified their conclusion on one or more of four central fears. The first was that Vietnam was rich in certain natural resources, that possession of these resources was essential to the health and prosperity of America and her allies, and that to allow these treasures to fall into Communist hands was unthinkable. In addition to the production of rice and rubber, mostly in the south, the resources most often enumerated were forest products, including several rare woods, and rich mineral deposits, mostly in the north: coal, tin, tungsten, zinc, phosphates, chromium, and manganese. The second contention lying beneath the general concern for American security was that Vietnam occupied a strategic geographic position that made its fate in the east-west struggle particularly critical. Saigon, after all, was within two thousand miles of Singapore, Jakarta, Hong Kong, Manila, and Bangkok. Vietnam lay athwart the busiest and most lucrative trade routes in Asia. Proponents of American intervention in Vietnam believed it mattered a great deal, both economically and militarily, whether a free or a Communist government controlled this territory.

A third belief underlying worry over American security interests, the famous "domino theory," was to assume immense importance in the debate over Vietnam. Although Truman had used the concept, Eisenhower, in a press conference on April 7, 1954, gave it classic expression. In response to a question about "the strategic importance of Indochina to the free world," the president (phrasing his answer with that trademarked diffuseness that for eight years both amused the reporters and filled them with despair) said: "Finally, you have broader considerations that might follow what you would call the 'falling domino' principle. You have a row of dominoes set up, you knock over the first one, and what will happen to the last one is the certainty that it will go over very quickly. So you could have a beginning of a disintegration that would have the most profound influences." Eisenhower mentioned the threat, in sequence, to the rest of Indochina, to Indonesia, to Japan, Formosa, and the Philippines, and even to Australia and New Zealand. Others would offer different lists of potential dominoes that might fall once Vietnam fell (India, Pakistan, Malaya, Okinawa). A few were even willing to go as far as Senator Thomas Dodd of Connecticut, who in a speech on February 23, 1965, warned that "if we fail to draw the line in Viet-Nam . . . we may find ourselves compelled to draw a defense line as far back as Seattle and Alaska, with Hawaii as a solitary outpost in mid-Pacific." Whether presented in moderate or in extreme form, the domino theory expressed one of the most commonly held fears among those Americans who urged intervention in Vietnam.

Finally, some of those stating the case for such intervention on national security grounds sometimes presented a fourth argument. The war in Vietnam, they pointed out, was of a different sort from those to which Americans were accustomed. Euphemistically called "wars of national liberation" by the Communists, these struggles were local insurgencies, characterized by guerrilla tactics, civil disruption, and deceptive propaganda spread through the countryside to inflame the peasantry. Such movements, caused often enough by grinding misery and real injustice, were assuming great importance in the modern world, especially in the undeveloped but modernizing societies of the Southern Hemisphere. Unfortunately, the Communists had proved to be particularly adept at exploiting these uprisings. With their discipline and secretiveness, with their skill in portraying themselves as uncompromising opponents of the rich and powerful (landowners, generals, businessmen, the religious hierarchy, colonial officials, and their native lackeys), with their seductive vision of equality and universal prosperity, with such heroes as Mao and Che Guevara, Communists were sometimes able to take over these movements and to deliver entire peoples to the Communist world.

A victory of this kind in Vietnam would encourage similar tendencies throughout Asia, Latin America, and Africa. Since the end of World War II the United States had demonstrated its willingness to contain Communism in Europe. Americans had shown again and again their readiness to contribute generously to the economic stability of countries around the world so that they might resist communism. In Korea the nation proved that it would not be intimidated by naked aggression, the full-scale invasion across a national boundary by Communist armies. Now it must show similar resolve and patience in this new arena; it must show the Communists the futility of these guerrilla wars of national liberation. The problems in such an undertaking were enormous, of course. For one thing the legitimate grievances and desires of native peoples had to be recognized, and meaningful reform had to be urged upon governments that had little interest in change. In addition, counterinsurgency was a hard kind of war—dirty, frustrating, slow, and with no clear moments of triumph. ("Th victory we seek," warned Kennedy's adviser Walt Rostow in 1961, will see no ticker-tape parades down Broadway, no climactic battles, nor great American celebrations of victory.") But failure to engage the nation in the attempt, would be an invitation to insurgent Communist elements in a dozen other places far from Vietnam. Anyone unable to see that our interests would be threatened and our safety seriously imperiled by such a development must be unusually naïve and cowardly.

Hence proponents of American participation in the Vietnam conflict argued strongly—even if sometimes along differing lines—the first traditional reason for an active foreign policy, the presence of factors of legitimate self-interest and the necessity to defend the country's security. They also placed heavy stress upon the second reason, arguing that the people of South Vietnam were facing a particularly immoral enemy. The allegations of immorality took two forms. First, advocates of American involvement insisted that from the start the North had plotted the overthrow of the anti-Communist government of the South and had pursued, in bold defiance of the customary practices of civilized nations, policies of subversion and armed aggression to accomplish its goal. And second, they charged that the Communist partisans had chosen to pursue this evil purpose by remarkably barbaric methods.

The charge that North Vietnam was bent on immoral policies of subversion and infiltration, engaged, in short, in an unscrupulous scheme to conquer a peaceful neighbor, was the official position of the American government from the early 1960s onward. President Lyndon Johnson capsulized the contention in a speech on February 17, 1965. America had entered the conflict, he said, in order to help defend "a brave people who are under attack that is controlled and that is directed from outside their country." On the same day, Vice President Hubert Humphrey went to the United Nations to complain about "the systematic attempts of foreign-backed subversives" in South Vietnam. Month after month, year after year, North Vietnam poured officers, men, weapons, and supplies into the South, making the war possible. In another speech Johnson called that aid "the heartbeat of the war." The State Department summarized and documented these charges in a publication of 1965 called *Aggression from the North: The Record of North Viet-Nam's Campaign to Conquer South Viet-Nam.* "South Viet-Nam is fighting for its life," the document began, and the attack upon its soil was "inspired, directed, supplied, and controlled by the Communist regime in Hanoi." The State Department explicitly denied that the trouble in Vietnam was a spontaneous rebellion: "In Viet-Nam a Communist government has set out deliberately to conquer a sovereign people in a neighboring state."

The charge that the Vietcong and their North Vietnamese allies fought with horrifying brutality was also asserted by advocates of American involvement. The State Department's White Paper of 1961, for example, charged the Communists with using "every available technique for spreading disorder and confusion in a peaceful society. . . . If mining a road will stop all transport, who cares that a school bus may be the first vehicle to pass? If halting rice shipments means that many people go hungry, perhaps they will blame it on the government." *Aggression from the North* echoed the accusation:

> Any official, worker, or establishment that represents a service to the people by the Government in Saigon is fair game for the Viet Cong. Schools have been among their favorite targets. Through harassment, the murder of teachers, and sabotage of buildings, the Viet Cong succeeded in closing hundreds of schools and interrupting the education of tens of thousands of youngsters. Hospitals and medical clinics have often been attacked as part of the anti-Government campaign. . . . Village and town offices, police stations, and agricultural research stations are high on the list of preferred targets for the Viet Cong.

Stories of unspeakable cruelty on the part of the Vietcong were regularly publicized: killing of innocent civilians in indiscriminate bombing, disfigurements, kidnappings, torture, random terror. In 1964 alone, the government reported, 436 hamlet officials were murdered, and 1,131 were kidnapped by Vietcong terrorists. These sinister and heartless tactics provided unmistakable proof of the enemy's utter depravity.

These two large, general defenses of American involvement—that national security was endangered and that the enemy was immoral—were tightly linked, in the minds of most Americans by a single, fearful, demonic specter: communism. After almost two decades of Cold War the word had come to symbolize for millions of Americans both everything that was endangering and everything that was immoral in world affairs. Insofar as communism represented international power, it was the shorthand word for the great force that threatened American safety. Insofar as it represented either a set of ideological principles or a standard of civilized behavior, it was the shorthand word for unmitigated and unrestrained evil. Unpersuaded by those who tried to draw nice distinctions between shades or kinds of communism (Chinese vs. Yugoslav, for example; or nationalistic vs. international), everyday Americans were satisfied to view communism as a monolithic monster that was attacking their nation on both fronts. Nothing was so dangerous to the nation's safety that it was impossible to imagine the Communists working night and day to accomplish it; and nothing was so immoral, either in theory or in practice, that it was impossible to imagine some Communist enthusiastically recommending its implementation. Thus the fact that Americans were resisting *communism* in Vietnam went a long way, by itself, toward justifying the effort. The mere use of the word was often thought sufficient, by advocates of American participation, to excuse themselves from embarking upon laborious elaborations of why the fight was necessary.

To these advocates, in short, the ancient requirements of "the just war" had been satisfied. Given the nature of communism, the struggle in Vietnam could be understood as both defensive and moral. Consciously or unconsciously, therefore, proponents of the war were able to make telling connections to the hallowed body of thought that had been used for centuries to justify going to war. They were also enormously strengthened in their contentions by being able to draw cautionary lessons from the central foreign policy experience of their generation, World War II. "The situation in Viet-Nam today," said Senator Dodd in his Senate speech of 1965, "bears many resemblances to the situation just before Munich. . . . In Vietnam today, we are again confronted by an incorrigible aggressor, fanatically committed to the destruction of the free world, whose agreements are as worthless as Hitler's." And in a comparison that would be repeated so often during the debate over Vietnam that "Munich" was elevated into a major symbol in the discourse, Dodd contrasted the wise and courageous policies of resistance with the foolish and craven ones of appeasement. When Vice President Johnson, in May 1961, went to South Vietnam and called Diem "the Winston Churchill of Asia," he no doubt intended to stir in Americans an affecting memory of dogged opposition to immoral force. To a slightly lesser extent, advocates of the war in Vietnam tried to make similar linkages to Korea: "North Viet-Nam's commitment to seize control of the South is no less total than was the commitment of the regime in North Korea in 1950," argued *Aggression from the North*.

These beliefs and arguments, however, with their assumptions and historical allusions, were not to be found solely in the minds of isolated government officials. They permeated American culture and were repeated in countless sermons, editorials, articles, and books. They constituted the conventional wisdom of ten thousand after-dinner speeches at the Rotary Club, the thing everybody could agree about over beers in a hundred thousand friendly bars, the comfortable shared faiths in a million neighborly chats across the back fence on warm spring evenings. After thirty years of repetition, they flowed out of people naturally. To most Americans they had the easy ring of self-evident truth.

Perhaps nothing did a better job of summarizing and reinforcing the familiar contentions of those who urged American involvement during the 1960s than the first major combat film of the war, John Wayne's *The Green Berets* (1968). In the opening scene combat-experienced soldiers are conducting a demonstration for the public at Fort Bragg, North Carolina. Three annoying reporters persist in badgering the soldiers with skeptical questions. The most aggressive of them says to the tough but highly articulate Sergeant Muldoon: "There are still a lot of people who believe that this is simply a war between the Vietnamese people. It's their war. Let's let them handle it." Muldoon has remained cool up to now, but this is too much. He strides to a display of captured Vietcong weapons, takes up a Chinese rifle, and slams it onto the press table. Then he does the same with another made in Russia. Then he takes a box of Czech ammunition and empties it in front of the chagrined reporter. "No sir, Mr. Beckworth. It doesn't take a lead weight to fall on me or a hit from one of those weapons to recognize that what's involved here is communist domination of the world."

If the film was careful to point out the high security stake for America in the Vietnam war, it was also careful to show that the enemy was utterly ruthless. In response to a question by another unconvinced reporter, Sergeant McGee, a battle-hardened black veteran, described the Vietcong's campaign of terror. "As soldiers, Miss

Sutton, we can understand the killing of the military. But the exter-
mination of the civilian leadership, the intentional murder and torture of innocent women and children . . ." He is rudely interrupted
by the reporter: "Yes, I guess horrible things happen in war, but that
doesn't mean to say that they need us or even want us." McGee looks
away from the hopelessly naive representatives of the press to the
wider audience of everyday Americans.

> I'll try to answer that question for you. Let me put it in terms we all can
> understand. If this same thing happened here in the United States,
> every mayor in every city would be murdered, every teacher that you've
> ever known would be tortured and killed, every professor you've ever
> heard of, every governor, every Senator, every member of the House
> of Representatives and their combined families all would be tortured
> and killed. And a like number kidnapped. But in spite of this, there's
> always some little fellow out there willing to stand up and take the place
> of those that have been decimated. They need us, Miss Sutton, and they
> want us.

During the film we learn that the Vietcong dip their booby-trap spikes
in poison, that they have brutally tortured an old village chief and
murdered his tiny granddaughter, and that they have killed a medical
officer who was delivering a baby in a nearby village. They are reported to have disemboweled another chief's teenage daughters and
made him watch as forty of them first raped his wife and then broke
all her bones with a steel rod—this last story, John Wayne said, was
told to him by General Stilwell.

The Green Berets inevitably called up memories of World War II in
the Pacific; John Wayne's presence alone probably had that effect for
the millions who remembered his heroic film exploits against the
Japanese in the 1940s. The sneaky Asians hiding behind every tree,
the grim humor of brave American boys in action, the way they be-
friended the liberty-loving natives and especially the children—all
were calculated to reawaken memories of stirring war films from a
quarter century before. The selfless courage under fire, the daring,
the grasp our men possessed of the values that were being contested
and tried there, the unashamed patriotism—all conveyed the message
that this war, too, was a worthy one, that the boys who fought it, so
far away from home, deserved the support, the sacrifices, the admiration, the gratitude of the American people. *The Green Berets*, which
was based on a popular novel by Robin Moore and which incorpo-
rated a well-known song, "The Ballad of the Green Berets," was

panned universally by the critics. It didn't matter. Millions of Americans loved it and were assured by it and flocked to see it; the picture grossed a handsome $11 million.

IV.

Although President Kennedy and his advisers understood both the growing complexity of the Vietnam situation and the mounting political stake at home, Vietnam was nevertheless not very high on the list of White House concerns during the Kennedy years. In the end, the administration chose neither full military involvement nor complete withdrawal. Seeing the Vietnam conflict as one battlefield in a worldwide struggle of immense importance, persuaded by the arguments of those who advocated firmness and commitment, Kennedy chose to increase American participation in what General Taylor called "a limited partnership" with the Diem regime. The terms of the partnership were straightforward: America would supply money, weapons, and some personnel in order to prevent a Communist victory in South Vietnam, and the Diem government would consolidate its power, vigorously oppose the Vietcong in the field, and institute much-needed programs of social, economic, and political reform.

There were 948 American servicemen in Vietnam in November 1961. The Kennedy administration tried desperately to keep that number low, sending, instead of men, millions of dollars worth of weapons and equipment. Not even America's most advanced military technology, however, could stop the progress of the Vietcong. By mid-1962, as part of a general buildup, there were more than five thousand American fighting men in South Vietnam, functioning mostly as advisers and pilots, but no increase seemed sufficient to turn the tide. Not even the "strategic hamlets" program, the forced relocation of South Vietnamese peasants into fortified villages, showed much success. By the end of 1962 Kennedy had committed more than eleven thousand military personnel, and by the time of his death, eleven months later, the total stood at better than sixteen thousand.

Meanwhile, President Diem dismissed every proposal for democratic reform. Trusting entirely in his iron-fisted brother, Ngo Dinh Nhu, and in his sister-in-law, the tactless and arrogant Madame Nhu, Diem turned his face against any liberalization of the regime. Certain that Washington would be unable to find an alternative to himself, Diem tightened his dictatorial control. Finally, the actions of the Buddhists in the spring and summer of 1963 and the violent repression by the Diem government brought the dictator's downfall. On May 8,

Diem's soldiers in Hue fired into a crowd that was protesting the government's recent order against displaying the Buddhist flag. On June 11, in one of those ghastly pictures from Vietnam that etched itself indelibly in the consciousness of Americans, a Buddhist monk in Saigon calmly seated himself in the street, poured gasoline over his body, and set himself on fire. In the next weeks, half a dozen other monks followed his example in order to dramatize their moral opposition to the government. At the end of August Diem's own special forces attacked Buddhist pagodas in cities throughout South Vietnam and arrested hundreds of monks. The country erupted in protest, much of it by university students. After eight years of quite substantial support for him, American officials began to regard Diem as a liability. When some South Vietnamese generals proposed a coup, the United States government acquiesced. On November 1 Diem was deposed; he and his brother were murdered; and a military junta headed by General Duong Van Minh came to power. Three weeks later the president of the United States was assassinated in Dallas, Texas.

During his first weeks in office, therefore, President Johnson faced a double problem regarding the formulation of a Vietnam policy. On the field, that embattled country was at the edge of chaos. The despotic but stable Diem regime was replaced by one that was despotic but unstable. In three months General Minh was deposed by another general, Nguyen Khanh; six months after that and Khanh's own Deputy Premier would be calling publicly for him to resign. Meanwhile, even usually optimistic American officials were conceding that the enemy controlled more than half the territory of South Vietnam. (A report of April 1964 estimated that the Khanh government controlled 34 percent of South Vietnam's villages; the Communists had 42 percent; and the remaining 24 percent were neutral.) South Vietnamese opposition to the war was growing as well, with Buddhist activists, students, editors, intellectuals, teachers, and politicians calling for a negotiated settlement, the "neutralization" of Vietnam in East-West politics, and a return to the Geneva Accords. American officials had some serious doubts by early 1964 about the ability and the will of the people of South Vietnam to resist the Communist threat.

At the same time, the new president confronted some stark political realities that plainly limited his choices in Vietnam. Like all presidents who come to office in the way he had, Johnson had tried to calm the nervous nation by pledging to continue the policies of his fallen predecessor. For the Democrats to enter the coming election, less than a year away, bearing the burden of a clear humiliation in Vietnam would be disastrous. Who had forgotten the howls of outrage the Republicans had hurled at Johnson's party over the loss of China only three elections before? Even if Johnson wished not to be encumbered by Vietnam, wanting desperately to be able to focus on his ambitious program of economic reform and civil rights, could the nation, having come this far, simply turn its back and leave? And if this brew of domestic factors was not complicated enough, Johnson had also to consider a growing public uneasiness over the war. A restiveness long discernible among our allies and at the United Nations was now becoming increasingly audible in the American population at large.

The Republicans' nomination of Senator Barry Goldwater, the strident, bellicose, and unpredictable conservative from Arizona, determined President Johnson's Vietnam strategy. In order to avoid the anticipated charges of capitulation to the Communists, the president rejected calls for a negotiated settlement of the war ("We do not believe in conferences called to ratify terror"). Ten days after the Goldwater nomination, moreover, Johnson increased American troop strength 30 percent, from sixteen thousand to twenty-one thousand advisers. At the same time, Johnson was careful to portray himself as the moderate, the man of reason in contrast to his warlike and irresponsible opponent. He wanted "no wider war," he said, and did not favor getting "tied down in a land war in Asia." He insisted that "Asian boys," not American boys, would have to determine the final outcome in Vietnam.

An episode that occurred in the middle of the presidential campaign of 1964 was destined to assume considerable importance in the debate over Vietnam. According to the government, on August 1 and 4 North Vietnamese patrol boats launched two unprovoked attacks on American destroyers in the Gulf of Tonkin. According to Hanoi, the first attack occurred because the *USS Maddox*, an intelligence gathering ship, had helped South Vietnamese troops conduct a raid on offshore North Vietnamese islands the night before. Hanoi claimed that the second attack never happened. Although some historians have given more credit to the North Vietnam version than to the American, neither Johnson nor the public was in a mood to temporize. Within hours of the second (disputed) attack, the United States launched air strikes against the North, destroying twenty-five patrol boats and some oil storage facilities. The administration also used the occasion to push through Congress the so-called Gulf of Tonkin Resolution. It stated that "the Congress approves and supports the determination of the President . . . to take all necessary measures to repel any armed attack against the forces of the United States and to prevent further aggression." It also declared that the nation was ready "to take all necessary steps, including the use of armed force," to protect the security of the region. After a perfunctory debate, the Senate passed the Resolution by a vote of 88–2 (only Ernest Gruening of Alaska and Wayne Morse of Oregon dissenting); the House talked about it for forty minutes and passed the declaration unanimously. It was as close as the United States Congress ever came to declaring war.

The election was a resounding victory for the Democrats, and the Johnson administration now turned its attention to a Vietnamese situation that was deteriorating with stunning rapidity. The Saigon government was in complete chaos. During the last months of 1964 and the first months of 1965, South Vietnam underwent a bewildering series of governmental changes, coups, and attempted coups. National leadership changed almost monthly. Ambitious generals vied with one another for power. Buddhist activists, using language that could only be called anti-American, stepped up their demonstrations and demanded immediate negotiations to end the war. Mobs stormed United States Information Service Libraries in Saigon and Hue. Meanwhile Catholics and others who favored fighting on tried, by diverse expedients and compromises, to ride out the storm. Interspersed among the various idealists were large numbers of frank opportunists motivated by personal ambition. Washington feared that a South Vietnamese government might emerge that would actually enter into negotiations with the Vietcong and ask the United States to leave the country. Meanwhile, the military situation grew ever more untenable. Maxwell Taylor had reported to the president as early as September 1964 that Saigon controlled only 30 percent of the territory of South Vietnam. The Vietcong were increasing their numbers every week, and every week the desertion problem in the South Vietnamese army grew more obvious and embarrassing. In August fully organized regular units of the North Vietnamese army began moving southward across the seventeenth parallel.

Johnson's response to this panorama of confusion and danger was to escalate the war. On February 7, 1965, he ordered bombing raids against the North in retaliation for a guerrilla attack on an American barracks that left eight GIs dead. Rejecting urgent calls for negotiations—from the Soviet Union, from France, from the United Nations, from significant elements within the civilian population of South Vietnam itself, and from increasing numbers of anxious Americans—the administration stepped up the pressure. By the end of February American planes were conducting daily runs against enemy targets in the South, and in the first week of March regular bombing of the North began without any pretense of being carried out in retaliation for Communist acts. During the same week, two battalions of marines arrived to provide security for the American airbase at Da-

nang: the first American combat troops in Asia since the Korean war.
A month later another twenty thousand marines were authorized for
Vietnam duty, and now all marines were cleared for offensive as well
as defensive missions. A few weeks after that forty thousand more
troops were approved. Finally, at the end of July 1965, after extensive
high level conferences, President Johnson announced that the United
States would increase its strength there to one hundred twenty-five
thousand men and that additional men would be sent at the request
of General William Westmoreland, the American commander in the
field. By the autumn of 1965, therefore, few could doubt that Vietnam was now an American war, not an Asian one in which Americans
were assisting.

Escalation required frequent justification by the president and his
spokesmen, and they responded by repeating the litany. Again and
again they insisted, without using the term itself, that the conditions
of "the just war" had been satisfied: the national security was endangered by ambitious aggressors; the enemies in Vietnam were immoral
criminals; and the clear duty was to fight. Both America's safety and
the nation's commitment to the principles of freedom were at stake.
In a news conference in April 1965 the president succinctly summarized, once again, the reasons for American participation in the Vietnam war:

> Independent South Viet-Nam has been attacked by North Viet-Nam.
> The object of that attack is conquest. Defeat in South Viet-Nam would
> be to deliver a friendly nation to terror and repression. It would en-
> courage and spur on those who seek to conquer all free nations within
> their reach. Our own welfare and our own freedom would be in dan-
> ger. This is the clearest lesson of our time. From Munich until today we
> have learned that to yield to aggression brings only greater threats—
> and more destructive war. To stand firm is the only guarantee of last-
> ing peace.

And yet, somehow, this time the message failed to convince completely. This time, for some reason, hundreds of thousands of American citizens—including many who had risen in support of these arguments since the late 1930s—found themselves uneasy over their
country's massive military presence in Southeast Asia. As the months
passed, instead of diminishing, the uneasiness grew.

3: THE CONTENTIONS

How Americans Disagreed about the War and Destroyed

the Consensus

I.

The central contention of those Americans who first decried participation in the Vietnam war was that it was immoral. This belief—that in Vietnam the United States was using its immense power in ways inconsistent with the principles, the values, the ethical standards of the American people—was at the core of the resistance to the whole enterprise. These moral reservations were particularly evident in the very earliest part of the debate, but even after other beliefs and arguments came to assume prominent places in the case being presented against the war, the nagging moral qualms of numerous citizens continued to play a crucial part in their criticism of American policy.

Of course there have always been some who have automatically opposed every war on moral grounds. They come to this position out of deeply held social principles or out of strong philosophic or religious beliefs. For them there is no such thing as a "just" war; for them the organized slaughter of other human beings is an intolerable affront to every moral principle, an assault upon the most fundamental of Christian teachings, a way of addressing disputes that is so barbaric and unjust that decent men and women must always and resolutely refuse to assent to it. Such antiwar activists have been present in American history at least since the end of the War of 1812 and, in the case of the Quakers, much longer than that. But if they have made their presence felt in each American conflict, their record in actually deterring their nation from international violence (as must be obvious to any student of the American past) has been mixed at best. In general, those who have opposed warfare on moral grounds, who stubbornly appealed to the better angels of our nature, were efficiently brushed aside whenever the emotions of American nationalism were fully aroused.

And if the whole career of American pacifism was marked by disappointment and feelings of futility, the peace movement suffered an especially difficult time right after World War II. The work of the Fascists persuaded many Americans that fighting, however regrettable, might sometimes be both necessary and moral. Men like Hitler and Mussolini had ways of making the advice of uncompromising pacifists seem naive, cowardly, and unwise; even before the bombs fell on Pearl Harbor, most members of the peace movement had abandoned rigid pacifism. Then, during the early 1950s, with another war raging in Korea, pacifists found themselves being battered by anti-Communist militants. Under the stinging attacks of Senator Joseph McCarthy and others, those working for world peace came to be regarded by many of their fellow citizens as men and women who were either unwittingly playing right into the Communists' hands or, even worse, taking their orders directly from the Kremlin itself.

Despite these setbacks, however, the peace movement had somehow revived by the early 1960s. The terrifying prospect of nuclear annihilation, the weariness with so many years of Cold War, the eroding faith in the government's ever-increasing reliance on military deterrence, and a new hopefulness about the United Nations or about winning over Soviet cooperation for a more harmonious world led many to enlist in efforts to bring about peace. These activists campaigned for an end to nuclear testing, for disarmament and a reduction of international tensions, for a strengthened system of world government. Meeting with a more favorable public response than might have been expected, they were emboldened. Older groups (such as the Fellowship of Reconciliation, founded by Quakers and others at the outbreak of World War I, or the Women's International League for Peace and Freedom) were revitalized. New organizations were formed: in 1957, both the Committee for Nonviolent Action and the National Committee for a SANE Nuclear Policy; in 1959, the Student Peace Union; in 1960, the Committee of Correspondence; in 1961, both the Women's Strike for Peace and the umbrella coordinating organization, Turn Toward Peace. These groups demonstrated, lobbied, wrote and distributed pamphlets, and worked for sympathetic candidates. Not surprisingly, those citizens who, on the basis of moral principle, rejected all warfare as an instrument of policy were among the first to register their objections to the beginnings of American involvement in Southeast Asia.

Whatever one might think of their general indictment of the folly, injustice, and immorality of war, these peace activists did not make the most effective moral appeal to an American public weighing the matter of Vietnam. The most telling accusations were leveled, not by those who condemned all wars on moral grounds, but by those who were revolted by this one in particular. Some of those protesting the morality of the Vietnam war might very well have registered similar reservations about all warfare, but most could conceive of wars, such as World War II, which they could have supported with a clear conscience. Against *this* war, however, they harbored special moral objections, and those objections clustered about three separate, but related, issues.

First, there was the matter of the war's legality. Not every legal war is moral, of course. It is possible to imagine a conflict in which all of the prescriptions of international law are scrupulously observed but which nevertheless fails to gain the approval of the consciences of mankind. But the reverse is not true. A war that is not legal, no matter how scrupulously it is conducted, is spoiled from the start, can never be morally justifiable. In one of the most intricately argued aspects of the entire Vietnam debate, experts on both sides of the question of American intervention battled over the legal issues. Those contending that the war in Vietnam was unlawful argued from two perspectives. On the one hand, they criticized American behavior with respect to an external standard: the government's policy in Vietnam, they said, failed to conform to accepted requirements of international law. On the other hand, they denounced American intervention by an internal measurement: the war, they asserted, failed to adhere to the demands of the Constitution.

According to these experts the United States had clearly violated international law by breaching the Geneva Accords of 1954. Respecting those agreements, it will be recalled, America pledged to "refrain from the threat or the use of force to disturb them," adding that the nation would "view any renewal of the aggression in violation of the aforesaid Agreements with grave concern and as seriously threatening international peace and security." Yet was it not perfectly plain that America had, from the outset, chosen to treat South Vietnam as an independent nation despite the firm insistence at Geneva that, as Article 6 of the Final Declaration stated, the line between north and south "is provisional and should not in any way be interpreted as constituting a political or territorial boundary"? Did not Article 4 prohibit "the introduction into Viet Nam of foreign troops and military personnel as well as of all kinds of arms and munitions"? Did not Article 5 stipulate that "no military base under the control of a foreign State may be established in the regrouping zones of the two parties"? Finally, did not Article 7 of the Final Declaration require that "general elections shall be held in July 1956"?

If the antiwar experts in international law placed primary emphasis on apparent violations of the Geneva Accords, they also stressed discrepancies between American policy and the United Nations Charter. Article 2 of that charter pledged that "all Members shall refrain in their international relations from the threat or use of force against the territorial integrity or political independence of any state, or in any other manner inconsistent with the Purposes of the United Nations." Critics also charged that American activities in Vietnam violated other sections of the U.N. Charter. Supporters of American policy, for example, pointed to Article 51, which permitted "the inherent right of individual or collective self-defense if an armed attack occurs against a Member of the United Nations." But critics protested that the charter required, in Article 53, that such use of force had to be previously authorized by the Security Council (which had never done so in the case of Vietnam) and that, in any event, neither North nor South Vietnam was "a Member" of the organization. In addition, they noted, Article 33 required that "the parties to any dispute, the continuance of which is likely to endanger the maintenance of international peace and security, shall, first of all, seek a solution by negotiation, enquiry, mediation, conciliation, arbitration, judicial settlement, resort to regional agencies or arrangements, or other peaceful means of their own choice." The international lawyers who opposed American policy in Vietnam pointed out that the government had never seriously explored any of these options.

A final battle was over the provisions of the South East Asia Treaty Organization (SEATO) agreement. Proponents of American involvement placed considerable weight on the obligation to intervene under the terms of that collective security pact; but critics countered, first, that such action required unanimity among the eight nations involved; second, that even if warranted, military action could not be taken in violation of the U.N. Charter, which required previous Security Council authorization; and, third, that in any case, the United States was not legally bound to respond with force. In short, critics alleged, the American government was acting illegally not only with respect to the Geneva Accords and the U.N. Charter, but also under the terms of the SEATO Treaty itself, the instrument under which it was pretending to be behaving lawfully. Wayne Morse of Oregon, one of the two senators who had voted against the Tonkin Gulf Resolution in 1964, was a former law professor and dean of the law school at the University of Oregon. "Some of my colleagues in the Senate and some members of the administration are not happy when I call my country an outlaw nation for its violations of international law in southeast Asia," he said in a Senate speech on February 3, 1966. "But we have convicted ourselves by our own illegal acts."

Beyond offering the gruff assertion that "we just don't *belong* there," most citizens who opposed the war probably never explored very deeply the complicated arguments of these legal authorities. Americans, after all, have never shown much patience for the niceties, restrictions, or abstractions of international law. Far more immediate and disturbing was the contention that those who prosecuted the war were doing so in violation of the nation's own fundamental law. Article I, Section 8, of the Constitution assigns to the Congress the power to declare war. That provision was intended to insure that under the American system of government a single person could not make a war; it was also intended to guarantee that a matter so momentous as war or peace would not be decided, except in the case of an emergency, without full public consideration, open debate, and a vote of the people's representatives. While it is true, critics of the war admitted, that the president is "the commander in chief" of the armed forces, that position does not include the authority to commit the country to a full-scale war single-handedly. The persistent refusal of the executive branch to ask for a formal declaration of war threw the Vietnam war into serious moral and legal doubt. To Senator George McGovern, writing in 1971, the usurpations by the presidency in these matters amounted "to an affront to the Constitution without equal in this century."

Opponents of the war rejected the rejoinder that Congress might have its say at any time simply by withholding funds for the continuation of the fighting. The hands of Congress, they argued, were tied. With American boys facing death in a foreign land, not even the harshest of the antiwar congressmen could, in conscience, deny them the resources required to defend themselves, even had such congressmen been willing to withstand the strictly political consequences of such a stand. Critics also rejected the argument that Congress had given its authorization for the war by passing the Gulf of Tonkin Resolution in August 1964, somehow approving by that act the tremendous escalation that occurred after 1965. The resolution appears to give a blank check to the president "to take all necessary measures." But that check was given to Lyndon Johnson in the midst of a campaign in which his was the moderating voice. "If laws are to be interpreted in the light of their legislative history," wrote the influential columnist Walter Lippmann, "the President is without legal and moral authority to fill in the blank check of August 1964, with whatever he thinks he ought to do in 1966." By 1968 the moral stature of the Gulf of Tonkin Resolution was further undermined as revelations about the actual incidents on the high seas emerged to contradict official accounts and as a number of individual senators and representatives who had voted for it expressed their dismay at what it had been used to permit.

II.

If the first ground for moral uneasiness about American intervention in Vietnam was doubt about the lawfulness of the enterprise, the second was closely related to this question of the war's legality. Many Americans wondered if their nation was not, in fact, engaged in the unsavory business of propping up a Saigon government that was under a more or less justifiable attack by its own people. Was this, as American leaders kept insisting, a plain case of aggression from the North, or was America merely meddling in a civil war that was none of its business? No question in the entire debate over Vietnam was more hotly disputed than this one because both sides could see that the moral authority of the undertaking depended directly upon what was believed. To opponents of the war the issues seemed clear cut. Insofar as the fighting involved northerners against southerners, they observed, all the participants were, after all, Vietnamese, members of a single nation both under the terms of the Geneva Accords and by the long, indisputable tradition of their history. Insofar as the fighting centered in the South, opponents of American policy contended, it was an indigenous uprising of ordinary men and women against a tyrannical and corrupt government that had, with American complicity, manufactured a nation of South Vietnam in order to rule over it. Infiltration from the North, they insisted, had not been an important factor until *after* the elections of 1956 had been called off and massive military aid from America threatened to overwhelm those fighting for their liberty against their rulers.

This issue—invasion or civil war—was directly related to the matter of legality because under international law the requirements for intervening in a civil war were quite different from those governing a conflict between two independent nations. In the former case, the central thrust of the legal authorities was to emphasize the private nature of the quarrel and to discourage the interference of outsiders. In the latter, when two independent countries were at war, any third nation could freely conclude a lawful alliance with either party in the normal way and come to the aid of its ally if asked. (This distinction was well understood by President Lincoln and the North a century before: by insisting that the conflict was merely a "rebellion," an "uprising" of disloyal citizens, Lincoln hoped to discourage European nations from entering into alliances with the Confederacy as if it were actually an independent nation.) To the opponents of the Vietnam war, the struggle in South Vietnam bore all the signs of a civil war caused by prodigious discontent with the Saigon government. And they were quick to assert that there was much about that government that might very well provoke an honest rebellion of angry citizens.

In fact, throughout the Vietnam controversy, those Americans who opposed the war had no more effective allies than the string of corrupt, ineffective, arrogant, stubborn leaders of South Vietnam who paraded across the stage like so many figures from some comic opera. In the beginning were Diem and the members of his family. A month before their downfall the respected reporter Stanley Karnow, who knew them all personally, described them in the generally conservative and widely read *Saturday Evening Post* as "a cross between the Borgias and the Bourbons. Narrow, devious, obstinate and imperious, they have functioned in an atmosphere of neurotic and sanctimonious egotism. They have plotted against their rivals, and played their own subordinates off against one another. They have preached puritanism but tolerated corruption, extolled democracy yet rigged elections, and jailed at least 30,000 political prisoners in 're-education' camps." The contempt for civil liberties, the merciless crackdown on dissent, the persecution of the Buddhists by a powerful Catholic family (Diem's elder brother was an archbishop), the whimsical royal decrees (banning the use of contraceptives, prohibiting divorce, gambling, or dancing in public), the heavy taxation—all were well known among the American reading public, and it did not require high imagination to believe that many South Vietnamese, including many non-Communists, would not particularly mind a change of government.

The period between the fall of Diem (November 1963) and the summer of 1965, the period of whirlwind changes among the petty schemers who laid claim, one after the other, to be leaders of South Vietnam, did nothing to establish confidence in the representative nature of the government America was defending. Then, in June 1965 there arose from the shadows of intrigue two career military officers who shared power in an uneasy competition with one another (the *Nation* referred to "the rivalry of puppets") until the end of the American presence in Vietnam. Nguyen Cao Ky, who himself had been born in the north, was the head of the air force; Nguyen Van Thieu, who had fought for the French until Dienbienphu, was an infantry commander who had helped to topple Diem. Both men were experienced in the Saigon world of plot and counterplot. Ky, decked out in his special uniform—a flying suit with a purple scarf and an ivory-handled pistol—professed a certain admiration for Hitler and earned a reputation for personal bad habits. Thieu was a steadier commodity, level-headed and efficient, if colorless. William Bundy, a presidential adviser, remembered that the pair "seemed to all of us the bottom of the barrel, absolutely the bottom of the barrel." Soon persistent rumors connected both men and their relatives with corruption and bribery, trafficking in narcotics, and the gross mishandling of American aid. "If we are defending liberty in South Vietnam," observed the well-known antiwar economist John Kenneth Galbraith, "the government must have some of the attributes of democracy as Americans understand it. A military junta fits badly into the picture."

In early 1966 major uprisings against the Ky government erupted in leading South Vietnam cities, strengthening the position of those Americans who were arguing that what was happening there was far closer to a civil war than it was to an invasion. Led by Buddhists, the demonstrations and riots were quickly joined by students, workers, intellectuals, Catholics, and even a few army officers. The protesters voiced even more harshly anti-American sentiments than usual, and a mob burned the United States consulate in Hue. The lead editorial in the antiwar *Christian Century* noted the internal turmoil:

> We can no longer lean on the ever fragile argument that we are in Vietnam because a freedom-loving people summoned us to their aid. . . . This illusion has now been thoroughly demolished by the anti-American demonstrations in Danang, Hue and Saigon, by proliferating "Yankee go home" signs in all parts of South Vietnam, by Buddhist demands for a South Vietnamese government which is something more than a puppet of the United States.

The unending instability of South Vietnamese politics—punctuated as they were by violent riots, anti-American demonstrations, self-immolations, hunger strikes, and civil disobedience—seemed to indicate that the people were in the throes of a serious internal squabble, a family quarrel, a civil war. American policy also appeared to be designed to sustain the hands of those whom the *Christian Century* styled "despised military dictators." That numerous Americans found such work to be morally indefensible will not be surprising.

Some Americans, therefore, thought that participation in the Vietnam war was immoral because of what seemed to be a dubious legal standing, both under international law and under the provisions of the federal Constitution. If an illegal war is automatically an unjust one, they argued, then the American presence in Vietnam was without the necessary moral sanction. Others condemned the war because it seemed to be an immoral effort to preserve a corrupt government, a government that had lost the confidence of its own people. How could Americans justify asking their young men to kill and to be killed in order to crush a rebellion of angry citizens, a rebellion, moreover, that seemed to many Americans not entirely unreasonable given the nature of the Saigon leadership? But whether reasonable or not, it was a rebellion that was clearly in the nature of a civil war and not the proper business of the American people. Waging war for such a purpose was not right.

But most Americans who opposed the war in Vietnam on moral grounds had a third reason. It was the nature of the fighting itself.

III.

The combat in Vietnam was reported at greater length, in more agonizing detail, and with more graphic words and stunning pictures than any war in human history. By 1963 the major television networks had full-time crews in Vietnam, and leading newspapers and magazines had stationed some of their most experienced reporters there. Before long eyewitness accounts from individual soldiers, from foreign observers, from government officials, celebrities, and antiwar activists were added to the flood of words and images that came pouring back to the United States from the field. Not all of that reportage was negative. Much of it, especially in the early years, emphasized the valor of the nation's fighting men and the hardships they were facing; as late as 1967 a Lou Harris poll for *Newsweek* reported that 64 percent of the American people believed that television coverage of the combat made them support the war more. The years ahead were to witness a steady erosion of that support as the dinnertime reports from the battleground wore steadily away at the sensitivities and patience of the people back home.

The American public was suddenly introduced to an awesome collection of ferocious weapons being brought to bear by the country's war machine: M-16 rifles that barked out a hundred rounds of ammunition each minute; 175mm artillery pieces that could lob their shells eighteen miles; aerial reconnaissance labs, equipped with infrared sensors that detected heat; computer-guided artillery and laser-guided bombs and see-in-the-dark radar; huge tractors and bull-dozers that efficiently cleared away forests. One plane, the AC47, called by the men "Puff the Magic Dragon," could slowly circle a target and fire eighteen thousand rounds per minute into it (a football field could be covered, one bullet into each square foot, in about three seconds). Flamethrowers, tanks, thousands of helicopters of various kinds, automatic grenade launchers, the most advanced communication and transport equipment in the world—all comprised a fearful array of death-dealing machinery. Just offshore steamed an immense armada manned, at its height, by seventy thousand men: aircraft carriers; destroyers and cruisers that each month hurled one hundred thousand five or eight inch projectiles at onshore targets; mine sweepers; amphibious assault ships; a battleship that, for four months in 1968, fired its sixteen-inch guns night and day into North Vietnam; even a fleet of one hundred eighty river patrol boats that operated on Vietnam's inland waterways.

Americans have always been proud of their know-how, their ability to apply scientific ingenuity and industrial methods to special problems, to find the right tools to do the job. To some, however, this particular exercise of national prowess seemed a little unclean, a little perverse, somehow unworthy of a great and principled nation. To these citizens it appeared as if their country, the wealthiest and most technologically sophisticated on the planet, had launched a furious war of destruction upon a primitive, peasant, essentially agricultural society. And some tactics and weapons came under such special condemnation that, for those who opposed the war on moral grounds, their continued use attained a kind of grotesque symbolic meaning.

No tactic was more widely debated or roundly criticized by antiwar spokesmen than aerial bombing. Raining death from the skies is such an imprecise art—the bombs always kill mothers and infants and frail old men as well as enemy soldiers; they inevitably destroy schools and hospitals and homes as well as legitimate military targets—that the practice has always carried a heavy moral burden. It will be recalled that President Roosevelt denounced the Fascists on this very point in his Quarantine Address of 1937: "Without a declaration of war and without warning or justification of any kind," he said, "civilians, including vast numbers of women and children, are being ruthlessly murdered by bombs from the air." Now America was doing it. And with what abandon. Neil Sheehan, former head of the United Press International Saigon bureau and then a Saigon reporter for the *New York Times*, calculated that "over the seven years from 1965, when sustained bombing raids against North Vietnam began, to the end of 1971, the United States dropped 6,300,000 tons of bombs and other aerial munitions on Indochina. This fact means that our country has loosed upon a region about the size of Texas three times the total tonnage of bombs dropped on Europe, Africa, and Asia during

World War II." An F-4 Phantom manned by two Americans, carried fourteen thousand pounds of explosives; a B-52 Stratofortress, manned by six, could drop more than a hundred five-hundred-pound bombs on each of its missions. The moral irony of the bombing was obvious whenever it was remembered that almost two-thirds of the total tonnage was dropped on South Vietnam itself, a country the United States was not attacking, after all, but defending.

Opponents of the war also condemned on moral grounds the kinds of bombs being used. Many of them were so-called anti-personnel weapons, engineered not to destroy buildings or other installations (which, in fact, some of these bombs could not do at all) but to kill people on the ground. Cluster bombs consisted of perhaps six hundred small "bomblets" (called "Pineapples" or "Guavas" because of their shapes). The casing blew open above ground, distributing the bomblets over a wide area; each bomblet then burst open, shooting two hundred fifty to three hundred fierce projectiles—shaped like nails or slivers or darts or balls—in all directions. Some of the bomblets were timed so as to delay their explosions in order to catch those rushing into the area to help the wounded. The United States also used "earthquake" bombs, mostly to clear landing areas for helicopters in the jungle, but also sometimes against people. They weighed seven tons each and were fixed to explode just before reaching the ground; they left no actual crater in the earth, but each of them could uproot trees for three hundred feet in every direction. Their shock waves annihilated all the plant, animal, and human life within ten times that radius.

Americans also developed and dropped from planes a wide range of chemical and biological agents that defoliated forests (so the Vietcong would have a harder time hiding), ruined crops (so that their food supply could be disrupted), and had severe toxic effects on human beings. The notorious Agent Orange was just one of these chemical herbicides, but it received special attention because large numbers of American fighting men who were exposed to it complained bitterly, afterwards, of suffering serious health problems. Sprayed onto forests, it entered into the plants, soil, and water. Approximately one-seventh of the land area of South Vietnam was subjected to these chemical weapons. Severe ecological damage was also caused by craters from five-hundred and seven-hundred-fifty pound bombs dropped from B-52s. These craters could be thirty feet deep and forty-five feet in diameter; they ruined the soil, caused erosion that severely hampered agriculture, and filled with water that provided breeding grounds for vermin. In South Vietnam alone there were perhaps ten million such craters.

No weapon used in Vietnam provoked more moral outrage, both among some Americans and among the citizenry of many other countries, than napalm. Jellied petroleum mixed with white phosphorus, it was packed into canisters and dropped from low flying planes. Upon impact the napalm, ignited by the phosphorus, covered up to a hundred feet in a withering fire storm that burned for several minutes at thousands of degrees Fahrenheit. When it splattered onto a human being it burned away whatever flesh it touched. It was extremely sticky so that when a panic-stricken victim tried to brush it off, he or she only spread it to other parts of the body. Napalm burned so intensely, moreover, that it consumed the available oxygen and produced carbon monoxide, and many who were not killed by burning died from asphyxiation. Those who survived the first few seconds might be poisoned by the phosphorus, which attacked the kidneys, liver, and nervous system. Those whom the napalm touched but did not kill were doomed to be horribly disfigured for the rest of their lives. Napalm had been used during World War II, principally in flamethrowers, and to a greater extent during the Korean war, but the United States may have dropped as much as four hundred million pounds of the substance on Vietnam between 1965 and 1972.

And if American weaponry disfigured many individual Vietnamese, other features of the American war effort disfigured the landscape and the society. Not only defoliation and cratering and the destruction of crops and homes and whole villages, but large scale disruptions of a stable, rural, peasant society also occurred. From a nation in which 85 or 90 percent of the people lived on the land, Vietnam became one in which suddenly 40 or 50 percent lived in cities of twenty thousand or more. Some were driven into terrible slums by the destruction of the countryside, by the desire to escape the bombs and the armies as the fighting rolled into their neighborhoods; some were herded into miserable, overcrowded "strategic hamlets" by forced relocation programs. Many were lured by the seductive opportunities opened by the introduction of millions and millions of American dollars. Thousands of young women became prostitutes. Other Vietnamese found places in the black market or in the drug trade or in the large-scale business of pilfering American supplies. Many performed menial labor, catering to the needs of the GIs in a dozen demeaning ways: cutting their hair, running their errands, procuring their women, doing their laundry.

The war required the intrusion upon a rural landscape of massive construction projects: warehouses for supplies, huge tank farms to store the fuel for planes and tanks and jeeps, barracks by the hundreds, military bases and airfields, pier and wharf facilities, thousands of stark concrete buildings for every purpose from housing radar to housing officers' clubs, huge power plants to generate the electricity for air conditioning and computers and food storage. Also, the staggering rate of inflation (in 1966 the money supply in Vietnam rose by 72 percent), the invasion of new consumer goods such as motorcycles and stereos, the substantial disruption of education, and the entrance of new habits and techniques and social relationships created entirely new patterns of life. Who among the various experts running the war, the critics asked, worried about the permanent effects of these things upon the economy, the institutions, the families, the culture of the people America had come to save?

Senator J. William Fulbright, the Arkansas Democrat and chair of the Senate Foreign Relations Committee, was a friend of Lyndon Johnson. He feared and distrusted the Communists, Soviet and Chinese alike. He believed in containment and gave support to the French in Indochina and to Diem in South Vietnam. He had shepherded the Gulf of Tonkin resolution smoothly through the Senate in 1964. By the end of 1965, however, William Fulbright had turned against the war, and although his conversion was largely on the basis of practical considerations, he demonstrated an acute awareness of the moral complaints of the dissenters. "There was always something about this war that has gone against the American grain," he noted in 1968. "The dissent was not born of something alien to American life and experience: it was born of traditional American ideas about decency and fair play and the sanctity of life."

Those supporting the war possessed a powerful master-symbol from World War II days: the example of "Munich," they repeated again and again, demonstrated the folly of appeasement, withdrawal, and passivity. Those opposing the war on moral grounds also appropriated a symbol from World War II: it was "Nuremberg." The trials for "war crimes" and for "crimes against humanity" that took place in that German city after the Nazi surrender seemed all too relevant to critics of the Vietnam war. Then the Allies tried, imprisoned, and hanged Nazi leaders for acts that were so brutal that the conscience of the civilized world cried out for justice. Now, it seemed to some Americans, a similar cruelty was being loosed upon the innocent by their own country, and a lively debate on the applicability of the Nuremberg precedent erupted. It ranged from an entire book, *Nuremberg and Vietnam: An American Tragedy*, written in 1970 by Telford Taylor, the Chief United States Counsel at Nuremberg, and ran the gamut of articles from James Reston, Jr.'s, "Is Nuremberg Coming Back to Haunt Us?" to Townsend Hoopes's "The Nuremberg Suggestion," to A. Frank Reel's "Must We Hang Nixon Too?" to Richard

Falk's "Ecocide, Genocide, and the Nuremberg Tradition of Individual Responsibility." Few commentators, no matter how vehemently they opposed the war, equated the American government with the Nazi war criminals, but the very fact that such a discussion was held was a measure of the moral unease that antiwar critics felt over the Vietnam war.

IV.

As powerful as the legal and ethical indictment against American behavior in Vietnam was, it did not entirely exhaust the moral reservations about the war harbored by some of its opponents. A whole class of moral criticism involved not the legal justifications for the war or the means of waging it, but the moral cost of Vietnam to the American people themselves. What were going to be the long-term consequences for a democratic society of the incessant exposure—whether directly, in the case of fighting men, or indirectly, in the case of everyday Americans safe at home—to such destruction, brutality, dislocation, and suffering? Was it possible to parade such military and social violence before the American people, day after day, night after night, without dulling the moral sensibilities of the citizenry? In this connection critics of the war tried to assess the moral and psychological impact of two very different kinds of killing that were occurring in Vietnam.

Some of the violence was coldly impersonal. Men in airplanes, soaring thousands of feet above the ground, pressed certain buttons and destroyed a village. They never heard the screams, smelled the burning flesh, or saw the mothers weeping piteously over the bodies of their children or the stunned old people whose homes had burst into fragments. The same "clean" delivery of death and devastation at long range and through advanced technology was experienced by thousands of others in Vietnam: strategic planners, artillerymen, offshore naval gunners, and, to a lesser extent, helicopter crews. Who was prepared to measure the effects of such work upon either the men who had to do it or upon the society that asked them to? How was it possible, opponents of the Vietnam war asked, to engage in impersonal killing and not be numbed to human suffering, made cynical about normal standards of morality and traditional American beliefs about the sacred value of a human life?

On the other hand, what about those young men for whom the killing was anything but clean: the combat soldiers on the ground, the "grunts" who slogged through jungle heat and tropical rains on "search and destroy" missions, who were the "bait," walking into deadly ambushes in order to draw the Vietcong out of hiding so that air strikes could be called in? For twelve agonizing months, they were locked into a world of terror and danger. They were nineteen-year-old boys, fresh from high school, and they witnessed things that no one should have to know. They saw the limbs of their comrades (or their own) blown off by mines, and they zipped their friends into black body-bags and loaded them onto helicopters. In the chaotic conditions of combat they sometimes discovered that they had poured their fire into unarmed civilians running from the scene, into old women or children. It was the kind of war that blurred the distinction between combatants and noncombatants, between the usual targets and those who might be concealing grenades under their peasant clothing. Everyone knew that the enemy mingled and hid in the civilian population and that apparently innocent Vietnamese might suddenly pose the most extreme danger. Was it any wonder that many GIs fell easily into a racist vocabulary of "gooks," "slopes," "slants," and "dinks" and that the "Mere Gook Rule" prevailed and that they laughed about "snake kills" and "turkey shoots" and "Cong-zaps" and that napalmed bodies were sometimes called "crispy critters"?

To the most radical antiwar critics, the soldiers were willing agents of a racist and imperialist foreign policy that had become America's chief way of dealing with the Third World in the twentieth century, just as in the nineteenth it had been the standard way to deal with American Indians. They were able to support their view by dozens of interviews with, and eyewitness accounts of, American boys who either admitted that they liked the war or reported that they had plenty of buddies who did—men who thrilled to the power of the big bombers, reveled in their own technological expertise, who actually enjoyed killing the gooks. Other opponents of the war, unable to subscribe to so sweeping a theory of American foreign policy or unwilling to assent to so brutal a description of American fighting men, tended to picture them as boys trapped in a war not of their own making, required to kill and be killed for unworthy or unclear purposes, victims of the senseless and immoral policies of their elders. But whichever picture one held, it was natural to wonder about the moral repercussions of the war on those Americans who took part in it.

The term *demoralization* has come to mean the loss of spirit, enthusiasm, will, purpose; but its obvious original meaning was the erosion of moral principle, an evaporation of moral restraints that led to corruption or perversion. Opponents of the war believed that a good many signs of demoralization existed among the fighting men in Vietnam—as if participation in so questionable a war resulted, somehow, in a general collapse of moral standards. The proliferation, in Saigon and other cities where GIs took rest and recreation, of entire districts of sleazy bars and the growth of a tremendous prostitution industry were signs of this collapse. A much-publicized problem of drug abuse among American boys in Vietnam contributed to perceptions of a general erosion of traditional morality. In addition to alcohol, soldiers could easily acquire barbiturates, hallucinogens like LSD, and amphetamines. A marijuana cigarette cost a dime, and perhaps as many as half of the GIs smoked pot, some of them daily: "In Vietnam, grass was smoked so much," wrote the historian Loren Baritz, "it is a wonder that a southerly wind did not levitate Hanoi's politburo." By the late 1960s such quantities of heroin, opium, and cocaine were being used by the troops in Vietnam that the government, fearing the impact of returning vet-addicts on American society, had to swallow the bad publicity and institute testing and rehabilitation programs.

There were other indications of demoralization in the military. A rate of desertion much higher than in Korea or World War II caused anxiety both among official authorities and in the population as a whole. Seventy-six thousand deserted in 1967 alone, and the rate of desertions from 1965 to 1971 shot up by more than 450 percent. Numerous instances of mutiny occurred where soldiers refused to obey orders they thought were too dangerous or silly. In 1971 a reporter for *U.S. News and World Report* observed that "the point has been reached where officers and sergeants sometimes hesitate to issue an order—out of apprehension that the troops may not obey and will 'cause trouble.'" The army was riven by disputes over everything from hair length to the legal rights of enlisted men. Even more serious, the relations between black and white soldiers exploded into periodic violence: "Past favorable publicity about integration of US troops here," wrote the *New Republic's* Vietnam correspondent, Zalin Grant, "has shimmered and disappeared like paddy water under a tropic sun." Blacks were more militant, more willing to organize, to voice objections about being passed over for promotions and assigned the most menial and the most hazardous duties ("Increasingly," wrote Grant, "blacks in Vietnam salute each other with the upraised clenched fist of Black Power"). Some white soldiers reacted with cutting racist remarks or developed a deepening racial resentment.

A particularly nasty evidence of the breakdown of traditional codes of military morality was called "fragging." Originally the term meant killing your own officer with a fragmentation grenade, but it came to mean the intentional murder of officers by any means. Some units pooled a "bounty" and gave the cash to the man who killed an especially hated or "dangerous" officer. Fragging had occurred in earlier wars, but this was different. Precise figures, not surprisingly, can never be known, but conservative estimates suggest that there were hundreds of attempts. Unlike previous wars, where the practice was generally confined to combat situations, fragging in Vietnam frequently took place in rear areas. Sometimes connected to narcotics and alcohol, fragging "has ballooned into an intra-Army guerrilla warfare," reported Eugene Linden in a 1972 article for the *Saturday Review.* "What was in World War I, World War II, and Korea an idiosyncratic yet understandable horror of war has become an obtrusive characteristic of our involvement in Southeast Asia." Linden, and other observers, placed the blame precisely where antiwar critics thought it should go. "'Fraggings' occur amid the detritus of a demoralized army: a world of heroin, racial tension, mutiny, and fear. They express the agony of the slow, internal collapse of our Army in Vietnam."

If some opponents of the war found evidence of moral deterioration in the armed services, some found it also in the conduct of the government itself. The American people have generally regarded their government with suspicion, of course, and have traditionally criticized the motives and methods of their politicians. But in the end, democratic government has to rest upon a bedrock of trust between citizens and their leaders, an assumption, on some level, that elected representatives are forthright and honest, that they tell the truth. But the pursuit of an immoral war in Vietnam, the critics charged, had resulted in some terribly dangerous practices by American officials. They too had become demoralized by the war, and for sordid political or military purposes they had cynically engaged in practices that many Americans, including some who were ready to support the war, found deeply disturbing.

Critics of government activities in connection with Vietnam contended that the American people had been lied to consistently about the war: Lyndon Johnson's assurance that he sought no wider war while he was actually planning one, the false reporting of the Gulf of Tonkin incident, Richard Nixon's hinting that he had a plan to end the war if he was elected. Some were willing to ascribe the embarrassingly optimistic official forecasts of imminent victory (all the upbeat talk about "turning the corner" or "home by Christmas" or "the light at the end of the tunnel") to mere ineptitude, sheer ignorance of the situation in the field. Others, however, saw these predictions as part of a policy of conscious deception, knowing attempts to beguile and mislead. Inflated official estimates of enemy dead, hiding American casualty figures from the public, secret bombing of Cambodia and Laos that lasted for months, the clandestine activities of the CIA and the FBI in spying on the free citizenry of the United States, the use of provocateurs and infiltrators, the attempts to control the media or to intimidate the peace movement—all indicated a government, according to the antiwar critics, that had turned away from established ethical practices and traditional constitutional guarantees.

Opponents of the war also accused Washington bureaucrats and Pentagon technicians of inventing a deceptive, euphemistic jargon coldly calculated to lull the American people by disguising the reality of the war, an exercise in manipulating the English language that would have been laughable had it not been so sinister. According to the critics, terms such as "body count" and "free fire zone" and "hostile civilians" were invented to cloak atrocity. Calling the men in Vietnam "advisers" and using words like "pacification" and "strategic hamlets," like "relocation" and "liberation," were acts hypocritcally designed to soften Americans to the horrors being committed in their name. Referring to artillery bombardments as "harassment and interdiction" or to air raids as "limited duration protective reaction strikes," were patent attempts to narcotize Americans into accepting brutality. Such self-conscious deception proved that the immorality of the enterprise could be found in clerks as well as in presidents, that the disease had spread like a cancer through all the echelons of the government.

Some were even prepared to argue that the cancer had spread through the entire body politic, that the ethical standards of the whole society had been weakened by the war. In his famous address at Johns Hopkins University in 1966, "The Arrogance of Power," Senator Fulbright thought he could already see "a marked change in the kinds of things we think about and talk about in America and there can be no doubt that the major cause of the change is the war." He worried about the wider effects of the "dehumanizing" work in Vietnam: "In the course of dehumanizing an enemy . . . a man dehumanizes himself. It is not just the naturally bellicose, the thwarted or the twisted personalities, that become dehumanized in a war. It is everyman: the good and decent citizen who looks after his children, who is considerate of his neighbors and kind to animals." The influential civil rights leader Martin Luther King, Jr., thought he detected a connection between the growing violence in American cities and the war in Vietnam:

> I knew that I could never again raise my voice against the violence of the oppressed in the ghettos without having first spoken clearly to the greatest purveyor of violence in the world today: my own government. . . . I have worked too long and hard now against segregated public accommodations to end up segregating my moral concern.

Justice is indivisible. . . . Now it should be incandescently clear that no one who has any concern for the integrity and life of America today can ignore the present war.

In 1971 Bill Moyers, the former press secretary to Lyndon Johnson, wrote a thoughtful essay for the *Saturday Review*, "Vietnam: What Is Left of Conscience," summarizing the fears of many people who connected the war with moral erosion at home. "We do not yet know the full extent to which the war in Vietnam has affected our moral sensibilities," he began, "but we do know enough to be troubled." Our soldiers, Moyers noted, had fought brutally in other wars, but Vietnam is the first time such fighting had been done with such a "nagging conscience." "We have abandoned propriety before; we have never before doubted the reason for doing so, as we doubt it now." The demoralization of the armed services was obvious enough, he continued, but those at home have also witnessed a decline of discipline and morale. "We have turned upon each other in spiteful and accusing fashion, which has resulted in violence, division, charges of intimidation and conspiracy, increased surveillance by the state of its citizens, and increased suspicion of the state by the citizen." Even worse, because Americans had to "forget propriety" there, they had stopped speaking out their indignation at injustice and suffering here: "Nations cannot abandon civility abroad and remain civilized at home."

V.

Not every American, obviously, was willing to subscribe to every particular of the moral indictment being offered against the Vietnam war. But at least some of the charges were plausible enough, vivid enough, well enough documented and publicized to raise serious doubts in the minds of many. Those who actively opposed the war were vocal about these matters and contended—often without much reservation—that the war in Vietnam was unjust, an unworthy exercise for a free, powerful, and decent people. No doubt even some of the conflict's staunch supporters quietly regretted, on moral grounds, certain aspects of it, wishing, for example, for fewer civilian casualties and less social dislocation or for less corruption among the South Vietnamese leaders that America was helping. For the millions of Americans who had not quite decided about the war or who were "soft" in their commitment and open to persuasion, the moral complaints being registered on every side must have been the cause of extremely troubling questions.

Since the mid-1930s, after all, considerations of national security and considerations of morality had gone hand-in-hand in the discussions of American foreign policy. Through all the years of confronting the Fascists, through all the years of confronting the Communists, the great majority of Americans could feel that the nation was pursuing purposes that were both necessary and principled, purposes that simultaneously maintained American safety and vindicated American ideals. Now those two strands in the ideology seemed somehow to have become separated, and it was at last possible to see that for more than a generation Americans had been drawn to a foreign policy consensus for very different reasons: some of them because they wanted to keep the country secure, others because they wanted to further certain moral principles and behavior in the world.

There are few situations in life that are more perplexing or paralyzing than those in which a person is attracted by two desirable goals, only one of which can be attained. Anyone who wants to remain faithful to a diet and is offered a piece of chocolate cake will understand in a small way the tearing nature of such a conflict. You cannot have both of these good things because in the act of choosing the one, diet or cake, you eliminate the possibility of having the other. It will not do to minimize the disintegrating quality of such an experience (using the term *disintegration* as it was originally meant: the loss of unity and wholeness). At such moments individuals are in a kind of war with themselves. And if the stakes are not trivial, but momentous and more or less irreversible ("Shall I marry the fetching Monique or would it be better to please Mom and Pop?"), the internal discord created in us can be bitter and angry, until we are so badly divided ("of two minds"), so torn by internal strain that our very mental health may be affected.

Is it too much to suggest that a whole society can also experience something very like this sort of a conflict, that it too can be so riven by wanting two good things and only being able to have one of them that it is also subject to serious discord, bitterness, and strain? At such moments is not the whole society in a kind of war with itself, and is not the very health of the body politic in some measure affected? During the late 1930s Americans had also desired two irreconcilable goals: that the western democracies should emerge victorious against the Fascists and that American boys should not become involved. Then too a spirited and abrasive debate occurred, a debate that was only quieted when a direct sneak attack upon American soil ended the disagreement and solidified the nation in patriotic unity. Now, a quarter century later, the nation was similarly pulled in two directions. Americans wanted to defend their vital interests as those interests had been authoritatively defined by a string of their presidents; they also wanted to behave in ways that were consistent with their values and ideals. Fulfilling one desire seemed to lead in the direction of continuing to fight in Vietnam, even to increasing the commitment there; fulfilling the other seemed to lead in the direction of withdrawing. And this time, no Pearl Harbor seemed likely to free citizens from the necessity to decide.

It is important to understand the terribly difficult nature of the choice being forced upon many citizens by this war. Americans traded harsh charges amongst themselves during these troubled years, and they frequently did so in very strident tones. Some of the most unrestrained opponents of the war were quite willing to brand those who disagreed with them militarists, baby-killers, tyrants, sadistic and eager perpetrators of atrocity. Meanwhile, some of the war's most convinced advocates did not hesitate to call the antiwar activists cowards, Communists, draft-dodgers, traitors to the flag and to the nation. There were numerous instances of antiwar activists greeting returning veterans with cruel verbal abuse, even pelting them with eggs, and there were numerous instances of prowar advocates spitting upon peaceful protesters, beating them up, or throwing yellow paint on them. Both sides were regularly guilty of trying to deny opponents the right to speak in public and, if that failed, of heckling, intimidating, and shouting them down. When we remember that inflated rhetoric and extreme gestures of animosity are often signs of serious social strain, we can begin to gauge the extent to which Vietnam tore at the nation as a whole. And if the dilemma ripped at the social fabric and imperiled the civility and mutual respect that democratic debate requires, it also touched the lives of countless individuals who were trying to arrive at personal decisions about Vietnam.

The conflict, both for individuals and for the community as a whole, was almost theological in nature. Once the two strands of the old ideology of international relations appeared, to many people, to separate, the question became one that seemed more appropriate for philosophers or professional moralists than for everyday citizens. Was *any* sort of behavior permissible in order to defend oneself? And if not, where did one locate the proper limits on action? What was the process by which a country could reasonably decide how to balance its desire for safety against its desire to abide by the principles of justice and morality? Such difficult matters were not easily weighed by average citizens, and it is not surprising that the debaters on both sides of the question sought ways of discussing Vietnam that did not force them to grapple with the hard choice at the center of the quandary.

The simplest and most obvious way of dealing with a conflict like this one, a conflict between two desirable, but apparently incompatible objects, is to weaken the lure of one of them. Some people (apparently) have the ability to convince themselves that chocolate cake is a highly exaggerated treat and that bean sprouts are just as tasty, and they are thereby freed to pursue their diets without inner tension. Others can persuade themselves that dieting is a highly dubious activity, that it cramps life and stunts pleasure, and they are freed to have their cake (and eat it too). It is not, however, only by a process of private negotiation and reevaluation that such conflicts get settled. Partisans on both sides quickly sense that their task is to help the process along by diminishing the desirability of one side or another. Thus Monique might cast certain aspersions upon Mom and Pop and suggest that it is time for you to grow up and follow your own heart, and the folks might aver that Monique is nothing but an empty-headed hussy.

In the debate over Vietnam this tactic was adopted by both the proponents and the opponents of the war. Each side devoted itself to the work of discrediting the central contention of the other. Each, in other words, tried to persuade undecided Americans that this sort of a disintegrating conflict did not exist in reality. It did not exist, each side insisted, because the other side had erected at the center of its argument an utterly false proposition. In fact, both argued, if the situation was viewed accurately, it would be apparent that the two strands of our ideology of international relations need not be seen as separating at all; the traditional combination of purposes was as workable and effective as it had been since the 1930s, and the choice before Americans was not difficult, but easy.

VI.

For advocates of the war, the task was to convince Americans that the two strands had not diverged because the war was *not* immoral. Part of that contention consisted of meeting directly the allegations of the war's opponents. For example, a group of able specialists in international law—from inside the government and from law schools across the nation—defended the position that instead of being illegal, the war in Vietnam was perfectly lawful. These lawyers offered several arguments intended to assure public opinion of the war's legality, but almost all of their reasons rested on two fundamental assumptions. The first was that North Vietnam and South Vietnam were, in fact, two independent countries. While it might have been true, as the wording of the Geneva Accords strongly suggested, that the negotiators, in 1954, *intended* that the division into "zones" was to be merely temporary, those negotiators had no power to determine for all time the future of the area. Since 1954, the prowar lawyers insisted, both the North and the South had become real nations in their own rights. Each had its government and ruled over a precisely defined territory. Each sent and received diplomatic envoys and was recognized by dozens of other countries. Each participated in numerous international organizations as fully accredited political units; each had its own army, its own flag, its own civil service, and all of the other trappings of genuine nationhood. North and South Vietnam, in short, were like East and West Germany or North and South Korea: political divisions generated by the Cold War that had become, at least for the time being, fully independent national bodies, regardless of either the sentiments of the inhabitants of the original entity (Germany or Korea) or the views of some outsiders who looked for eventual reunification. And if North and South Vietnam were actually nations, they had the rights of other nations, including the right to self-defense and the right to enter into alliances.

The second assumption of those experts in international law who defended the American presence in Vietnam was that what was happening in the independent nation of South Vietnam was in considerable part a matter of foreign aggression and not merely an indigenous civil war. According to Leonard C. Meeker, the legal advisor to the State Department, North Vietnam had been sending hostile infiltrators into the South since 1957. "All of this activity—the training, the equipping, the transporting, the assigning—was directed from Hanoi. It did not just happen within South Viet Nam." Thus the lawyers who supported American intervention accepted the analysis of the government that aggression from the North had taken place, and American intervention was to be judged by the normal standards of defensive, rather than offensive, warfare. In the light of these two assumptions, prowar lawyers were able to construe the documents and principles at the center of the legal debate far differently than did their antiwar colleagues.

They were able to argue, for example, that because of its policy of subversion and infiltration, North Vietnam had been the party guilty of breaching the Geneva Accords, thereby freeing America and South Vietnam from the obligation of adhering to the limits imposed in 1954. Similarly, once it was assumed that an armed attack was made on South Vietnam, Article 51 of the United Nations Charter came into play. That article, it will be recalled, stated that "nothing in the present Charter shall impair the inherent right of individual or collective self-defense if an armed attack occurs against a Member of the United Nations." The experts who defended the legality of the war denied that Article 53 constrained the use of force until the Security Council approved; they insisted that the document meant what it said, that "nothing in the present Charter" (including Article 53) should interfere with the right of self-defense. They also argued that there was plenty of precedent for applying the principle to nonmember countries: our NATO arrangement, for example, had encompassed several countries that were not yet members of the United Nations, nor was South Korea a member when the United Nations came to her defense in 1950. Finally, the prowar students of international law asserted that the SEATO Treaty did not require unanimous agreement of the signatories before any one of them could respond to a Communist attack, and that although South Vietnam had not been a signatory of the SEATO Treaty, it was included by unanimous consent, in a protocol to the original agreement.

As far as the internal question of legality was concerned—the question of the constitutionality of the war under America's own fundamental law—the lawyers defending the Vietnam intervention mounted a vigorous response to the antiwar critics. The president of the United States, they argued, possessed ample authority both in the Constitution and in precedents set throughout the twentieth century for the commitment of American troops into combat. His role as commander in chief implies the power to make and to pursue effectively decisions aimed at protecting the nation and its legitimate security interests. That presidents in the past have done so seemed beyond dispute. A long list of such presidential initiatives could easily be produced, the most compelling case being President Truman's commitment of a quarter of a million men to Korea without any formal expression of congressional approval. But John Norton Moore, a distinguished professor of law at the University of Virginia and one of the most prolific and persuasive of the legal experts defending the legality of the war, argued that "Congress did support and participate in United States involvement in the Indo-China war." That conclusion, he argued, was obvious to anyone who read the congressional debates on the Gulf of Tonkin Resolution, who noted the overwhelming rejection of subsequent efforts to repeal it, or who considered the congressional approval of the various appropriations bills for the war.

But if those supporting the Vietnam war attempted to undercut the position of their opponents by attacking specific contentions of the antiwar lawyers, they did not confine their defense of the war's morality to these arguments alone. They also tried to discredit the charge of immorality by taking higher ground. Their task, after all, was to denigrate the central argument of the critics, to convince undecided Americans that the charge of the antiwar activists about the war's immorality was entirely specious. Thus they argued not only that the Vietnam war was justifiable on legal grounds, but that it was, in other ways, a completely moral and idealistic undertaking. Like World War II, it found the American people fighting on the right side, for the right reasons, and for a set of noble, generous, and worthy purposes.

In the first place, these advocates of the Vietnam war insisted, America's motives for entering upon this duty were singularly untainted. "We want nothing for ourselves," said President Johnson in 1965, "only that the people of South Vietnam be allowed to guide their own country in their own way." Arthur Goldberg, the United States ambassador to the United Nations, spelled out the things America did not want:

> Our aims in giving this assistance are strictly limited. We are not engaged in a "holy war" against communism. We do not seek to establish an American empire or a sphere of influence in Asia. We seek no permanent military bases, no permanent establishment of troops, no permanent alliances, and no permanent American presence of any kind in South Viet Nam. We do not seek to impose a policy of alignment on South Viet Nam. We do not seek to overthrow the Government of North Viet Nam.

The United States wanted not a single inch of Vietnamese territory, not a single commercial favor. It wanted only to preserve the rights of small nations to determine their own futures, to defend against a Communist takeover, to help the brave people of Vietnam fight for their freedom. Indeed, a large part of the effort was devoted to winning over the hearts and minds of the people, and as soon as this dreadful war was over, America had comprehensive plans for the economic development of the region. The American people could be expected to help build schools and hospitals and roads, to help improve agriculture, to assist in repairing the damage done by the war.

Supporters of American policy in Vietnam admitted that, of course, a certain amount of brutality was connected with the struggle; it is in the nature of wars that terrible acts are perpetrated by both sides. But to focus on battlefield behavior as an index of the morality of the enterprise was to address the question at the lowest possible level. There were higher moral values being vindicated by the American presence in Vietnam. What about the morality of keeping one's

word? Presidents since Harry Truman had pledged the country's support to the defense of freedom in Vietnam. Were those pledges to be broken simply because they were difficult to fulfill? What about the morality of proving oneself a reliable ally to the family of nations that comprised the free world? Other friends of the United States were wondering what weight to give to America's assurances, what reliance to place upon its solemn commitments. And perhaps most important of all, what about the morality of maintaining an unembarrassed and unencumbered force for freedom, ready to endure any sacrifice and to pay any price to resist the threat of Communist aggression? When the moral questions were examined from this higher perspective the war appeared far from immoral. Advocates of the war thought that their undecided fellow citizens need feel no internal conflict whatsoever, that any American could support this war with a clean conscience because the two strands of the American ideology of foreign relations had not separated at all. The United States was engaged in Vietnam, as always, in the linked effort to defend both its national security and its democratic principles.

VII.

For opponents of the war the task was to convince Americans that the two strands had not diverged because the safety of the United States would *not* be affected by any conceivable outcome in Vietnam. The American people had no genuine security interests at stake there, they insisted, because virtually nothing that happened in that remote little country could touch in any important way the vital interests of the United States of America. The tone of this part of the debate over Vietnam was set, in large part, by a group of theorists who regarded themselves as no less realistic, no less immune from the influence of merely moralistic or sentimental arguments, than were the most hardheaded foreign policy experts within the Johnson or Nixon administrations. As was the case with the prowar advocates, part of their effort was devoted to countering directly the contentions of their opponents. They launched a powerful attack on several of the central tenets of the world view that, they believed, had drawn America into this disastrous and misguided war.

To begin with, they argued that the widespread belief in a unitary and centralized Communist conspiracy was false and pernicious. To whatever extent such primitive thinking dominated American opinion, to whatever extent it was an underlying assumption of those formulating Vietnam policy, to precisely that extent was the opinion and the policy based on a dangerous myth, a "devil theory." The notion that every outbreak against a ruling class was somehow supervised by the Kremlin was paranoid and naive. People rebelled for their own reasons, not Moscow's. Any realistic analysis of the Communist world, moreover, revealed deep divisions. The Soviet Union, Yugoslavia, Poland, Czechoslovakia, China, Cuba—they might all be Communist countries, but a fear of their possessing a unified set of views or purposes would be silly. "Today it is belaboring the obvious," wrote the prominent political scientist Hans Morgenthau in April 1965, "to say that we are not faced with one monolithic Communism whose uniform hostility must be countered with equally uniform hostility, but with a number of different Communisms whose hostilities, determined by different national interests, vary."

Therefore, critics of the Vietnam war argued, it was ridiculous to suggest that America had to stand firm in Vietnam in order to stop "the spread of communism" or in order "to show the Communists" that wars of national liberation will not work. The truth was that while the opposition to the Saigon government was led by Communists, the war was being fought for local and nationalistic reasons. No doubt the Kremlin aided and sympathized with Saigon's opponents, but it never had the power to start the war, and it did not have the power to call it off. A special scorn was reserved for those who tried to argue, after the explosive public split between the Soviet Union and China, that the latter was behind the trouble in Vietnam. The idea that North Vietnam was taking its orders from Mao or that the Chinese had designs upon Vietnam as a puppet state ignored the fact that the North was receiving far more help from Moscow than from Peking. It also ignored the entire history of Vietnam, which was largely a long struggle to keep the Chinese at bay, and the deep ethnic animosity felt by the Vietnamese against the Chinese. "China is the hereditary enemy of Vietnam," wrote Morgenthau, "and Ho Chi Minh will become the leader of a Chinese satellite only if the United States forces him to become one."

Those critics who argued that the national security was not at risk in Vietnam also attacked proponents of the war at two of their most heavily relied upon points: the Munich analogy and the domino theory. Theories that posited so neat and predictable a career for aggression—moving, orderly, from one contiguous nation to the next— were too simplistic. If the trouble sometimes spread like that, as it did in Hitler's case, it did not always. China, for example, was a huge domino that had been Communist since 1949. Was there any sign that the contagion was spreading to India, Pakistan, Burma, the Philippines, South Korea, Japan? Conversely, what was the neighboring domino that had knocked Cuba over into the Communist camp?

Nations fell to communism, the antiwar critics argued, for a host of reasons, most of them internal. Poverty, hunger, tyranny, hopelessness, an entrenched and uncompromising ruling elite—these were far likelier to cause a takeover than the presence of a Communist next-door neighbor, and it was toward combating these domestic evils that American policy and foreign aid should be directed. The soundest way to prevent Thailand, say, from going Communist was to help build a prosperous, stable, contented society there, not to imagine that communism was like a red flood that had to be dammed up in Vietnam so that it would not overflow other places. In short, the opponents of the war insisted that reliance on the Munich analogy was misguided, and the domino theory was so tenuous that many, even within the government, had given it up by the mid-1960s.

George F. Kennan was a former ambassador and probably the most thoughtful, articulate, and highly regarded analyst of American foreign policy in the period after World War II. He was widely regarded as the author of America's containment policy in Europe and as one of the closest and most judicious students of Communist behavior. It was only natural, therefore, that the Senate Foreign Relations Committee, hearing testimony on the war during their much publicized hearings of early 1966, should want to hear his views. His opening statement provided an apt summary of the beliefs of those realists who opposed the war in Vietnam:

> The first point I would like to make is that if we were not already involved as we are today in Vietnam, I would know of no reason why we should wish to become so involved, and I could think of several reasons why we should wish not to. Vietnam is not a region of major military, industrial importance. It is difficult to believe that any decisive developments of the world situation would be determined in normal circumstances by what happens on that territory. If it were not for the considerations of prestige that arise precisely out of our present involvement, even a situation in which South Vietnam was controlled exclusively by the Viet Cong, while regrettable, and no doubt morally unwarranted, would not, in my opinion, present dangers great enough to justify our direct military intervention.

As far as the matter of American prestige was concerned, Hans Morgenthau wondered how much of it America had gained "by being involved in a civil war on the mainland of Asia and by being unable to win it." In fact, he asked, "Does not a great power gain prestige by mustering the wisdom and courage necessary to liquidate a losing enterprise?" Finally, to the contention that other free nations regarded the war as a test of the United States' willingness to help them, should the need arise, the critics answered that it was difficult to believe that any of them could want America to visit upon their soil the same devastation it was currently visiting upon the landscape of its friends in South Vietnam.

But those who criticized the war on the basis of national security requirements were ready to go much further than the mere assertions that America had no important interests in South Vietnam or that America's prestige would be enhanced more by dignified withdrawal than by stubborn pursuit of an irrelevant purpose. Just as the prowar advocates insisted that Americans look above the morality of the battlefield toward the demands of a higher morality, so too did these analysts insist that their fellow citizens consider a higher realism, the overarching effects of the war upon the country's security. In an age when nuclear weapons stood poised for ultimate use, where was the realism, they asked, in an ever-widening, ever-escalating war, rapidly careening out of control with no end in sight? Other analysts wondered whether the vast commitment of American resources in Vietnam did not, in fact, weaken or—just as dangerous—*appear* to weaken the nation's ability to fulfill its commitments and respond to emergencies in areas of the world much more critical to its security. Who knew what reckless leader of another country might come to believe that with America bogged down in Vietnam this would be a very good time to embark upon some bold adventure? Was the slaughter America was causing in Vietnam damaging its reputation in the rest of the Third World; could the United States not expect, because of Vietnam, a rash of anti-American words and actions from other small and undeveloped nonwhite nations? Was it not possible, in other words, that this effort in Vietnam—perceived in Asia, Africa, and Latin America as reckless and racist—might have the effect of undermining national security by alienating other nations from American purposes and policies?

Those who criticized the war on the grounds of national security asked other tough questions as well. Was it wise for America to pursue so unrelenting a policy in the face of the doubts and clearly expressed wishes of its closest friends and allies? Was American policy in Vietnam endangering harmony within a western alliance that was the keystone in the arch of the nation's strategic planning? Was not the main foreign policy task of this generation, moreover, to drive a wedge between the two great Communist powers, the Soviet Union and China? If so, how was it possible to justify pursuing a course in Vietnam, an unrestrained attack on a small Communist state, that seemed calculated to drive the two giants together? Finally, these realists argued, the security of the United States of America depended, more than on any other single factor, upon the health, prosperity, and unity of its people. But the war, by threatening to undermine these things, endangered the national safety far more than would a Communist regime in little Vietnam. The war brought a skyrocketing inflation rate that caused anger and economic dislocation. The Great Society reforms of Lyndon Johnson were withering, all but abandoned, because money going into war machinery could not go to improved education, more decent cities, better race relations, a repair of the industrial and transportation infrastructure, and the eradication of poverty. By 1967 the federal government was spending more each month for the war than was being spent to combat poverty at home in a year. In short, antiwar realists, like their opponents, believed there was no reason for any American to feel torn by the choice in Vietnam. They too implied that the conflict was illusory—illusory, in their view, because the official version about how this mad adventure affected the national security that everyone desired was so wrong-headed and shortsighted.

And what about American unity? Who could measure the effects of the Vietnam war on the patriotism and common feeling that had always provided the best foundation for American strength, the surest guarantee of the national health and safety? Who could look at the country in the late 1960s and not recognize that the debate over this war—over its necessity, its morality, its wisdom—had poisoned the society, had made many doubt the credibility of their government, had filled Americans with suspicions about the motives and values and ideals of one another? Even if the war was as moral as its proponents insisted, was it worth the cost?

4: THE CONFLICTS

How Americans Fought Some Small Civil Wars in

Their Own Country

I.

Like other momentous debates in American history, the debate over the war in Vietnam was, at least in one respect, thoroughly national. For the most part, the assertions that people hurled at one another transcended the normal lines that separate into groups any society as large and diverse as the United States. The issues could be fervently argued by San Diego lawyers and Cleveland blue-collar workers, by college students and housewives, by bus drivers and dentists, by Methodists, generals, and members of the Klan. There might be strenuous disagreement, but at least everybody understood the terms of the discussion. In this way it was essentially different from the quarrels that affected, however profoundly, only a portion of the population: what was the proper age to receive Baptism? were right-to-work laws fair? should university professors be granted tenure? what were the merits and what were the dangers of rock-and-roll? The commonality of the Vietnam debate, the extent to which its language could include and arouse citizens whatever their private affiliations, was one of its most notable features.

On the other hand, the debate over Vietnam cannot be fully understood if it is seen as an exercise in primitive, Athenian democracy—as if, somehow, all the participants had gathered themselves on some vast hillside for the purpose of engaging the issues. America is too large, too varied and divided, to be imagined as a single community. Its people are segmented—by their economic and social standings, by how they earn their livings or how far they got in school, by their religions, by how old they are, by all the philosophic, social, ethnic, and political attachments they inherit or acquire as their lives proceed—into dozens of formal or informal subcommunities. The Vietnam debate was given some of its special flavor by the fact that it so often occurred between and within particular subcommunities. No matter how universal the vocabulary, the debate over Vietnam centered in groups. Some of those groups, influenced by the other positions to which they subscribed or by the need to oppose old rivals, were able to achieve a relatively easy consensus on the war. Far more interesting and revealing were those subcommunities that found themselves so bitterly and irreparably torn that little civil wars sprang up within them.

II.

One group that had a relatively easy time with the issue of Vietnam was the Republican party. Whatever initial tensions existed among Republicans over the war were present, in large measure, because of two strong and not entirely compatible positions they had staked out for themselves in the twenty years after 1935. In part these positions were the products of the philosophic and political views of their membership, views generally more conservative than those of the Democrats; in part Republican doctrines grew out of the need to combat Democrats. From 1933 to 1968 Republicans held the White House for only eight years, and they ran the Congress for only four. They were required, therefore, to probe for weaknesses in the policies of their opponents, to distinguish themselves from the party in power, to give voters reasons to entrust power to them.

Republicans carried into the 1950s and early 1960s a strong strain of isolationism. Reservations about overseas involvement had a long history in America, of course, but the old disposition to limit overseas commitments received new impetus among the Republicans in the late 1930s and again in the late 1940s as they sought to gain votes by opposing the foreign policies of Roosevelt and Truman. Isolationist sentiments centered in the West and the Middle West and in the 1950s were given sharpest expression by the wing of the Republican party led by Robert A. Taft of Ohio, Everett Dirksen of Illinois, and Charles Halleck and William Jenner of Indiana. But Republicans were also very determined anti-Communists, strenuously opposed to Marxism as an economic and philosophic system and genuinely alarmed at the growth of Soviet influence. They were also ready to use the issue of Communist expansion to whatever political advantage they could. Thus charges that Roosevelt had been naïve in dealing with the Russians at Yalta or that Truman had lost China by his inadequate appreciation of the Communist menace were staples of Republican oratory through the 1950s. The anti-Communist strain in Republican ideology could be found not only in such extremists as Joseph McCarthy, Barry Goldwater, Richard Nixon, and Ronald Reagan, but in more moderate spokesmen such as Eisenhower, Nelson Rockefeller, George Romney, Gerald Ford, and many others. Even those Republicans whose instincts were isolationist denounced the Russians with enthusiasm; indeed, so pervasive was the hatred of Communism that virtually no Republican (and virtually no Democrat) could have publicly appeared to be unconcerned.

If, when it came to Vietnam, there was a conflict between the Republicans' isolationism and their anticommunism, it was quickly resolved in favor of the latter. Three months after Lyndon Johnson assumed the presidency, Senate Minority Leader Dirksen once again enunciated the position: "It is high time our Government recognized that Communist aggression never stops and never will until we formulate policies to meet the realities presented by a cold, relentless, and inhuman enemy." In the struggle for the Republican nomination in 1964, the conservative Goldwater and the moderate Rockefeller, whatever their other differences, were entirely agreed on the need to stand firm in Vietnam and united in condemning Johnson's half-hearted pursuit of the war. The Republican platform assailed him for "appearing to set limits on America's willingness to act" and for denying our troops modern equipment. "We are at war in Vietnam," exclaimed Goldwater in his acceptance speech, "and yet the President . . . refuses to say—refuses to say, mind you, whether or not the objective over there is victory." Every Republican in both houses of Congress voted for the Gulf of Tonkin Resolution.

Throughout the mid-1960s Republicans debated the war within fairly narrow boundaries. "If President Johnson has reaped a harvest of protest among Americans who deplore his war policy in Vietnam, it is not from any effort by the national leaders of the Republican Party," observed Karl Purnell in the *Nation* in January 1966. "Not only do Republicans blandly accept the White House commitment of American soldiers to Vietnam, they are even rushing desperately into the President's arms with declarations of approval." On one side were those Republicans who thought it best to support the Democratic president's purposes in Vietnam, to maintain a low profile on the subject, and to refrain from making the war a campaign issue. On the other side were those calling for greater military action against the enemy and no substitute for victory. Advocates of both positions could agree to focus their public statements on how the war was being waged. Thus Republicans condemned the "vacillation," the absence of a clear objective, the unwillingness to support to the fullest American boys in the field, and the refusal to be honest with the country about the administration's failures in Vietnam. The party was proud of its own resistance to communism and ready to contrast its patriotism with Democratic wavering. While campaigning for Republican congressional candidates in 1966, Richard Nixon declared:

> Republicans have stood behind the President in his efforts to deny reward to aggression. Republicans have refused to undercut the United States in Asia for partisan gains. It has been the President's party that has harbored those who have counseled appeasement of Communist aggression in Vietnam. It has been the 25 Democratic senators and 90 Democratic congressmen whose cries for peace at any price has given heart to Hanoi—and thus been directly responsible for encouraging the enemy, prolonging the war and lengthening the risk of American casualties.

By the time of Nixon's own election in 1968, only a few Republicans in the Senate and elsewhere counted themselves opponents of the Vietnam war. The venerable George Aiken, who had been Vermont's maverick senator since 1940 and a member of the Foreign Relations Committee since 1954, began to criticize the war in 1966. He was joined by fellow Republican Senators John Sherman Cooper and Thurston Morton of Kentucky, Mark Hatfield of Oregon, and Charles Goodell and Jacob Javits of New York. The most outspoken House Republican against the war was Paul ("Pete") McCloskey of California, a Korean war hero who mounted an ineffective campaign to unseat Nixon in 1972. The high point of Republican opposition to the war occurred in May 1967, when a group of young staff members of the Republican Senate Policy Committee prepared an extensive white paper critical of national policy and raising troubling questions about the future of American involvement. That document was quickly shelved by the Republican leadership and never discussed in Congress.

At their convention in 1968 the Republicans had to hammer together a position of their own for the platform. In what political commentator Theodore H. White has called "a masterpiece of political carpentry," party leaders of varying shades of opinion found themselves close enough to compromise. They toned down the most bellicose language of an original draft, condemned the Johnson administration for its many failures and for having "wasted our massive military superiority and frittered away our options," promised a program for a peace that would be "neither peace at any price nor a camouflaged surrender of legitimate United States or allied interests," and praised the courage of the men who were fighting in Vietnam. Thus the Republican party was able to remain relatively unscathed by the Vietnam issue as the war became the responsibility of their own party with Nixon's victory in 1968.

If the Republicans were able to achieve a general consensus over the war, the Democrats were literally shattered by it. More than any other single factor, the issue cost the Democrats two presidential elections and an ascendancy in American politics that, with the exception of the Eisenhower years of the 1950s, had lasted since the Great Depression. Perhaps it was natural that the party that had hammered together, under Roosevelt and Truman, the double-sided ideology of American foreign relations should suffer most when that ideology seemed to fragment into its separate parts. For almost three decades the Democrats were able smoothly to combine appeals to national security with appeals to international morality. Now, as this combination of objectives was being subjected to terrible stress, Democrats began to suffer serious fragmentation.

The first, tentative sign of uneasiness among Democrats was when two of them voted against the Gulf of Tonkin Resolution in the Senate. The Senate rebellion spread and became centered among the Democrats of the powerful Foreign Relations Committee. After the chairman of the Committee, J. William Fulbright, moved into opposition in mid-1965, other members found it easier to do likewise. Fulbright, after all, had been a respected senatorial spokesman on foreign affairs since the late 1940s. If he felt angry and betrayed by the president's policies, it was entirely possible that those policies were flawed. Among the influential Democratic members of the Foreign Relations Committee who spoke out against the war were Frank Church of Idaho, Eugene McCarthy of Minnesota, Joseph Clark of Pennsylvania, Claiborne Pell of Rhode Island, and Albert Gore of Tennessee. They were joined by others in the Senate, men such as George McGovern of South Dakota, Gaylord Nelson of Wisconsin, and Robert and Edward Kennedy, brothers of the late president, who represented New York and Massachusetts. In late January 1966 fifteen Democratic senators wrote to ask Johnson not to resume bombing North Vietnam after a pause that had begun the previous Christmas Eve. When Johnson ignored them, the Fulbright committee opened damaging hearings on Vietnam in February. The rebellion of the Senate Democrats had a vocal, but less powerful counterpart in the House, and soon dozens of representatives were asking hard questions about American policy in Southeast Asia.

The "civil war" in the Democratic party was not confined to the United States Congress. Johnson had gathered an informal group of experienced former officials, men whose intelligence, knowledge, and judgment he trusted—the elder statesmen of the Democratic party. Called "the Wise Men," the group consisted of former Secretary of State Dean Acheson, former ambassador to the Soviet Union Averell Harriman, Foreign Service veterans George F. Kennan and Charles Bohlen, Justice Abe Fortas of the Supreme Court, former Justice Arthur Goldberg, retired General Omar Bradley, former National Security Adviser McGeorge Bundy, and a handful of others. Meeting in the fall of 1967, they warned Johnson about possible difficulties should the war continue for very long, but they nevertheless urged him to persevere. At the end of March 1968, only five months later, members of the group met again to assess the situation in view of the enemy's new offensive, a request from the military for a major increase in the number of troops, and the rising tide of protest at home. This time, although divided, the majority of the Wise Men advised their chief to wind down the war and disengage from Vietnam. They based their advice on such practical considerations as the likely length of any war fought to a conclusion, the heavy odds against achieving a non-Communist, independent South Vietnam, and the unappetizing domestic effects of continuing the struggle.

Clark Clifford was a lifelong Democrat. He practiced law in St. Louis until World War II, when he moved quickly from the Naval Reserve to become, first, Truman's naval aide and then the president's special counsel. He helped to implement Truman's containment policy against the Soviet Union in the late 1940s. After another decade of legal practice he joined John Kennedy's campaign as a major strategist and became a close adviser to both Kennedy and Johnson. He had vast experience with the CIA, made numerous trips to Vietnam to report to the White House, and was a staunch and able defender of the war. In early 1968, when Robert McNamara resigned as secretary of defense, Johnson persuaded Clifford to step into the position. Clifford undertook a process of intensive study, discussions with European and Asian allies, and interviews with military and civilian officials. Slowly he turned against the war. He urged Johnson to place a cap on our involvement, stop the bombing of North Vietnam, and open peace talks as soon as possible. The break between Democrat Clifford and those Democrats who continued to support the war was typical of the fragmentation of the party under the pressure of this issue.

If one could see the tension among Democrats by looking at Congress or by noting the defections of high advisors, one could also see it by going to almost any Democratic precinct meeting in the United States in 1968 or again in 1972. Those little exercises in grass-roots democracy—where everyday Democrats gathered to decide who would represent them at county and state conventions and, from there, at the national convention that was to pick their presidential candidate—were suddenly packed, better attended than ever before in American history. In church basements, lodge halls, school auditoriums, and crowded living rooms all over America, party members came and talked things over, sometimes quietly and good naturedly, sometimes with the embarrassment that comes from not having much practice in speaking out their views in public, sometimes with animation and anger and eloquence. Not all the talk among these Democrats was about Vietnam, of course; there were other issues. But a lot of it was. And they found that they were deeply divided over this war. When the time came, they went into little huddles and chose representatives from among their neighbors who promised to support Gene McCarthy or Hubert Humphrey or Bobby Kennedy or George McGovern or George Wallace.

The divisions over Vietnam in the major parties were never easy to categorize. Among Republicans, the moderates—those least hostile to civil rights, social welfare, and domestic reform—were the likeliest to oppose the war. But the case of the prowar moderate, Nelson Rockefeller, demonstrated that even this vague rule had its exceptions. Among the Democrats no generalization seemed very useful. Conservative and southern Democrats tended to support the war— but Fulbright was from Arkansas and opposed civil rights legislation, Albert Gore was from Tennessee, and Fred Harris was from Oklahoma. Eugene McCarthy, the most visible Democratic opponent of the war in 1968, had a mediocre record as a domestic liberal. The quandary was hardest of all for liberal Democrats. Their heroes, after all, could be found on both sides of the Vietnam question. Who had better records for supporting New Deal social and economic reforms, for advocating the needs of the poor, or for civil rights than Johnson and Humphrey? And yet, on the other side of the war issue stood such staunch liberals as Robert Kennedy, Frank Church, George McGovern, Gaylord Nelson, and many others. Neither regional ties nor age helped predict who would favor and who would oppose this war. In 1968 the leading prowar candidate for the Democratic nomination was Humphrey, and the leading antiwar candidate was McCarthy; one was fifty-seven, the other was fifty-two, and both were from Minnesota. Little wonder then that this single, perplexing issue—decided privately, one Democrat at a time and on the basis of private definitions of value, loyalty, and patriotism—almost destroyed the party.

III.

Most politicians, whatever their party affiliation, like to picture themselves as men and women of action, more or less immune from airy speculation, relatively unaffected by abstract and theoretical considerations, taking their cues instead from the hard realities. The British economist John Maynard Keynes had a different view. "Practical men, who believe themselves to be quite exempt from any intellectual influences, are usually the slaves of some defunct economist," he wrote in 1936. "Madmen in authority, who hear voices in the air, are distilling their frenzy from some academic scribbler of a few years back." The opinions of often obscure intellectuals, Keynes cautioned, "both when they are right and when they are wrong," often have profound effects: "Indeed, the world is ruled by little else."

In fact, by the mid-1950s an influential subcommunity of public policy intellectuals existed in the United States, the descendants of those who counseled Wilson during the 1910s and advised Roosevelt or staffed the New Deal agencies of the 1930s. After John Kennedy took office, they were much in evidence. They were social scientists or foreign policy experts, scholars, historians, political observers, writers, eminent journalists, intellectual specialists of one kind or another. Some were attached to leading newspapers or to one of the periodicals that specialized in serious political discussion. Others taught at prestigious colleges; still others were drawn into government service as policy advisers, consultants, speech writers, State Department area experts, or behind-the-scene architects of programs or policies. Many shuffled between the academy and the capital and a few of these—Henry Kissinger, Walt Rostow, Hans Morgenthau, McGeorge Bundy, John Kenneth Galbraith, Arthur Schlesinger, Jr., and others—exercised considerable influence upon the powerful and, as a result, achieved a kind of personal celebrity. Freed from the need to please constituents or win elections, these policy intellectuals wrote their books and articles, made their speeches, conferred with political leaders, and sometimes knew the heady satisfaction of seeing their views repeated and implemented by those in high places. This community of thoughtful and intelligent men and women did a good deal to shape the debate over Vietnam; in turn, the community of intellectuals was itself radically changed by the war.

By the early 1960s a quite remarkable consensus had emerged among the great majority of these intellectuals. Even their disagreements were debated on the basis of a set of broadly shared assumptions, assumptions that came almost to take on the aura of unquestioned truths. The central article of faith was that Communist expansion was the single most obvious outside threat to American security, prosperity, and happiness. That communism, besides being a considerable danger, was also a great evil, few of these intellectuals were disposed to deny. The proper response to this threat, they thought, was to contain it within its present boundaries. And the task of containment could only be accomplished by a strong, resolute, and energetic foreign policy. It followed from these beliefs that America's armed forces must be prepared for any eventuality; that the conduct of foreign policy should be in the hands of a strong president; and that, if it was to succeed, such a policy would have to be based on the most accurate, unblinking, and expert assessment of power realities. When the country thought seriously about the rest of the world, there was no place for wishful utopianism or sentimental moralism. Of course the precise application of these general principles was open to debate because each policy intellectual could reinterpret these common beliefs in various ways with each new foreign crisis. But the noteworthy thing in 1960 was not how much these intellectuals might occasionally bicker, but how much they agreed upon as they discussed international affairs. In general, all liberals and most moderate conservatives were able to subscribe to the doctrine. Whatever fundamental criticism of the consensus existed came either from a handful of intellectuals on the far left or from an even smaller band on the far right.

By 1960, as we have seen, both pacifism and the political left were recovering strength after the beating they had taken in the 1950s. They were greatly energized by a rising generation of bright young academicians. Although these intellectuals spoke of a "new" left free of the dogmatic sectarianism of the "old" left of the 1930s, they too fell to attacking each other and were soon embroiled in bitter partisanship. Nevertheless, a spirited critique of American domestic and foreign policies issued forth from such small-circulation periodicals of the left as *I. F. Stone's Weekly, Monthly Review, Liberation, National Guardian, Studies on the Left,* and *Dissent.* Led by such well-known writers and scholars as Michael Harrington, Irving Howe, Paul Goodman, Stoughton Lynd, William A. Williams, C. Wright Mills, and Noam Chomsky, the left assailed the standard Cold War assumptions in general and the war in Vietnam in particular. Instead of an effort to preserve the freedom of the Vietnamese people, the war was seen by the intellectuals of the left as nothing more than the latest chapter in the long and bloody story of American imperialism. It was caused by the same set of economic and political motives that had always dictated American policies toward underdeveloped nations. These policies were so greedy and brutal, so obviously directed by the wealthiest and most powerful people in the country and so obviously for their own benefit, that decent Americans were compelled to oppose the war and lend their sympathies to the brave Vietnamese who wanted only to make a better life for themselves and their children.

The intellectuals of the right were fewer in number and less well known than those on the left, but their views were probably more in harmony with those of most everyday Americans. In 1960 the intellectual right was composed mostly of Eastern European refugees from communism, a few former radicals of the 1930s, some southerners, and a handful of ultraconservative Catholics. Their leading spokesmen were Russell Kirk, Friedrich Hayek, Richard Weaver, Peter Viereck, James Burnham, Frank Meyer, and William F. Buckley. Like the leftists, they formulated a thorough critique of both liberal domestic and foreign policies, and like them, they too experienced factional infighting—most significantly between libertarian opponents of big government and the anti-Communist hard liners who wanted a federal government powerful enough to combat the Russians. They too produced lively books and had their own periodicals: *Modern Age, Freeman, American Mercury*, and *New Individualist Review* (not founded until 1961). Certainly one of the most important moments for the postwar right had come in 1955, when William Buckley launched the popular *National Review* and gathered around it a group of shrewd, combative, and articulate writers. Just as the left criticized Vietnam policy because it was the sad continuation of an immoral tradition (imperialism), so too did the right attach its critique of the policy to a sad and immoral tradition: that of inadequate responses, since 1945, to Communist aggression, the tradition of containment rather than triumph, of self-imposed limitation, of reliance upon the United Nations or on lethargic allies. The intellectuals of the right demanded full commitment in Vietnam, support of Diem, and a fight to the finish.

The chief effect of the war on the subcommunity of public policy intellectuals was to fragment the old consensus, driving many of its adherents either steadily toward the left or steadily toward the right. Those destined to drift leftward had already shown some signs of restiveness by the time of the Gulf of Tonkin incident, but the movement was slowed by the profound fear of a Goldwater victory in November 1964. With the escalation of the war in 1965, the erosion became obvious. No doubt some of the public policy intellectuals who moved leftward did so on moral grounds, appalled by the increasing violence and brutality of the war. But many turned to the left for a more practical reason. They became convinced that the war could not be won. National ambitions in Vietnam were too closely identified with the Communists and too stubborn for America to overcome without employing unacceptable military measures; the quest for a democratic and honest administration in Saigon was doomed to failure. To pursue a mindless escalation under these circumstances, especially when the chance of Soviet or Chinese intervention loomed in the background, was senseless. Once cut adrift from the assumptions of the consensus, it was natural that some—particularly among young intellectuals who were not tied by long experience to the Cold War assumptions—would move farther to the left, begin to connect American policy with imperialism and the defense of vested economic and political interests, and eventually subscribe to some more radical analysis of the war. Moving out of the consensus as the 1960s proceeded and into ever harsher criticism of the war were such periodicals as the *Nation*, the *New Republic*, *Commonweal*, and the *Partisan Review*. An influential new journal, the *New York Review of Books*, founded in February 1963, became an important vehicle for the left's critique.

Meanwhile, other policy intellectuals drifted rightward. Unable to abandon, as if it were somehow no longer valid, the premise that Communist expansionism threatened American freedom and safety, many were angered by what seemed to be an inadequate, even cowardly, response to the aggression of North Vietnam. They demanded more strenuous measures, fewer restraints, less talk of negotiated settlement, and more talk of victory. But it was much more than merely the lukewarm conduct of military operations that drove some intellectuals to the right. So much of the protest against the war seemed to represent a profoundly troubling attack upon the values, the institutions, the faiths that had made America the most successful country in history. Not only the evaporation of patriotism, but the erosion of discipline, the whining complaints about free enterprise capitalism, the orgy of hedonism, sexual promiscuity, and drugs, the debilitating permissivism of the counterculture—these seemed like certain signs of moral decay and national decline. Those who were alarmed at these warnings rushed to reassert the old truths and, in the process, deserted the liberal consensus and moved to the right. In the fall of 1965 a group of distinguished New York ex-leftists—Daniel Bell, Seymour Lipset, Nathan Glazer, Irving Kristol—started a new quarterly, the *Public Interest*, to give voice to their views. They were able to make common cause with those rightists who, only a few years before, stood alone, outside the consensus. The case of the illustrious magazine *Commentary* is worthy of note: it began the 1960s as an effective proponent of the liberal consensus; it began the 1970s criticizing domestic and international liberalism and defending the war in Vietnam.

Thus did the public policy intellectuals in Washington find themselves increasingly isolated as some erstwhile colleagues moved to oppose the war while others demanded more strenuous and uncompromising action.

For the future of American political discourse, the most important result of this fragmentation of the center was the abuse suddenly poured upon *liberalism* by intellectual critics, both left and right. It was almost as if they had diabolically conspired to transform what had once been a term of respectability into a shorthand word for all that was ineffective, pusillanimous, and soft-headed. As late as April 1966 John K. Galbraith could begin his keynote address to the Americans for Democratic Action with a ringing declaration: "These, without doubt, are the years of the liberal. Almost everyone now so describes himself. . . . A liberal stand on issues is synonymous with a sound and intelligent position." Within a very few years, almost nobody would be talking like that, and the sudden decline of the reputation of liberalism constituted one of the most dramatic reversals in the history of the American political lexicon. While the debate over Vietnam and the flight from the liberal consensus of 1960 by public policy intellectuals was not entirely responsible (generalized criticism of social and economic programs, welfare, civil rights, big government, and inflation also helped to account for it), Vietnam certainly played an important part.

For reasons not hard to understand, a selection process operated in the government. Those intellectuals and experts who questioned Vietnam policy—who were "negative" or "skeptical" or "pessimistic"— were gradually removed from sensitive positions or, in some instances, removed themselves. In November 1961, for example, Undersecretary of State Chester Bowles, a former ambassador to India, was fired by the Kennedy administration because he advocated a negotiated settlement. Few Americans knew more about Indochina than Paul Kattenburg. He had worked as an analyst on the region through the 1950s and made countless trips to South Vietnam. He had known Diem for ten years. In 1963 he was the Vietnam desk officer at the State Department. At a high-level meeting on August 31 he declared that supporting Diem was a disastrous policy, that the Vietcong were much stronger than had previously been reported, and that the administration should give serious consideration to getting out. Kattenburg was quickly transferred to a less important job, and then to one that had nothing whatever to do with Vietnam policy. By late 1967 Secretary of Defense Robert McNamara's view of the war had changed; he came to doubt the effectiveness of the bombing and brooded over the continued escalation and the mounting casualties.

He advised Johnson to stop bombing the North, limit the number of troops sent over, and work for a negotiated settlement. By November the secretary and the president had agreed to part company. In March 1968 Arthur Goldberg voluntarily quit as ambassador to the United Nations and proceeded to denounce the war. These cases were by no means isolated. And the inevitable result of this winnowing process was what Kattenburg termed "closed-system decision-making," a style of thinking that was "impervious to contrary views and inputs from outside the inner circle."

While Vietnam policy was being made by a circle of intellectuals and experts who worked in Washington—men wed to containment and the use of power, and speaking the bold language of determination and optimism—another group of writers was at work raising some troubling questions. Journalists were often criticized by opponents of the war for unquestioningly repeating government press releases. But if some reporters were content to parrot official versions of the war, an influential group of war correspondents was sending disturbing reports back home to the American public. This coterie of journalists, men and women operating in the long tradition of investigative reporting, filed stories that struck at the heart of official accounts. The war, they said, was brutal, cruel, and bloody; it therefore raised hard moral questions about the proper use of American power. The war, they said, caused enormous hardships for the everyday people of Vietnam whom we had come to help. The enemy, they said, was tough, resolute, and thoroughly dedicated to its cause. The American-supported Saigon government was corrupt, and the South Vietnamese army was a joke. There was no real prospect for a speedy end to it all.

An early model for this sort of reporting was an intrepid Frenchman named Bernard Fall. He had been in his late twenties when he first went to Vietnam in 1953. At the time he was killed by a Vietcong land mine in February 1967, he was a respected authority on the country and its people. He poured out two hundred fifty articles for leading American magazines and wrote a half dozen books about the war. Never satisfied with official press releases, Fall wanted to walk over the ground himself: "He risked and lost his life," his *New Republic* obituary said, "because he could not long be content with secondhand reports." He covered the war from the point of view of the combat soldier or the Vietnamese peasant, and he constantly warned that the United States was making many of the same mistakes that France had made in the early 1950s. Bernard Fall set a standard for a handful of influential American journalists. David Halberstam covered the war for the *New York Times* from 1960 to 1964 and shared a Pulitzer Prize with Malcolm Browne of the Associated Press for Vietnam reporting. Neil Sheehan of United Press International, John Hughes of the *Christian Science Monitor*, Bernard Kalb and Morley Safer of CBS, Michael Herr of *Esquire*, Jonathan Schell of the *New Yorker*, Stanley Karnow of the *Saturday Evening Post* and then the *Washington Post*, all won high praise for the quality of their reporting. Free-lance writers such as Gloria Emerson, Frances FitzGerald, Mary McCarthy, and Martha Gellhorn contributed numerous articles to widely read American magazines. Harrison Salisbury's trip to Hanoi, for the *New York Times*, earned him considerable official ire. I. F. Stone and Seymour Hersh, although based in America, wrote tellingly about the war. These American journalists, together with distinguished foreign colleagues (Jean Lacouture, Francois Sully, Peter Arnett, Wilfred Burchett, and many others) and a host of skilled photographers, provided over the years an alternative and a rather more pessimistic view of the war than the version emanating from official sources.

In addition to their dispatches and articles, these reporters also wrote some widely read books that inevitably shaped the picture of the war in the minds of literate Americans. Starting with Fall's graphic accounts, *The Two Vietnams* (1963) and *Vietnam Witness* (1966), the most important book-length accounts of the war came from journalists. Halberstam's *The Making of a Quagmire* and Browne's *The New Face of War* both appeared in 1965. Burchett, an Australian reporter with strong Vietcong sympathies, published *Vietnam: Inside Story of a Guerilla War* in 1965 and *Vietnam North* in 1966. Other journalistic accounts of the North were Salisbury's *Behind the Lines* (1967) and McCarthy's *Hanoi* (1968). In 1967 and 1968 Schell's gripping accounts of the destruction of South Vietnamese villages, written for the *New Yorker*, were published in book form as *The Village of Ben Suc* and *The Military Half*. In 1970 Hersh's *My Lai 4* appeared as did *The Road from War*, by the experienced Far East reporter Robert Shaplen. In 1972, the last year of American participation in the war, two huge sellers were Halberstam's *The Best and the Brightest*, the story of policy-making under Kennedy and Johnson, and *Fire in the Lake*, a sensitive exploration of the clash of two cultures, by Frances FitzGerald.

Of all the popular accounts by journalists written during the war, only Marguerite Higgins's *Our Vietnam Nightmare* (1965) was likely to give much comfort to the war's supporters. Higgins was an experienced war correspondent and married to an Air Force general. She went to Vietnam in 1963 and contracted a tropical disease that ended her life in 1966. "Reporters here," she wrote the editor of *Time* magazine, "would like to see us lose the war to prove they are right." In regard to most of the reporters, Higgins was probably wrong; at least

at the beginning they seemed to have approved of the war's purposes
and to have hoped for an American victory. They were appalled,
however, by how the war was being fought, by the suffering of the
people, and by the venality of the Saigon government. The position
of many of them might well have been indicated by the title of a 1966
article by Neil Sheehan, "Not a Dove, But No Longer a Hawk." Nevertheless, taken as a group, the books of these journalists seemed to
constitute a searing indictment of American policy. William Buckley's
National Review scented a bit of a conspiracy: "When you look around
the bookstores," the journal complained in April 1969, "when you
read the reviews, you realize that the market is flooded with books on
Vietnam but that they all—with the single possible exception of the
late Marguerite Higgins's on-the-scene reports—are opposed to the
U.S. defense of South Vietnam. And you wonder why? Is it that no
prominent hawk has written such a book or that such a book can't be
published?"

As distressing to proponents of the war as the disillusionment of
the reporters who were covering it was the defection of journalists
with little or no direct experience of Indochina, but with immense
prestige and credibility. Perhaps the most respected and influential
political columnist in the United States was Walter Lippmann. Despite
courting by the White House, despite Lippmann's personal admiration for the president, the writer broke with Johnson in the spring of
1965. He accepted the bombing of the North as a necessary prelude
to negotiations, but became persuaded that Johnson was not opening
a meaningful negotiating position. His columns grew increasingly
critical of the war, and personal relations with the president became
frigid. By mid-1968 Lippmann's doubts were being echoed by many
other prestigious newsmen, newspapers, and magazines: James Reston and Anthony Lewis of the *New York Times*, Joseph Kraft of the
Washington Post; Frank McGee of NBC, Walter Cronkite of CBS, *Harper's*, *Atlantic Monthly*, and the *Wall Street Journal*—all had either
moved into the camp of the skeptics or started giving respectful attention to those who had. Humorist Art Buchwald, ridiculing the dogged
optimism of the administration in the face of continued frustration,
wrote a parody entitled "'We Have Enemy on the Run' Says Gen. Cus-
ter at Big Horn."

That the civil war within the intellectual subcommunity was not
confined to those who specialized in public policy questions was
shown early in the debate. In June 1965 the White House announced
a day-long "Festival of the Arts" to honor the men and women who
had made distinctive contributions to the fine arts in America. Johnson, always self-conscious about his relations with high-toned intellec-

tuals and a little resentful at the ease with which Kennedy had managed such relations, thought the event might build a useful bridge. The first sign of trouble occurred when the Pulitzer Prize winning poet, Robert Lowell, made public a telegram to Johnson stating that he would not attend because of his opposition to the president's Vietnam policy. The *New York Times* carried the rebuff on the front page. Other invited guests followed suit, and when the day finally came, the atmosphere in the White House rose garden was chilly and uneasy. One guest, the radical critic Dwight Macdonald, passed around a petition stating that presence at the event did not necessarily mean disavowing Lowell's position or approving the president's policy. Part of the day's program was to include authors reading selections from their works. When it was John Hersey's turn, he chose to read from his 1946 book, *Hiroshima*, a nonfictional account of the aftermath of the first atomic bomb. Less than a month after Lyndon Johnson had resumed bombing North Vietnam, and with Mrs. Johnson sitting in the hushed audience, Hersey quietly introduced his work: "Let these words be a reminder. The step from one degree of violence to the next is imperceptibly taken, and cannot be easily taken back. The end point of these little steps is horror and oblivion."

IV.

Another segment of American society that was deeply divided over the war and where debate was especially intense was organized religion. In every society, of course, religion has a multiplicity of tasks. Besides the daily work of offering comfort, assurance, and consolation, religion has acquired over the centuries some critical social functions. One of the chief of these is to provide a code of morality, a set of principles that can help to direct people's behavior toward one another and toward the world. In countries where a single religion predominates, that faith can often impose elaborate and binding rules; it can also provide additional symbols of patriotism and unity—one thinks of the ancient Israelites, the pre-World War II Japanese, or the modern Iranians. In societies such as America, however, where hundreds of denominations carry out their labors side by side, the picture becomes far more complicated.

In the first place, each denomination gives its followers a means of identification, membership in a community of the like-minded, a kind of social location in the midst of a swirling and heterogeneous nation. Americans are Roman Catholics, Seventh Day Adventists, Mormons, Jews, or Methodists, and these loyalties help to fix them in particular ways, help them understand what they are and what they are not.

Even if there are large areas of agreement over the requirements of the moral life, the existence of so many denominations tends to emphasize diversity and division rather than agreement and unity. In the second place, these hundreds of denominations are in a kind of competition with one another for adherents. Among its other results, this competition can sometimes have the effect of watering down moral pronouncements. (In the antebellum South, for example, a minister who mounted his pulpit and, Sunday after Sunday, sternly denounced the institution of slavery on moral grounds could be fairly certain that the slaveholders in his congregation would be sorely tempted to find themselves a more understanding and congenial pastor.) Thus there operates in American society an intimate interplay between the currents of public opinion and the moral teachings of religious leaders. Finally, most moral issues present themselves to us with subtlety and ambiguity. More than one answer is nearly always available, and each answer can come fully clothed in persuasive moral language. This is especially true in societies, like America, where there is no single, recognized source of moral truth. All of these factors operated in the discussion of Vietnam, as Catholics, Protestants, and Jews wrestled with the morality of the war.

There were several reasons why Jewish Americans might have been inclined to support the Vietnam war. Jews voted Democratic in overwhelming numbers, and their loyalty to Lyndon Johnson was strong. They had a hearty animosity toward the Soviet Union because of its harsh treatment of fellow Jews, and to whatever extent Vietnam could be portrayed as an effort to frustrate Soviet ambitions, Jews might have been expected to be supportive. Some Jews believed, moreover, that Vietnam was a test case for Israel: if the United States did not keep its commitments to one, small, independent nation struggling for its survival, would it keep its commitments to another? After the Israeli-Arab war in 1967, and the heightened dependence on American good will that Jews felt acutely, this argument had special force, and President Johnson was not above raising the matter pointedly in private chats with Jewish leaders. When Nixon came to power some Jews, fearing he might hold aid to Israel hostage for a sympathetic Jewish stance toward the Vietnam war, counseled discretion and a low profile. Finally, some Jews feared that a too visible opposition to American policy might unleash a reaction of anti-semitism from the most avid and irrational of the right-wing proponents of the war.

Nevertheless, despite these inducements to support the war or at least to acquiesce in it, American Jews were the most likely of the three major religious groupings to oppose it. According to the Social Research Center of the University of Michigan, Jews consistently outpolled Catholics and Protestants in favoring either immediate withdrawal or a negotiated end to the war. In 1964, for example, 50 percent of American Jews chose one of those two options as opposed to 33 percent of Protestants and 34 percent of Catholics; in 1966, 63 percent of Jews wanted withdrawal or negotiations as against 43 percent of Protestants and 49 percent of Catholics. The Gallup organization, similarly, found Jews lagging significantly behind Catholics and Protestants in expressing support for the war: in October 1968, for example, only 16 percent of Jews expressed support of the war; but 37 percent of the Protestants and 42 percent of the Catholics did. By the start of 1970 Gallup reported that 15 percent of Jews favored the war as against 30 percent of Protestants and 36 percent of Catholics. In that year three social scientists (Milton J. Rosenberg, Sidney Verba, and Philip E. Converse) concluded that Jews were "more distinctively dovish than any other simply defined group in the electorate."

The high representation of Jews among the war's opponents was partly a reflection of the fact that they disproportionately belonged to those groupings in the general population that tended to oppose the war: in greater percentages than members of other faiths, Jews were part of the fragmenting liberal Democratic consensus, graduates of leading colleges and universities, holders of graduate degrees, and located on both coasts and in metropolitan areas. In any case, from 1965 onward Judaism's most prestigious and influential rabbis and most powerful national organizations—the American Jewish Congress, the Union of American Hebrew Congregations, the Synagogue Council of America, the Central Conference of American Rabbis, and others—took strong antiwar stands. With only a few exceptions, leaders of the Jewish community condemned the war on moral grounds. Among the most active spokesmen against the war was one of Judaism's most revered theologians and teachers, Rabbi Abraham Joshua Heschel, of the Jewish Theological Seminary. In his widely circulated speech of 1967, "The Moral Outrage of Vietnam," he raised the questions being asked by many Jewish spokesmen: "Has our conscience become a fossil? .... If mercy, the mother of humanity, is still alive as a demand, how can we say Yes to our bringing agony to the tormented nation of Vietnam?"

American Protestants are so numerous and diverse that it is hard to think of them as constituting a single community. Thus generalizations about Protestantism and the Vietnam war have to be offered very cautiously. At least one proposition, however, appears to have considerable validity: that differences between Protestants over Vietnam were intimately tied to differences over other social, political, and theological matters. It would not be correct, therefore, to suggest that a civil war erupted within American Protestantism over the question of Vietnam; there already was a civil war going on. It was being waged over many issues, and by the late 1960s one of those points of contention was American policy in Vietnam.

The war tended to be supported by those Protestant ministers who were also fundamentalists, evangelicals, opponents of civil rights and social welfare legislation, and most deeply suspicious of communism at home and abroad. Among the most extreme voices in the prowar camp were such fiery right-wing evangelists as Carl McIntire and Billy James Hargis, publications like the *Christian Crusade*, and single-minded organizations like the Christian Anti-Communist Crusade. But not every Protestant minister supporting the war was a firebrand or an extremist. Most of them were more moderate, willing to believe in the essential morality of the American effort in Vietnam, able to subscribe to the patriotic sentiments that accompanied such ventures. In general, moreover, they tended to think that the main business of religion was not frenetic social activism in this world, but preparing individual men and women for salvation. Their model, in many ways, was the enormously effective evangelist, Billy Graham. While indicating, in one way or another, general support for the war, Graham tended to avoid or minimize the issue (once pointing out, for example, that more Americans were killed in car accidents than in Vietnam). He also often mixed into his sermons expressions of proud patriotism and disparaging remarks about dissenters and protesters.

In mid-1968 Harold E. Quinley, a student of religious opinion, polled more than fifteen hundred California clergymen of the nine largest Protestant denominations. Of those calling themselves fundamentalists, 91 percent said that they favored either the continued bombing of North Vietnam or actually increasing America's military effort. Of the Southern Baptist ministers (representing the nation's largest Protestant denomination), 97 percent favored one of those two options; so did 70 percent of the ministers of the conservative Missouri Synod Lutheran church. The option of complete withdrawal was favored by 2 percent of the Southern Baptists and by 3 percent of all those who described themselves as fundamentalists. By contrast, Quinley found the ministers of the so-called "mainline" Protestant churches to be more moderate in their views. Favoring continued bombing or escalation were 41 percent of the ministers of the Lutheran Church in America, 40 percent of the Episcopal, 42 percent of the Presbyterians, 25 percent of the Methodists, and 23 percent of the United Church of Christ. The mainline clergy, moreover, were much readier to espouse complete withdrawal: it was favored by 40 percent of the ministers of both the United Church of Christ and the Methodists. Of those who described themselves as theologically liberal, 42 percent favored leaving Vietnam.

Even leaving aside such avowedly pacifist denominations as the Society of Friends or such liberal ones as the Unitarian Universalist Association, the war in Vietnam had thousands of opponents among the leaders of American Protestantism. They spoke through such large circulation periodicals as *Christianity and Crisis* and the *Christian Century* as well as through many smaller magazines and journals. The powerful National Council of Churches, an ecumenical fellowship of three dozen Protestant and Eastern Orthodox denominations representing almost 40 million members, issued its "Message to the Churches on Vietnam" in December 1965 and followed it with regular antiwar statements. Within particular Protestant denominations, moreover, laymen and clergy formed many energetic organizations, caucuses, and lobbying groups devoted to such causes as civil rights and peace.

Critics of the Vietnam war within American Protestantism had many influential and articulate spokesmen. William Sloane Coffin, a World War II veteran and a CIA expert on the Soviet Union, became a Presbyterian minister and chaplain of Yale University; he was an early and extremely active critic of the war. Martin Luther King, Jr., the best known civil rights activist in the United States and a Baptist minister, began preaching against the war in 1967. There were many others: Richard John Neuhaus, a Lutheran pastor and theologian; John C. Bennett, president of the Union Theological Seminary; Episcopal Bishop Harvey Butterfield; and John Wesley Lord and James K. Matthews, Methodist bishops of Washington, D.C., and Boston. Antiwar Protestants also included a galaxy of renowned writers on religious affairs. Among them were Lutherans Peter Berger and Martin E. Marty; Robert McAfee Brown, a professor of religion at Stanford; Harvey Cox of the Harvard Divinity School; and Reinhold Niebuhr, perhaps the most eminent American theologian and writer on Christian ethics. At the start of 1970 Pastor Neuhaus could declare that American religious leadership "has succeeded in making opposition to the Vietnam war respectable. . . . It is overwhelmingly clear that American religion has not rallied to the flag in support of the Vietnam war."

But Neuhaus was quick to add that "the image of relentless religious opposition to the war is misleading." If there is a second generalization possible about American Protestantism and the war, it is this: at any given point in the debate, a higher percentage of clergymen could be found in opposition to the war than was the case for

their parishioners. Polling data from the Gallup organization indicates that more rank-and-file Protestants supported the war than opposed it until late 1967 (49–27 in May 1965; 46–37 in May 1966;
47–39 in May 1967). After that point fewer could be found for than
against the war (43–47 in December 1967; 37–54 in October 1968;
31–58 in January 1971; 29–60 in May 1971). How did it happen that
the image of a militantly antiwar Protestantism could coexist with a
reality that included a substantial body of prowar opinion, even until
the very end?

Quinley, basing his opinion on his study of California clergymen,
offers a possible answer: "the image of the clergy as one of the most
militant opposition groups to the war in Vietnam derives . . . from the
much greater tendency of those who are opposed to the war to engage in highly visible public activities." Those supporting the war
tended to do so quietly. Southern Baptists, for example, were practically unwilling to have the issue raised in national debate. According
to Neuhaus, "those who support or are undecided about the war pursue an avoidance course." They unprotestingly conformed to government policy. In part, conservative and fundamentalist Protestants
were led to this stance by their suspicion of social activism, their emphasis on personal salvation, and their strong traditions of church-
state separation. Meanwhile, opponents of the war were delivering
sermons and writing articles. They led marches, offered sanctuary in
their churches to deserters and draft resisters, campaigned to accord
conscientious objector status to those who opposed only particular
wars. Finally, the antiwar ministers were more often members of the
more "respectable" denominations; they tended to be better educated, better established than their prowar opponents. This combination of factors may have magnified their influence and, particularly
in the early days of the protest, made their views appear to be more
representative than they really were.

American Roman Catholics were consistently more favorable to the
war than were Protestants. In May 1966, for example, Gallup found
that 46 percent of Protestants and 57 percent of Catholics approved
of the war. Not until the spring of 1968 did most of the Catholics
polled by Gallup indicate that they opposed it, and thereafter, although Catholics were still more supportive, the gap between Catholic
and Protestant opinion narrowed. In January 1970, for example, 30
percent of Protestants still favored the war while 36 percent of Catholics did. Two reasons for such strong Catholic support immediately
suggest themselves. First, the Christian community in South Vietnam
was almost entirely Roman Catholic, and its defense must have

seemed even a greater duty for American Catholics than for other Americans, almost in the nature of a brotherly responsibility. Second, no discussion of the foreign policy views of Catholics can get very far without acknowledging the powerful strain of anticommunism that was always a part of the ideology. This strain was especially apparent among Catholics of eastern European lineage, many of whom were themselves refugees from nations under the oppressive control of the Soviet Union. Catholics shared with Protestants a philosophical animosity against atheistic Marxism, but Catholics' feelings were intensified by a deep resentment against the tangible persecution of their church by Soviet commissars. The liberal Catholic magazine *Commonweal* speculated, in an editorial of January 1972, that greater Catholic support of the war might also have stemmed from "the still-lingering urge of the descendants of an immigrant church to prove their patriotism," and from what it called "the ingrained Catholic stress on respect for authority."

The Catholic hierarchy enthusiastically favored the war during the reign of President Diem, when loyalty to a devout coreligionist merged easily with ideological abhorrence of international communism. Even after 1963, however, the Vietnam effort was approved by many high Catholic church officials. It certainly had the warm support of one of the nation's best known and most influential religious leaders, Francis Cardinal Spellman of New York. A friend of Diem and a former schoolmate of his brother, Archbishop Ngo Dinh Thuc, Spellman was the Vicar General of the Armed Forces and had visited South Vietnam often. His remark, "my country right or wrong," was probably the most widely quoted statement of any Catholic prelate regarding the war. Until his death in December 1967, the war had few more unqualified supporters among prominent American clergymen. He once called it "a war for civilization" and thought that "less than victory is inconceivable." Among the two hundred fifty or three hundred American bishops there were many others who shared Cardinal Spellman's view, and many others who preferred to remain silent on the issue. In early 1966 the *National Catholic Reporter* queried the bishops about their views of the Vietnam war; only six replied. *Commonweal* was outraged: "the near total silence must be judged a scandal. Vietnam, in our opinion, is the number one moral problem confronting the American people, and those entrusted with moral leadership might be expected to address themselves to it."

When they did speak, the bishops were cautious, balanced, and, in some cases, ambiguous. Thus Cardinal Shehan's "Pastoral Letter on Peace and Patriotism" (June 1966) listed the moral restraints that must govern any just war, endorsed conscientious objection, and urged that we always be ready for "reasonable and honorable negotiations." Within weeks, however, Shehan issued another statement, insisting that it be included with the first. The second statement criticized those trying "to interpret my pastoral as a condemnation of American presence in Vietnam." Similarly, Cardinal Cushing prayed for peace at Christmastime 1967 ("For God's sake we must bring this war to an end"), but refused to support the idea of selective conscientious objection or counseling help for Catholic men who had moral qualms about the war. In November 1966, the National Conference of Catholic Bishops issued one of its few statements about the war. After repeating the standards of "the just war," the statement said: "While we do not claim to be able to resolve these issues authoritatively, in the light of the facts, as they are known to us, it is reasonable to argue that our presence in Vietnam is justified." The *New York Times* printed the story under the headline "Catholic Bishops Back War Policy." In 1968 the bishops endorsed selective conscientious objection, but they then, for a number of years, fell officially silent on the issue. Gordon Zahn of the University of Massachusetts, an antiwar Catholic, titled his review of church teachings on Vietnam for *Commonweal*, in October 1971, "The Scandal of Silence." (Writing in the *Saturday Review* a month earlier, Zahn was even harsher toward the bishops: "By their silence they have made themselves and their church accomplices to murder.")

On the other hand, a few bishops and auxiliary bishops were early critics of the war. Two of them—James P. Shannon of St. Paul and Bernard M. Kelly of Providence—resigned their positions, at least in part over the Vietnam issue. Among others who opposed the war but remained in the church were Bernard Flanagan, Floyd Begin, Ernest Unterkoefler, James V. Casey, Joseph Durick, Carroll Dozier, and Thomas Gumbleton. As the war dragged on more bishops spoke out against it. The *ad hoc* group calling itself the American Catholic Coalition for Peace had six bishops among its members. In May 1971 fourteen New England bishops joined in a strong antiwar statement, and six months later the National Conference of American Bishops finally concluded that "whatever good we hope to achieve through continued involvement is now outweighed by the destruction of human life and moral values which it inflicts."

If, from Professor Zahn's perspective, the response of the church's higher clergy was ambiguous, culpable, and tardy, other Catholics, he thought, deserved high praise: "The church has given witness, of course, but it has come from a different source, from the priests, nuns and lay people who rejected the pattern of silent complicity and, often enough, risked ecclesiastical disapproval as well as civil penalty for their efforts." He was referring to that extremely aggressive movement, sometimes called ultraresistance, that was also part of the Roman Catholic response to the Vietnam war. Through much of the twentieth century there had been an element of social activism, pacifism, even of radicalism, within the American church. At first a small minority that gathered around Dorothy Day's *Catholic Worker* movement in the 1930s, these few managed a token resistance to World War II and were enormously encouraged and strengthened by the papacy of John XXIII and especially by his 1963 encyclical, *Pacem in Terris.* If there was a single American teacher and theoretician for this embryonic movement, it was Thomas Merton, the gentle Trappist monk whose writings on pacifism inspired many Catholics who would take leading parts in the antiwar movement. And if there were any living symbols of ultraresistance in the church, they were the Berrigan brothers.

Both were priests. Daniel was a poet, writer, and professor of New Testament in Syracuse. Philip, two years younger, was a combat veteran of World War II and, after his ordination in 1955, a civil rights activist. The two helped found the Catholic Peace Fellowship in 1964. In October 1967 Philip Berrigan and three others entered the Selective Service Office in Baltimore and poured containers of blood over the files. Seven months later both brothers and seven others walked into another Selective Service Office in Catonsville, Maryland, took armloads of records into the parking lot where they burned them with homemade napalm, and then quietly awaited arrest. The trial of "the Catonsville Nine" attracted national attention, and crowds of supporters gathered outside the courtroom each day. Rather than submitting to imprisonment for what they deemed an act of conscience, the two went underground in April 1970, continuing to write and give interviews. The FBI apprehended Philip two weeks later and Daniel in August, and both went to prison. In 1971 the two men, with five others, were charged with plotting to kidnap Henry Kissinger and blow up heating tunnels under Washington, D.C. The jury deadlocked on the serious charges, and they were later dismissed. However, Philip was convicted of smuggling letters out of prison through Sister Elizabeth McAlister, a peace activist whom he later married. Naturally, the activities of the Berrigan brothers were hotly debated both inside and outside the Roman Catholic church. Most Catholics, of course, found their opinions unacceptable and their actions grotesque; even some who agreed with them about the war regretted the extreme nature of their acts. But they also had hundreds of admirers and loyal followers among dedicated members of the church. The controversy over the Berrigans may be taken as the most dramatic sign of the deep division within American Catholicism over the war in Vietnam.

In addition to these divisive antiwar activities within particular denominations, opponents of the war also launched many interdenominational peace activities. An organization calling itself the Clergymen's Emergency Committee for Vietnam formed in early 1965 in response to the initial bombing of North Vietnam. On April 4, twenty-five hundred rabbis, ministers, and priests signed a paid advertisement, "In the Name of God, Stop It!!" That summer a group of clergy visited Vietnam and reported back their impressions of the misery and destruction being caused by American policies. In 1968 a Clergy for McCarthy Committee promoted Eugene McCarthy's candidacy for the presidency. Clergy from many denominations were also active in secular organizations such as Negotiations Now! The most active, prestigious, and influential interfaith antiwar effort, however, was Clergy and Laymen Concerned About Vietnam. Organized in 1965, the group was led by such well-known figures as Rabbi Heschel, Daniel Berrigan, Martin Luther King, Jr., Robert McAfee Brown, Michael Novak, a Catholic from Stanford, Jacob Weinstein, head of the Central Conference of American Rabbis, Eugene Carson Blake, secretary of the National Council of Churches, and a great many others. The CLCV eventually had more than thirty thousand members, most of them clergy or religious leaders. The group was self-consciously moderate, hoping to enlist all shades of antiwar opinion, but it sponsored fasts and demonstrations against the war, distributed literature, and joined other groups in various antiwar activities.

If public policy intellectuals tended to argue about Vietnam in terms of practical politics and power realities, the religious debate centered around the matter of the war's morality. Lively discussions sprang up among clergymen and theologians reviewing American policy in terms of the ancient criteria of "the just war," and dozens of books and articles explored whether various aspects of the war did or did not conform to those moral standards. Discussions of "just war," it will be recalled, were usually divided into two parts. The first part judged whether the initial recourse to war was justifiable (*jus ad bellum*). As far as Vietnam was concerned, this part of the dialogue duplicated the one going on between prowar and antiwar lawyers and turned on the same questions: had aggression been committed? was South Vietnam a real nation? was the struggle there a civil war or a conflict between independent nations? And like the lawyers, religious leaders rested their final judgments about the morality of entering the war on their answers to these questions.

The second half of the question of "just war" (*jus in bellum*) centered on how the war was being fought. Lawyers entered this discussion too, but it was primarily religious leaders who scrutinized and debated various aspects of the fighting in the light of "the just war" categories. Chief among the controversial issues were the bombing of populated areas, the sometimes indiscriminate killing of civilians including women and children, the designation of "free fire zones," the use of particular weapons such as napalm and chemical herbicides, offshore bombardments, the treatment of prisoners, the attacks into neutral Laos and Cambodia, certain procedures such as "body counting," and certain tactics such as "search and destroy" missions. Each measure was exhaustively explored in moral terms: was it necessary? was its destructiveness roughly proportional to the threat facing the nation or its fighting men? did it adequately distinguish between the innocent and the guilty?

The most articulate, reasoned, and persuasive spokesman for the view that the war, in general, did satisfy the requirements of justice was Paul Ramsey, a distinguished professor of religion at Princeton. In several books and numerous articles Ramsey put the case for the justice of the Vietnam war. There may have been instances, Ramsey acknowledged, when the government used excessive force or appeared to be waging war "against a society" rather than against the enemy, but on the whole, he concluded, the chief onus for whatever evils occurred rested upon America's enemies—particularly on their use of such tactics as disguising themselves as innocent peasants, conducting their operations in populated areas, or hiding themselves among civilians. Ramsey's view was supported, in general, by other students of the question: David Little (Yale), Quentin Quade (American University), Ernest Lefever (a minister associated with the Brookings Institution), and Joseph Allen (the Perkins School of Theology).

Not surprisingly, their position was vigorously challenged by numerous clergymen and theologians of all faiths. Their position—that the firepower employed was entirely out of proportion both to the provocation America endured and to the actual risk the nation faced, that insufficient care was exercised to discriminate between innocent men, women, and children and enemy combatants, and that particular weapons and tactics were immoral by any fair standards of civilized behavior—was also espoused in numerous books and articles appearing in the general press as well as in the periodicals of particular denominations. Sometimes their indictments of the war's morality were phrased in the traditional terms of "the just war" debate; often,

however, the indictment was more generalized, an outraged criticism
of the war and of those religious men and women who supported it,
from the perspective of accepted standards of Judeo-Christian ethics.
Not untypical in this respect was an editorial statement from the
Christian Century in January 1967:

> People who have discharged their personal anxiety by transferring all
> authority to Big Brother in Washington, who have solved the dilemmas
> of war and peace by gulping down a my-country-right-or-wrong creed,
> who as Christians acquire easy consciences when a Cardinal Spellman
> or a Billy Graham endorses the war in Vietnam as a holy enter-
> prise—such people are displeased when by the slightest hint their cler-
> gyman puts the issue to them. They have made their peace with the evil
> thing. Reassured by the national leaders and the popular apostles of
> Christ that it is Christian to sear the flesh of the infant, the aged, the
> helpless, convinced that they serve God by killing, maiming and burn-
> ing human beings, the people complacently go to war with their minds
> at peace.

Such denunciations were matched by the prowar side, where feelings were every bit as intense and language just as spirited. The denunciations of the Communists and their Vietcong and North Vietnamese representatives were also fervent. And they were equaled by
criticism of those Americans who used extreme means to oppose the
war, who burned American flags or advocated revolution, who ex-
emplified by their lifestyles a sinful hedonism and a bold disregard
for decent behavior. Thus did the war in Vietnam nourish, if it did
not sow, bitter seeds of discord amongst religious men and women in
American society.

V.

Another segment of American life profoundly touched by the debate
over Vietnam was higher education. So fierce, colorful, and well publicized did the protest against the war sometimes become on college
campuses that many citizens must have thought—and many must still
believe—that opposition centered there, that without college students
and professors there might have been very little trouble at all. Unfortunately, the common view that conflict over Vietnam was largely between young people on campus and older generations in the general
population is a terrible oversimplification that must be examined with
great care.

That many older Americans opposed the war with vehemence and energy is amply suggested by individual examples. Among the very first to protest America's conduct in Vietnam was the British philosopher Bertrand Russell, who was in his early nineties. A. J. Muste, the dean of American pacifism, had been laboring for international peace since World War I and was eighty years old when Lyndon Johnson escalated the war in 1965; he worked for an end to the fighting until his death in 1967. Walter Lippmann was seventy-six when he broke with Johnson; the veteran Socialist, Norman Thomas, was eighty; Reinhold Niebuhr, seventy. The famous pediatrician and author of books on child care, Benjamin Spock, was well into his sixties when he joined the peace movement and became—at six feet four and dressed in conservative business suits—a conspicuous figure at antiwar demonstrations. George Kennan was sixty-two when he denounced the war before the Fulbright committee; Rabbi Heschel was fifty-eight when he helped to form Clergy and Laymen Concerned about Vietnam. Thousands of others, advanced in years and not much resembling the stereotyped picture of the ill-kempt, youthful, college-based "peacenik," protested against the war in Vietnam both as leaders of the movement and as rank-and-file followers.

In fact, if one was considering only a person's age, older Americans were far more likely to oppose the war than were younger ones. The Gallup organization divided those it polled into three categories: young (under 30); middle-aged (30 to 49) and older (over 49). In August 1965, after the early escalations of the Johnson administration, Gallup noted that 76 percent of young Americans supported the war compared to 64 percent of the middle group and 51 percent of the older. Three years later, in August 1968, the war was still supported by 45 percent of the young, but by only 39 percent of the middle and 27 percent of the older groups. In May 1971 the figures were 34-30-23 percent respectively in support of the war. John E. Mueller, a careful student of public opinion, bluntly concluded in 1973 that "no case can be made for the popular proposition that 'youth' was in revolt over the war. . . . The poll data argue that, although *some* young people may have been deeply opposed to the war, 'youth' as a whole was generally more supportive of the war than older people."

Indeed, thousands upon thousands of young people, including many on every college campus in the United States, approved of the war. For some the support was quiet and unanalytic, a product of inertia or of an unquestioning faith in the wisdom of America's leaders or of traditional ideas of patriotism and duty. For many, however, support for the war stemmed from weighing the issues and deciding that the prowar arguments were stronger. The Young Democrats supported the war uneasily through mid-decade (although even before Nixon became president the group had turned decisively against it in many places). The Young Republicans, with their hundreds of thousands of members and perhaps a thousand local chapters, generally supported the war to the very end. The most effective conservative group composed largely of college students was the Young Americans for Freedom. Well funded, sponsored by leading conservatives, the organization started in 1960 on a platform of free enterprise, anticommunism, and strong national defense. YAF was a militant, active, and imaginative voice in support of the war. It held counterdemonstrations, worked in politics, wrote and distributed prowar materials. Other small, local, conservative groups sprang up in many places: the Silent Majority against Revolutionary Tactics (SMART) in San Francisco, the New Emergency against Violence and Expressed Revolution (NEVER) in Colorado; the Student Committee for a Responsible University (SCRU) at Penn State, and a dozen others.

Here again, the polls undercut the popular view that college campuses were hotbeds of revolutionary sentiment and antiwar agitation. It must be remembered that there were close to twenty-five hundred institutions of higher education in America during the 1960s. Many of these were small, conservative, and relatively quiet. Some were two-year colleges serving a local community; some specialized in night classes for working adults; some were affiliated with one or another religious denomination; some were vocational, professional, or technical institutes. Probably fewer than half of all campuses experienced organized antiwar activity during the 1960s. One study of 1973 estimates the number that did at "somewhere between 10 and 40 percent." Likewise, many Americans of the 1960s would have been surprised to learn that college-educated citizens supported the war in much greater numbers and with much greater consistency than did those who were less well educated. In August 1965 Gallup reported that 69 percent of the college educated supported the war, as opposed to 64 percent of the high-school and 50 percent of the grade-school educated. Three years later the respective figures were 42-37-26; and in May 1971, 31-30-21.

Nor were college professors an especially radical or pacifist segment of the population, another popular myth that cannot stand close examination. An extensive survey of 1969, to which more than sixty thousand professors responded, revealed that only 18 percent favored immediate withdrawal from Vietnam. Another 40 percent wanted the establishment of a coalition government there, while a third favored gradual de-escalation and the prevention of a Communist takeover. Other surveys confirm these findings. After polling the faculty on their own campus in February 1967, two University of Michigan sociologists discovered that, while many professors vehemently and vocally opposed the war, "the largest single bloc . . . was *not* the doves, as current folklore would have it, but supporters of the Administration policy." Sociologist E. M. Schreiber concluded in a 1973 paper that "faculty opinion on the war was not markedly more anti-war than mass public opinion." In general, professors in the social sciences were most against the war, followed by humanists, then natural scientists. Those in professional and vocational fields such as agriculture, business, engineering, and education tended to support the war in greater numbers than did their colleagues.

All this having been said, the view that antiwar opposition centered on college campuses was so generally believed that it is hard to dismiss it entirely, to wash it away in a flood of surveys and statistics and smugly conclude that the public's perception was simply dead wrong. After all, by June 1970—once again, according to the Gallup organization—Americans considered "campus unrest" to be the number one problem in the nation. No doubt there were many reasons besides Vietnam for this national uneasiness about colleges and universities, their students and faculties; but the images of students wildly protesting against the war, burning draft cards, occupying buildings, boycotting classes, picketing both university and government officials, and endlessly marching and striking was an important ingredient. How are we to account for this apparent discrepancy between the scientific evidence against a campus rebellion on the Vietnam issue and the widespread public perception that colleges and universities were at the heart of the uproar?

In the first place, it is important, in reading the polls, to distinguish college educated respondents from those young people actually enrolled in college during the 1960s and early 1970s. The former category, of course, included those who might have graduated thirty or forty years earlier, men and women now, presumably, relatively well established, prosperous, and tending to be more conservative than other Americans. By the 1960s, moreover, colleges and universities had been opened to numerous outsiders, young people from economic classes and races that had not always had easy access to higher education. These newcomers were more likely to dissent from traditional conservative campus attitudes, to register greater opposition to the war in Vietnam, than those who had, at some time in the past, been to college. The simple factor of male students being susceptible to being drafted and actually sent to fight in Vietnam, while difficult to measure, cannot be ignored as a source of opposition to the war that was present in the current generation but absent in older college-educated Americans.

Second, authorities agree that it is crucial to distinguish between college students in general and those who were attending so-called leading or elite schools. When polling encompassed students spread among all institutions of postsecondary education, the results tended to show rather strong support of the war. But when it was confined to the one hundred fifty or two hundred most prestigious institutions, those with more than merely locally gathered student bodies and merely local academic reputations, the results were far different. While support for the war was never absent from these leading colleges and universities, antiwar sentiment was particularly strong, grew stronger as the war dragged on, and at particular moments in the late 1960s and early 1970s became almost overwhelming. (Indeed, skeptical conservatives often charged that at these elite colleges antiwar demonstrations had degenerated into a sort of campus fad, roughly comparable to swallowing goldfish in the 1920s or stuffing phone booths with human bodies in the 1950s.) Graduate students at the leading institutions tended to be strong opponents of the war and faculty members at these schools, more critical of official policy in Vietnam than were those at less prestigious colleges.

Finally, opponents of the war on America's leading campuses were able to project an image of even wider discontent with the war than was probably actually the case. In this respect their success resembled that of antiwar ministers who were more critical of the war than their congregants. Student protesters succeeded, moreover, for some of the same reasons as the ministers. They were more vocal, more visible, more energetic, more deeply aroused, more profoundly engaged by the issues of the war than were those students who could satisfy the need to have a position by just repeating that they supported the government. Some of these campus activists (as well as some older recent students who had a flair for appealing to the young) gained a sort of national celebrity, almost a kind of stardom, for their abilities to awaken and persuade, enlist and organize. Rennie Davis, Tom Hayden, Abbie Hoffman, Mark Rudd, Carl Oglesby, Jerry Rubin, Angela Davis, Tod Gitlin, Allard Lowenstein, and a handful of others were in great demand as campus speakers. The media hung on their words and reported their activities, their shocking language and bold ideas, the bizarre way they dressed, to a fascinated and sometimes breathlessly appalled general public.

Every major campus, however, had its corps of less well known, but committed, articulate, and tireless antiwar students. They devoted themselves to criticizing American policy, debating the issues, finding new and dramatic ways to make their protest known and effective. They wrote fiery letters to the campus newspaper or started their own underground papers. They organized demonstrations against the presence on campus of the ROTC, or of recruiters for the military or the CIA or those industrial concerns like Dow Chemical, the maker of napalm, whose products were being used in Vietnam to destroy human life. They organized "teach-ins," "sit-ins," boycotts, pickets, marches, and strikes. They stuffed the envelopes, distributed the campaign literature, and rang the doorbells for Eugene McCarthy and Robert Kennedy in 1968 and George McGovern in 1972. They arranged for the buses, painted the angry posters, and provided the bodies for the huge national demonstrations against the war.

These student activists held widely differing political opinions. Some were middle-of-the-road or liberal; others were leftists of various kinds, shading off, in a few cases, into the most extreme forms of radicalism: men and women who claimed to follow the teachings of China's Mao or Cuba's Che Guevara and who advocated and sometimes perpetrated revolutionary violence. Activists of all shades of opinion soon learned the advantages of combining appeals against the war with other causes, and most campus demonstrations were not only about Vietnam, but about issues such as the environment, civil rights, and reform of the curriculum and other school policies. Dozens of campus groups were engaged in these efforts. Some of them were old organizations into which the student movement had breathed fresh life, others were called into being by the war. Thus protests against the war might be sponsored by organizations as mild as the Young Democrats or as radical as the the Young People's International Party (the Yippies), the Young Socialist Alliance, Progressive Labor, or the DuBois Clubs. No doubt the best publicized and one of the most effective of these groups was the Students for a Democratic Society (SDS). Founded in May 1960 at the University of Michigan, SDS set out to further the cause of civil rights and to organize poor urban neighborhoods for purposes of social activism. In 1962 it issued the famous Port Huron Statement, a manifesto written by Tom Hayden and calling for democratic change throughout American life. At its height in 1969, SDS probably had around four hundred campus chapters and was extremely active in mounting protests against the war. Thereafter, the organization was torn by factional infighting and broke up into competing groups.

The presence on leading American campuses of large numbers of activists raised difficult questions for faculty members and administrators. Some of those questions dealt with matters of the school's academic and governance policies; others, however, were related directly to the war in Vietnam. Many professors realized that the decision to give a male student the C he had earned instead of a B might mean sending him into combat and to possible death. The moral intricacies of such a choice were complex and troubling, especially if the faculty member thought the war was immoral or unnecessary. What should be the school's attitude toward secret, government-sponsored, and war-related research undertaken by members of the faculty? Was the university obliged to divulge the names of those students who belonged to radical organizations or to respond to other official requests for information about a student? (What books did she borrow from the library? What was his grade point?) Should the college's president speak out on the war? Should the faculty take a vote expressing its opinion on American policy in Vietnam? Should individual professors write letters to the editor? Should those letters be written on university stationery? All these questions and a host of others were warmly debated on campuses across the nation during the war. It may be argued that the impact of Vietnam on American higher education was traumatic, shaking, and, at least in some respects, permanent.

To whatever extent the debate over Vietnam took place between students at America's best colleges and universities and older generations in the general public (remembering always the thousands and thousands of exceptions to that facile and partly mythical generalization), both sides suffered from a kind of historical amnesia. On the one side were those young Americans who preserved no memories of Hitler and World War II. They represented a generation that knew not the satisfaction their parents had known in fighting a war that could present such powerful claims on both their desire for national security and their devotion to high moral and democratic principle, a war that was warmly approved by the great bulk of their fellow citizens. Many of their elders, for whom that experience was not only vivid but in some ways the central public event of their lives, were bewildered and appalled at the sight of so many young people resisting the call to defend the nation's banner (to say nothing of occasionally burning it). Some of them issued grave and gloomy warnings about the decline of the American spirit and the end of American ascendancy. But it was not only the young who had failed to learn their country's history. Many older Americans seemed unable to remember that the nation's wars had much more often been resisted than applauded, that *their* war against fascism was the exception, that those youngsters who demonstrated their unhappiness with the war in Vietnam and who insisted that it be fully justified in moral and practical terms were more like former generations of skeptical Americans than they were different from them.

VI.

It may seem inappropriate to think of women as making up a subcommunity within American society. Not only are women more than half the population, they are also, besides being female, many other things: journalists and Southern Baptists, college students and workers and business executives, whites and blacks. One would never argue, after all, that men constitute a subcommunity in American society. Nevertheless, it is probable that within every single category, women were more opposed to the war in Vietnam than were men—that is, women fundamentalists were more opposed than male fundamentalists, black women more opposed than black men, women workers more opposed than men in the same factory. Most commentators attempt to account for this difference by reference to the social and educational inculcation of traditional gender roles. Girls in American society tend to be taught to nurture, to protect, and to sanctify human life, to avoid quarrels and seek compromise; boys tend to be instructed about manliness and honor and are offered military models of heroism. ("Only a male orientation would keep us in Vietnam," argued the Boston theologian Mary Daly in 1971, "because we don't want to look like we're running away.") In any case, Gallup discovered that in May 1965, 58 percent of white men indicated support for the war, but only 48 percent of white women did; in April 1968 the figures were 48–40; and in April 1970, 41–30.

Many of the leading antiwar activists of the 1960s were women, continuing a long tradition in the history of the American peace movement, and two of the earliest groups to rise in protest against the Vietnam war were the Women's International League for Peace and Freedom and Women Strike for Peace. In general, those women who thought of themselves as committed feminists also opposed the war: Betty Friedan, Bella Abzug, Gloria Steinem, Robin Morgan, Bernadine Dohrn, Shirley Chisholm, and many others. When the National Women's Political Caucus formed in July 1971, included among the women's issues to be addressed (equal opportunity, abortion, day care) was a policy against the war in Vietnam. As might have been expected, women who took more conservative social positions and who were readier to advocate traditional roles for women, women who were about to mount a vocal and effective campaign against the Equal Rights Amendment, tended in larger numbers to support American policy in Vietnam. Phyllis Schlafly, the leading woman conservative of the 1960s and 1970s, had originally opposed sending American troops to Vietnam but once they were there, she vehemently denounced the failure, as she saw it, to pursue a policy aimed at gaining a clear victory.

Constructing a political agenda to which a sizable majority of American women might have subscribed was, clearly, never a real possibility. The bitter debate over the ERA revealed how fundamental were the differences that divided women. They struggled principally over the proper role for members of their sex, over the nature of the home and the family. It is wrong even to suggest, therefore, that Vietnam was at the heart of their political quarrel, that without the war the women of the United States might have somehow come together as a community in pursuit of common objectives. But it is surely correct to assert that for women, as for other subcommunities in the nation, differences over Vietnam added to the enmity and accentuated the distrust between citizens.

There were at least two reasons why black Americans might have been expected to support the war in Vietnam, at least in its early phases. First, the black community felt a substantial loyalty to Lyndon Johnson. The Democrats had garnered more than 80 percent of the black vote in 1964, but the loyalty to Johnson transcended mere party regularity. Johnson had proved to be one southern white who was deeply sympathetic to the aspirations of black people. He had pushed through the landmark Civil Rights Act of 1964; he spoke often and movingly about the moral necessity for achieving a society of equal opportunity for all citizens; and he was the father of the Great Society programs that were designed to eradicate poverty, improve education, and provide medical care for all Americans. He had also appointed blacks to federal office in unprecedented numbers. When the critics of the war loosed their furious attacks on the president, therefore, they were assailing a man for whom many blacks felt a certain gratitude, one whom many blacks hoped would continue to lead the great national struggle for racial equality.

A second reason why black Americans might have been pulled toward greater support for the war was that a high proportion of the fighting and dying in Vietnam was being done by young black men. In the mid-1960s blacks comprised around 11 percent of the population, ages nineteen to twenty-one; through 1966, however, 22 percent of the enlisted men killed in action were black. Some combat units were reported to be more than 50 percent black. The armed forces seemed to be one of the most thoroughly integrated institutions in American society, and in a nation still tainted by pervasive racial discrimination, opportunities for blacks in the military appeared to be much better than in northern cities or on the sharecrop farms of the rural South. Thus 45 percent of blacks in the military signed up for a second tour of duty, as compared to 17 percent of whites. To whatever extent the antiwar movement expressed animosity toward the fighting men in Vietnam or seemed to imply an unwillingness to back the boys up, blacks might have been expected to demur.

And yet, despite these strong reasons to support the war, blacks tended to oppose it in greater than average numbers, and black women were among those who were least favorable to the Vietnam war of any segment of the American population. According to the Gallup poll, in March 1966, 53 percent of black men approved of the war compared to 65 percent of white men, and 43 percent of black women approved compared to 54 percent of white women. By April 1970, 27 percent of black men and 41 percent of white men still approved, while only 19 percent of black women and 30 percent of white women did so. In part this relative lack of support can be accounted for by the fact that blacks were disproportionately found among other segments of the population that opposed the war or were indifferent to it: the very poor, those in metropolitan areas, and those with less education. In part, however, black Americans turned against the war for reasons of their own.

In the first place, once the war was turned over to the Nixon administration, in January 1969, lingering loyalty to the White House evaporated. Introduction of the lottery system for draftees meant that blacks were now being inducted at a rate (12.9 percent) only slightly out of proportion to their numbers in the population, and their death rate fell as well, until, at the end of the war, black Americans accounted for 12.7 percent of all deaths in Vietnam. This balancing of the war's racial burden may have negated one potential reason for blacks to manifest a disproportionate support for troops in the field. In addition, by the late 1960s widely publicized revelations began to circulate in the black community, indicating that the armed forces were not as free of prejudice as had been thought. In October 1966 a study showed that only 1.6 percent of the members of all American draft boards were blacks. By 1967, it was revealed, only 5 percent of blacks fit for service could get deferments while 95 percent of whites could. Only 3.5 percent of the officers in the army were black, and even fewer black officers could be found in the other services. Before the end of the decade returning black vets told harrowing tales of racism among the whites with whom they served, and some ugly incidents of racial violence had exploded among American servicemen in Vietnam.

Meanwhile, many black Americans had been caught up in the quickening pace of the civil rights crusade. The excitement of that dramatic movement affected black attitudes toward the war in several ways. Repeated complaints about the institutionalized racism of American society tended to make some blacks more skeptical of appeals to patriotism and calls to defend the flag. Influential civil rights leaders—Bayard Rustin, Floyd McKissick, Stokely Carmichael, and others—argued that young blacks should be fighting for freedom in the United States and not in Vietnam. Some in the movement also feared that the commitment in Vietnam was diverting scarce resources from the social programs of the Johnson administration and that the war climate was inevitably strengthening those conservative elements in America that had so often opposed civil rights for blacks. A few of the most radical argued that the war was just another case of whites killing nonwhites and that blacks entering into the exercise were, in Carmichael's words, merely "mercenaries of a white government . . . fighting their colored brothers in Vietnam."

Finally, the rejection of the war by two transcendent heroes of the black community, and the resulting abuse to which each was subjected, influenced many blacks to withhold their own support from it. Muhammad Ali, the flamboyant heavyweight champion of the world, became a Black Muslim in 1964 and applied for conscientious objector status: "I ain't got no quarrel with those Vietcong anyway; they never called me nigger." When his application was denied, he refused to report for induction and in June 1967 was sentenced to prison (the Supreme Court overturned his conviction in 1974). The defiance of Ali was savagely condemned by many whites, but his brash militancy elevated him into a symbol of manly resistance to white society and endeared him especially to numerous young blacks. Even more important was the opposition of Martin Luther King, Jr., the man who had come to personify the conscience and courage of the civil rights movement. He spoke out vigorously and with his usual eloquence against the war in 1967, emphasizing what he considered its brutal immorality. After his assassination in 1968, his widow, Coretta Scott King, became a leading antiwar activist.

The attitudes of American labor provide an interesting parallel to those of college and university students. In the latter case, as we have seen, opinion about the war was much more evenly divided than popular perception suspected. Because of the vociferousness, the energy, the level of commitment, and the occasional, but well-publicized, resort to violence of the antiwar students, most Americans erroneously believed that nearly all students opposed the Vietnam war. In the case of labor, the exact opposite appears to be true. Opinion among white workers was divided, but those who supported the war were somehow able to create the image of a working class that was solidly behind the policies of Lyndon Johnson and Richard Nixon.

There is, of course, a strong stereotype of white working class political feeling. According to this stereotype, workers may be liberal on bread-and-butter economic issues, but they are much more conservative when it comes to civil liberties, the rights of minorities, and foreign policy. On these matters, according to the common view, workers tend to favor easy answers, ones that can be reduced to simple slogans. They also tend to be belligerent and "macho," supporting solutions that involve action and that seem to be direct, tough, decisive, no-nonsense. As far as foreign policy is concerned, workers are generally thought to espouse old-fashioned patriotism, strident anticommunism, and a more frequent resort to force. They are, therefore, less patient with limited wars and more bellicose and intolerant when it comes to protesters, compromisers, and intellectuals. These attitudes are believed to derive from workers having less education, less interest in politics, and paying less attention to books, newspapers, magazines, and television news.

There was plenty of evidence for this stereotype of labor belligerence during the Vietnam years. Peace demonstrators were regularly told by jeering urban laborers to "Go back to Russia." Hardhats sometimes hurled their contempt and hatred (or weightier objects) down from the steel rafters of construction projects. Other workers would sometimes line the sidewalks along the route of peace marches. They carried posters that read "America, Love It or Leave It," flung vulgar insults at the women, and dared the men to step over to the curb and settle this thing like real men. These workers were far more threatening to opponents of the war than the police, and often only the police stood between the demonstrators and these taunting, brawny, infuriated men who "talked with their muscles." The worst instance of violence was in May 1970, when some New York City longshore-men, construction workers, and seamen—armed with hammers, pli-ers, or wire-cutters—tore into a crowd of peaceful demonstrators. The police were helpless (some said they stood by approvingly) as the workers smashed faces and stomped heads. They rampaged through City Hall and broke into nearby Pace College, where they beat the students without mercy, men and women alike. More than a few New Yorkers were reminded of the street work of Hitler's brown-shirts. When, three weeks later, Peter Brennan, leader of the construction workers, presented President Nixon with a hardhat, few missed the symbolism. The New York City episode was unusually vicious, but it was not by any means the only case of blue-collar violence upon those with whom they disagreed about the war. Such incidents reinforced the stereotype of the tough, mindless, simplistic, impulsive working-class patriot.

For many Americans of the 1960s, labor's attitude toward the war could be neatly summed up in the person of George Meany, the presi-dent of the AFL-CIO and, by virtue of his office, labor's preeminent spokesman. For decades a blunt anti-Communist, Meany had prob-ably favored sending the troops to Vietnam to aid the French in the early 1950s. Joseph C. Goulden, his biographer, wrote that "Meany supported Johnson unflinchingly on Vietnam. . . . [and] spoke more on Vietnam than on perhaps any single issue during 1965–1968." There is little reason to doubt Goulden's conclusion that on Vietnam "no unofficial American clung closer to Johnson than did Meany." He charged that antiwar activities, both inside and outside the labor movement, were "prefabricated" in Moscow and Peking or planned in Hanoi. Under his dominating influence, the AFL-CIO issued nine statements endorsing American policy between the Gulf of Tonkin Resolution and February 1968. The federation's national conventions ringingly endorsed the war. Nor did Meany's support lessen once President Nixon took over.

Nevertheless, despite outbreaks of labor anger against peace dem-onstrators or the staunchly prowar stance of Meany and other labor leaders, there is evidence of working-class discontent with the war. As was the case for other Americans, moreover, this discontent grew more vocal and angry as the war dragged on. Figures on the extent of working-class opposition to the war vary greatly. In the fall of 1967 the AFL-CIO's Committee on Political Education polled movement leaders and found strong support for the war: 1,448 endorsed gov-ernment policy; 1,368 favored escalation; 471 favored de-escalation; and 276 wanted withdrawal. On the other hand, figures from the Uni-versity of Michigan's Survey Research Center, both in 1964 and in

1968, tell another story. They indicate that there was almost no statistical difference between laborers and those labeled lower-middle or upper-middle class. In the 1968 poll, for example, 19 percent of working-class respondents favored pulling out of Vietnam, but so did 21 percent of the lower- and 19 percent of the upper-middle classes. Favoring a cease-fire were 40 percent of the working class, and 41 and 43 percent of the lower- and upper-middle classes. The SRC poll reported almost identical opinions from union and nonunion labor. These figures caused one social scientist, James D. Wright, to conclude that "as a group, workers were no more hawkish than those in white collar occupations."

By 1970 there were obvious signs within the labor movement of an open rebellion against Meany's position on Vietnam. "We do not believe that the leader of our great American trade union family speaks for that family in supporting the President in the present war dilemma of our nation," declared the official journal of the Amalgamated Meat Cutters and Butchers. Leonard Woodcock, president of the powerful United Auto Workers, and Jacob Potofsky, president of the Amalgamated Clothing Workers, both came out against the war. More than four hundred west coast union leaders signed a full-page ad in the *San Francisco Chronicle*: "We want out of Vietnam—Now! We've had it!" The signers were officers of the Teamsters, the International Longshoremen, the Building Trades Council, the Metal Trades Council, the Carpenters Council, and of many other unions. A few national unions and more than a few locals took official antiwar stands. A National Labor Committee to End the War was organized by Potofsky; so was a National Rank-and-File Action Conference in order to "get labor moving . . . to end the war."

There were many reasons for the labor revolt against the war. For some it was simple resentment against Meany's claim to speak for the entire movement. Others were uneasy about the fact that the working class's traditional allies—liberal Democrats, intellectuals, student activists—had come out against the war and that labor was, by the early 1970s, becoming increasingly isolated on the issue. Some feared the effects of the war on their own economic position; inflation, unemployment, and rising taxes were always among workers' worst fears, and there were signs that all three were taking their toll. Many believed the war was diverting attention and resources from the much-needed social and urban programs that would benefit workers directly. A few suspected that the war was merely a way to enrich big business, the corporate moguls, and, drawing on a venerable antibusiness rhetoric, opposed the war on that ground. For a number of reasons, therefore, American workers also experienced a little civil war in their ranks;

within this subcommunity, as within so many others, a deep division
had opened.

In his book about the campaign of 1968, *The Selling of the President*,
Joe McGinnis recounted a conversation between two Nixon aides:

> Then they talked about fund raising.
> "The first [Eugene] McCarthy telecast raised a hundred and twenty-
> five thousand dollars," Ruth Jones said.
> "Who gave the pitch?" [Frank] Shakespeare asked.
> "Paul Newman."
> "Oh, well, that made a difference."
> "It was a personal involvement pitch. Dick Goodwin wrote it for
> him."
> "We'll use the same pitch," Shakespeare said, "but we don't have as
> strong a man."
> "Who do we have?"
> "Bud Wilkinson."

There are celebrities in American society who the eminent sociologist
C. Wright Mills described as "The Names that need no further identification." Wherever they go, Mills added, "they are recognized, and
moreover, recognized with some excitement and awe. Whatever they
do has publicity value." Celebrities are created by the mass media, and
they tend to be actors or singers, rock stars or sports heroes or comics,
talk-show hosts or talk-show guests. For some reason, large numbers
of Americans appear to be susceptible to persuasion by such "personalities," which is why they can be found advising the public about
which candidate to send money to, or about what beer, what car, what
tennis shoe, or what insurance company to use. Celebrities also had
opinions about what was going on in Vietnam. They became another
group (a genuine "group" in the sense that they all seemed to know
one another by first name and all seemed to lunch at the same restaurants and were always firing off rounds of golf with one another) that
was badly split over the war.

Because of their proven ability to attract and persuade, celebrities
were much in demand as sponsors of or participants in both prowar
and antiwar exercises. Their names were prominently featured in advertisements that supported or condemned the war, and before it was
over some of them had established considerable reputations for their
devotion to one side or the other in the debate. There is no iron-clad
rule about the way they divided over the war, but in general those
celebrities who were older, who were prominent during World War

II, who had special appeal to that generation, tended to be in the ranks of those supporting the war in Vietnam. Younger celebrities tended to be found in the antiwar camp. But it is important to emphasize that there were many exceptions.

Advocates of the war could claim two celebrities who were at the very apex of their professions. John Wayne's movies had earned more money than those of any other Hollywood star, and in 1971 Bob Hope enjoyed the highest Nielsen ratings in television. Both men were enthusiastic supporters of the American presence in Vietnam. Wayne's *Green Berets,* as we have seen, attempted to model the conflict on World War II and repeated many of the most common prowar arguments. Wayne had little patience for those who opposed the war: "I think they oughta shoot 'em if they're carrying the Vietcong flag," he told an interviewer in December 1967; "As far as I'm concerned, it wouldn't bother me a bit to pull the trigger on one of 'em." Bob Hope, who had been entertaining troops overseas since the 1940s, also had a dim view of the protesters. Decent young Americans who did not riot or demonstrate, Hope thought, were "taking the rap for a lunatic fringe that gets mixed up with outsiders and subversive forces." The comedian was convinced that the war, while painful, was necessary. "If we weren't [fighting in Vietnam]," he said in January 1967, "those Commies would have the whole thing, and it wouldn't be long until we'd be looking at them off the coast of Santa Monica."

Other well-known figures supported the war beside Wayne and Hope. A host of popular entertainers felt comfortable enough about the views of Humphrey in 1968, or about those of Nixon in 1968 or 1972, to support them for the presidency of the United States. Among them were actors Charlton Heston, James Stewart, Chuck Connors, June Allyson, Clint Eastwood, Zsa Zsa Gabor, Fred MacMurray, Art Linkletter, Virginia Mayo, Gene Autry, and Lorne Greene. Also enlisted were singers Frank Sinatra, Tony Martin, Robert Goulet, Rudy Vallee, Pat Boone, and Frankie Avalon, and comedians Jimmy Durante, Ray Bolger, and Red Skelton.

But it was probably the antiwar side that won the battle for celebrities. Dozens of them lent their names to the movement; they raised funds, signed ads, appeared at demonstrations, and endorsed peace candidates. Although some of them were old timers who appealed to the World War II generation (Gregory Peck, Frederic March, Bette Davis, Burt Lancaster, Lauren Bacall, Myrna Loy, Gene Kelly, Henry Fonda, Artie Shaw, Melvyn Douglas, Jack Lemmon, and others), many of them were rising young stars who had immense appeal for middle-aged and younger Americans. Included among the actors who opposed the war in Vietnam (or who, at least, were willing to campaign for Eugene McCarthy, Robert Kennedy, or George McGovern) were Dustin Hoffman, Warren Beatty, Shirley MacLaine, Ryan O'Neal, Diahann Carroll, Tony Curtis, Gene Hackman, Walter Matthau, Robert Vaughn, Raquel Welch, Marlon Brando, Paul Newman, Sidney Poitier, Tony Randall, George C. Scott, and a great many others. Numerous singers and musicians became involved: Sammy Davis Jr., Leonard Bernstein, Carol Channing, Mahalia Jackson, Andre Previn, Mitch Miller, Theodore Bikel, Diana Ross, Andy Willliams, Joel Grey, Bobby Darin, Eartha Kitt, and Aretha Franklin. It would have been difficult to find a folksinger anywhere in the United States of America who favored the war in Vietnam. Among other celebrities who opposed the war or who worked for peace candidates were writers Joseph Heller, James Baldwin, Norman Mailer, Lilian Hellman, Robert Lowell, Arthur Miller, Neil Simon, and William Styron; comedians Woody Allen, Dick Van Dyke, Elaine May, Don Adams, Bill Cosby, and Steve Allen; and a contingent of well-known figures as diverse as Erich Fromm, Stan Musial, Charles Addams, Carl Reiner, and Jules Feiffer.

Indeed, in the early phases of the 1968 campaign the struggle to enlist celebrities was not so much between the antiwar and the prowar camps as it was between those who worked for Robert Kennedy and those who worked for Eugene McCarthy. In May, *Time Magazine* helped its readers out by running, under the title "Notable Names for Bobby & Gene," two parallel columns of illustrious personalities who had announced for one or the other of the peace candidates. In all, there were more than one hundred sixty names, and most Americans probably would have had an easier time recognizing them than they would trying to name members of Congress or the Supreme Court. Some stars were in a quandary. Barbra Streisand, for example, was claimed by both of the presidential hopefuls. "With two candidates now advocating peace," she explained, "I am trying to hear and learn as much as I can so I can make an intelligent decision." The assassination of Kennedy, five weeks later, propelled many stars into the McCarthy or the late-starting McGovern camps by default.

Two celebrities who became so closely identified with the antiwar movement as to emerge as symbols of the protest were singer Joan Baez and actress Jane Fonda. In her mid-twenties as the war began to escalate, Baez was gifted with a crystalline voice and was at the start of a promising career as a folksinger and recording artist. She used her talents to further several social causes and was particularly absorbed by the antiwar movement. She refused to pay her income taxes as a protest against the government's use of the money in Vietnam.

She married a well-known draft-resister, David Harris, and was herself arrested for picketing an army induction center in California. Baez sang and spoke on dozens of campuses and at dozens of demonstrations against the war. Fonda, the daughter of one of the nation's most revered actors, also combined her career with spirited social activism. She spoke frequently around the country, married SDS founder Tom Hayden, and helped fund, in 1971, the so-called "Winter Soldier" investigations into American atrocities in Southeast Asia. That same year she proposed a Bob Hope–like tour of army bases so that she might entertain the boys with a somewhat more radical message; when the authorities refused her request she and others played at local GI coffeehouses to packed and cheering crowds. Her most spectacular antiwar act, however, and one that many Americans could never quite forgive her for, was her trip to North Vietnam in the summer of 1972. She visited American prisoners of war, made a radio broadcast to American troops, and was promptly dubbed "Hanoi Jane."

Decisions about the war among the celebrities were sometimes deeply personal. Gregory Peck came out against American policy despite the fact that his son served as a combat marine in Vietnam. And Frank Sinatra made the opposite choice, eventually campaigning for Nixon, despite opposition to the war by his wife, Mia Farrow, and such close friends as Sammy Davis, Jr., Peter Lawford, and Shirley MacLaine. But except for being less private, the divisions caused by Vietnam among the "Names that needed no further identification" were not unlike those being created elsewhere. All across America people of the same political party, the same religion, and the same profession, people on the same campus, in the same union, and of the same family found themselves at odds about this. In a hundred small ways the social cement that holds a nation together showed signs of crumbling, and many sensitive observers, no matter how they felt about the war, were afraid for the country.

VII.

The debate over Vietnam, raging within and between the subcommunities of America, did not take place in a vacuum. It was profoundly affected, provided its distinctive tone, even—in some ways—made possible, by the cultural climate of the time. By general agreement Americans have manufactured a shorthand designation for that climate: "the sixties." And like all such shorthand designations (particularly those that blithely divide American history into decades and then pretend that each of these arbitrary ten-year periods has unique characteristics), this one too has become distorted by simplistic stereotypes. To many Americans "the sixties" conjures up pictures of long-haired hippies ingesting God only knows what harmful, disgusting, and illegal substances; half-crazed radicals at work making bombs in their basements; and rebellious youth defying the establishment, joining cults, hitchhiking to gigantic and pagan rock festivals, and studying nothing so hard as how to bring grief to their bewildered parents. These images have been slow to die, no doubt because they are lovingly perpetuated both by those who invest that time with a romantic nostalgia and by those who recoil in horror and tell cautionary tales about the unspeakable excesses.

Sober analysts of the 1960s caution against these stereotypes. First, they remind us, the pictures associated most readily with the 1960s really come into prominence only at mid-decade; nor do they automatically disappear on the final day of 1969, but extend, in some places, far into the 1970s. Even more important, the so-called counterculture— that widely publicized rejection of traditional American faiths about technological progress, sexual propriety, materialism, and the nature of the good society—was largely the preoccupation of a small segment of middle- and upper-middle class youth. It seems that the bulk of Americans of the 1960s were not so different from those of the 1940s or 1950s, not so different from those of the 1970s or 1980s. The shifts in sentiment and culture that did appear were rather more modest than either those who applauded them or those who hated and feared them like to insist.

It is possible, nevertheless, to isolate, cautiously, some propensities that were especially accentuated in the years after 1965. That it was a time of heightened social activism would be hard to deny. The civil rights movement, beginning during the last half of the 1950s, captured the imaginations of millions of Americans. The examples of courage and determination on the part of young blacks and whites during the early 1960s inspired others to pursue their rights in American society. Soon women, Native Americans, Chicanos, homosexuals, farm workers, and the urban poor were demanding an end to second-class citizenship. The activity that began in the various struggles for equal rights spread to a dozen other issues: tighter control over business, conservation, preservation of the environment, provision of medical care for those who could not afford it, reform of education, and disarmament and world peace. By the time it was over, historians were ready to concede that Americans had just been through a period not unlike the 1830s, the 1910s, or the 1930s, a period when many fundamental beliefs and institutions were called before the bar of public opinion and required to justify themselves.

To the extent that such activities habituated Americans to social protest, this part of the cultural climate of the 1960s aided the efforts of the antiwar movement when the time came to protest the war in Vietnam. Large numbers of Americans had grown more or less accustomed to organized action on behalf of change. They had already witnessed, in Alabama and Mississippi, the contorted faces of citizens as they angrily asserted differing visions of proper social policy. They had already seen, in the name of other causes, the bold willingness to question and resist the government itself. The constitutional defenses of free speech had all been enunciated before they were required to defend antiwar activities. The dramatic techniques of protest—marches, sit-ins, pickets, civil disobedience and submission to arrest, political lobbying and campaigning—were no longer so new or startling. In these ways, the movement against the war was the beneficiary of the climate of the 1960s. In turn, the massive effort against the war further encouraged other such pursuits and fed back into the more general social ferment.

Such pervasive reform activity implied a willingness to challenge and resist authority, a readiness not just to question policies, customs, and institutions, but to oppose the powerful figures who made the policies, enforced the customs, and represented the institutions. Many observers detected just such a shift in view during the 1960s, a shift that seemed especially noticeable after the relatively unquestioning patriotism and conformity of the 1940s and 1950s. Even if the extent of the rebellion came to be overstated, there was plenty of evidence that skepticism had become fashionable. From bumper stickers that read "Question Authority" to popular novels and movies, the disposition to resist those in power seemed everywhere ascendant by the early 1960s. John Yossarian, the hero of Joseph Heller's immensely popular novel, *Catch-22* (1961), specialized in thwarting the bumbling and insensitive Army officers placed in control of his life. Randall P. McMurphy, the central character of Ken Kesey's *One Flew over the Cuckoo's Nest* (1962), devoted himself to disrupting the dictatorship of the Big Nurse, a tyrant hired by society to enforce order, efficiency, and adjustment. Hollywood responded to this cultural climate—and greatly reinforced it—with films that ridiculed authority or exalted rebels against the absurd world that authority had made. Millions flocked to see *Dr. Strangelove* (1964), *Bonnie and Clyde* (1967), *The Graduate* (1967), *Cool Hand Luke* (1967), *Easy Rider* (1969), *Midnight Cowboy* (1969), *Butch Cassidy and the Sundance Kid* (1969), and *M*A*S*H* (1970). The tone of irreverence, combined with admiration for rebels who remained true to their own visions, was echoed in fashion, popular music, hairstyles, and the drug culture.

This willingness to ridicule and resist authority carried a more ambiguous legacy for the antiwar movement than did the impulse toward social reform. On the one hand, the possibility that those in power might be vicious, corrupt, and ridiculous and that their policies might be wrong-headed, immoral, and unjust is almost a prerequisite for organization and protest. It is hard to imagine resistance to the war taking the shape it did without so strong a suspicion of the political, military, and economic leadership of America. On the other hand, it soon became apparent that resistance to authority could just as easily be directed against the movement to end the war itself. Criticism of leaders was never confined to those managing the war; it was easily transferable to those opposing it. From start to finish, therefore, numerous opponents of the Vietnam war proved congenitally unable to follow orders, to suppress, even for a moment, their own individual instincts, to drop some personal preference in the name of a group purpose. The unrestrained bickering among those who opposed the war was often as ferocious as the quarrels between the war's opponents and its supporters. This internal bickering was also a product of the 1960s' celebration of the unhampered individual, freed from the constraints of other people's authority.

And when the climate of the 1960s led to the conclusion that the modern world was inherently and incurably absurd (rather than merely being seriously, but not irreparably, misguided), the reaction was bound to be, in many instances, not to fight, but to flee. Thousands upon thousands of Americans, young and old, drew exactly that conclusion. As thoroughly suspicious of authority as their activist cousins, they took the war in Vietnam to be just another instance of the stupidity, brutality, and futility of it all. For many of them the appropriate response was to withdraw, to escape, to pursue private rather than social avenues of relief. They retreated (contending all the while that it was an advance) into drugs, sexual experimentation, eastern religion, meditation therapies, and isolated rural utopias. Sure that social effort was fruitless, that political organization was just another way to enforce conformity upon free individuals, they removed themselves from the struggle. To the regular frustration of the antiwar activists, with whom they shared both the hatred of authority and the judgment that the war was wrong, they were more or less lost to the cause of peace.

But individuals and groups opposed to the war in Vietnam determined to proceed anyway. Aided more than hampered by the cultural atmosphere of the 1960s, encouraged by the discovery that there were whole subcommunities within the nation that shared their feelings, willing to challenge the normally undisputed power of the president to conduct foreign policy, they set about to broadcast their reservations and to organize their opposition.

5: THE CONFRONTATION

How Americans Debated the War in Vietnam

I.

The first public criticism of American *purposes* in Vietnam (as opposed to even earlier misgivings about the adequacy of the means being employed to achieve those purposes) no doubt came as part of a general indictment of American foreign policy. Probably some already established radical or pacifist group, while making known its views on a range of policies it considered dangerous or immoral, paused to argue that the government's policy in Vietnam was just one more example of sinister American activity that imperiled world peace. By the late spring or early summer of 1963 such denunciations were occurring regularly. Despite the gradual awakening of public interest in Vietnam, however, it is not entirely surprising that these first criticisms were almost wholly ignored. They were offered, after all, by people located at the outermost fringes of the nation's politics, a region of national life that few Americans have ever taken very seriously.

Even in the minds of those committed few, moreover, Vietnam, in mid-1963, did not occupy an especially central place. They had more important things to think about. The civil rights movement claimed much of the attention of those who were also likely to be concerned about Vietnam; it reached a kind of crescendo on August 28, when two hundred fifty thousand people gathered in Washington to register their commitment to a society of racial equality. Energies were also being absorbed by other causes: working against poverty and for social welfare, combating the military-industrial complex, reforming education; agitating for a general democratization of American life.

As far as foreign affairs were concerned, much more interest was generated, among pacifists and radicals as well as among everyday Americans, by other matters. The arms race, general disarmament and a test-ban treaty, Cuba and Laos, ongoing rivalries with the Soviet Union and China, Pope John XXIII's hopeful new encyclical, *Pacem in Terris*—all seemed to produce more emotion or require more effort than Vietnam.

Despite these other engrossing concerns, however, some scattered (and entirely ineffectual) objections to government policy in Vietnam surfaced even before the November deaths of Diem and Kennedy. At the somewhat ritualistic rallies held by pacifist and radical groups during Easter week or in early August to commemorate the dropping of the atomic bomb on Hiroshima, America's role in Vietnam started to receive more protracted and critical attention. The horrifying pictures of monks burning themselves to death and the televised violence against Buddhists during the summer also sparked mild protest. The residence of Saigon's representative to the United Nation was picketed by a handful of New Yorkers, and when Madame Nhu, Diem's sister-in-law, embarked on an American tour to drum up support for the regime, she was treated a little roughly by some SDS members and others on a few college campuses. At this early stage opposition was expressed almost exclusively in moral terms. Most public policy intellectuals seemed generally satisfied with the goals of American policy, but more and more of them were developing reservations about the chances for success with Diem in control.

For all practical purposes the movement against the Vietnam war took shape during the twenty months between the start of 1964 and the end of the summer of 1965. Dramatic and troubling events kept forcing the issue before the public. That parade of ineffective and corrupt South Vietnamese leaders, after Diem, caused many Americans to wonder about the wisdom and morality of the undertaking. The Gulf of Tonkin incident, the ensuing resolution, and the elevation of the war into a campaign issue in the fall of 1964 certainly focused attention on the conflict. The rapidly deepening involvement after Lyndon Johnson's inauguration—the start of retaliatory bombing against North Vietnam in February 1965, the beginning of wide, nonretaliatory bombing of the North and the arrival of the first marines in March, and the authorization of a direct combat role for them in early June—must have bothered numerous Americans. Above all, the enormous escalation of the American presence caused even the drowsiest citizen to see that something grim and important was happening. At the beginning of 1964 there were 16,300 American military personnel in Vietnam, and they were largely restricted to advisory, transport, technical, and guarding duties. At the end of the summer of 1965 there were 132,300; there was frank acknowledgment that more were on the way (a total of 184,300 by the end of the year); and they were engaged in every facet of a brutal, casualty-producing land war in Asia. The movement against that war escalated with a kind of inevitability alongside the war itself.

During the first half of this twenty-month period, the protest remained largely the work of pacifists and radicals. Through 1964 they conducted a series of antiwar activities that began, slowly, to capture notice: letter writing and lobbying campaigns during the spring, a few newspaper ads signed by young men declaring that they would not fight in this war, a "May 2nd Movement" that gathered medical supplies for North Vietnam and issued "A Declaration of Conscience," prayer vigils outside the White House in July and in New York in October. These steps, and a few others like them, were organized by groups such as the Women's International League for Peace and Freedom, the Progressive Labor Party, the Young Socialist Alliance, the Student Peace Union, Students for a Democratic Society, the Society of Friends, or the Socialist Workers Party. When they needed leaders of experience and reputation, they turned to such people as A. J. Muste, I. F. Stone, Bayard Rustin, Joan Baez, David Dellinger, Norman Thomas, Tom Hayden, the Berrigan brothers—all veterans of the civil rights crusade, of years of lonely pacifist or radical causes, or members of the rising generation of student activists.

But by the end of the period three critical developments had taken place. First, the protest against the war succeeded in enlisting large numbers of nontraditional participants: college professors and students not especially known for radicalism, liberal Democrats, housewives, clergymen, lawyers, journalists, and some union leaders. By the autumn of 1965 sizable antiwar demonstrations could be mounted on either coast. The SDS Easter protest against the war drew more than fifteen thousand people to Washington in April; the first Vietnam Day at Berkeley, on May 21, attracted around twenty thousand; the International Days of Protest, October 15–16, saw demonstrations in dozens of cities that may have involved as many as one hundred thousand Americans. The second change in the antiwar movement was just as significant. In the beginning the protests had come mostly in reaction to particular events in Vietnam; thus the first bombings of the North in February 1965 provoked campus protests, a picket line at the White House, a small demonstration at the United Nations, and ads in the *New York Times*. By the end of the summer of 1965, however, the movement was able to sustain itself as a continuing presence that was not dependent upon fresh incidents. It became possible, therefore, to announce antiwar activities well in advance and be relatively confident of significant participation.

A third development of inestimable importance was the experimentation with a wide variety of techniques for publicizing opposition. Excluding only a certain propensity for violence that later came to characterize some antiwar elements, almost all the methods that would ever be used were tried, at least in embryonic form, by the fall of 1965. Some had been employed in earlier wars, in labor disputes, or in the civil rights movement; others were invented especially for this war, or so fully elaborated and matured as to make them seem new. Before these months were over Americans witnessed not only lobbying and letter-writing campaigns, vigils, and signed advertisements, but tactics that were more unsettling: widespread draft resistance, including after late July the public burning of hundreds of draft cards; demonstrations at familiar public landmarks; sit-ins, such as the one at SDS's Easter march on Washington; submission to arrest and other forms of civil disobedience; lying down in front of troop trains, as was attempted in Oakland, California, in early September; even meeting directly with the enemy, as was done by members of the Women's Strike for Peace in Jakarta, in mid-summer. One method that captured much public attention was the "teach-in." In its classic form it involved canceling the normal work of a college or university and, in its place, holding seminars, lectures, debates, and spirited discussions on the war. The first one occurred at the University of Michigan on March 24, 1965. By the end of the school year, two months later, teach-ins had achieved a vogue on campuses across the nation; before the war ended, hundreds of leading colleges and universities had conducted one or more of them.

Also apparent by the autumn of 1965 were some internal tensions that were to plague the antiwar movement until the end. Should Communists, other revolutionaries, and those who openly favored the enemy be excluded from antiwar activities or welcomed to participate? How could those insisting on peaceful methods of protest be encompassed within the same effort as those favoring less passive, more energetic, or even violent means? Should the movement demand immediate withdrawal or less radical positions: an end to escalation, cessation of bombing, negotiations, and an "honorable" solution to the war? Each of these internal debates turned upon a central strategic question. Should the antiwar movement aim to increase its financial, political, and moral support among millions of ordinary Americans? If so, excluding Communists, shunning violence, and advocating moderate measures short of immediate withdrawal might make sense. Or should the movement be the work of a vanguard of idealistic, uncompromised, and courageous individuals whose task was to point the way. If so, then it might occasionally have to go beyond tactics designed to win superficial popularity and middle-class acceptability.

In early August 1965, after extensive protests against the war in connection with the twentieth anniversary of Hiroshima, the first phase of the antiwar movement culminated in the formation of a new organization. All shades of opinion were able to come together, at least for the moment, to create the National Coordinating Committee to End the War in Vietnam. That body set out to organize the work of more than thirty antiwar groups. To those within the movement, it was probably clear that, however hopeful it might be on other grounds, the new committee could not hope to paper over all the internal strains in their enterprise. To those supporting the war, on the other hand, the Committee to End the War must have appeared to be at least a formidable opponent in the battle over public opinion and national policy, and at worst a highly dangerous collection of traitors.

It is hard to know precisely when decision-makers first realized that they were going to have a problem with public opinion. The critics of the war seemed, at first, so utterly without credibility that answering them might actually have had the unwanted effect of enhancing their stature. Besides, which policy-expert in the early days dreamed that the conflict would reach the stage it eventually did? A little show of force, they assumed, a few promises of subsequent American aid, a concession or two at some bargaining table, and America's opponents would see reason. Once Ho Chi Minh "sobers up and unloads his pistol," as Johnson put it, the whole thing would end with the public amply satisfied by the resolute stand against communism. In addition, those in power were fully aware of the uncertainty of public opinion when it came to foreign affairs. Johnson's rating in the polls rose dramatically, for example, both after halting the bombing in late 1965 and after resuming it a month later. (After studying the data in July 1966 the sociologist Seymour Martin Lipset concluded that "most Americans are, in fact, doves *and* hawks.") Policy-makers also recognized the terrible ignorance of the American people about the rest of the world. One poll of the mid-1960s revealed that one out of four Americans was not aware that Communists ruled China. In the face of this innocence, ambivalence, and lack of knowledge, many in Washington believed that constructing a responsible foreign policy might have to be done without constantly taking the pulse of public opinion. Finally, both the overwhelming support for the Gulf of Tonkin Resolution in August 1964 and Johnson's landslide election victory in November assured proponents of the war that public opinion was generally supportive and certainly manageable.

By the start of 1965, however, and the decisions to raise the stakes in Vietnam, policy-makers realized that something positive would have to be done to avoid the erosion of public approval. The initial response of the Johnson administration was to insist that bombing North Vietnam and introducing the marines constituted neither radical escalation nor a new kind of policy, but were logical extensions of what had been the country's policy since the 1950s. The State Department issued its official justification, *Aggression from the North*, emphasizing the enemy's ruthless immorality, in late February, three weeks after the start of the bombing and nine days before sending in the marines. Those hoping that Johnson's calming tone and the State Department's documentation of North Vietnam's belligerence would be enough to contain the protest were badly disappointed. Journalist I. F. Stone's answer to *Aggression from the North* refuted the document at every key point and was widely circulated; militants in the Senate refused to be silenced; telegrams pouring into the White House were more than ten-to-one against the bombing; and teach-ins and other antiwar activities around the nation accelerated rather than diminished.

Against this background the president traveled to Baltimore on April 7 to deliver a major address on Vietnam at the Johns Hopkins University. In that brief and emotional talk Johnson touched virtually all of the themes that comprised the defense of administration policy. He emphasized the purity of American motives: "We have no territory there, nor do we seek any. . . . Our objective is the independence of South Vietnam, and its freedom from attack. We want nothing for ourselves." He sounded both of the notes that had rallied Americans to action since the late 1930s, implying that participation in this war was amply sanctioned by the traditional categories of just warfare. The enemy was clearly immoral: "The first reality is that North Vietnam has attacked the independent nation of South Vietnam. Its object is total conquest. . . . And it is a war of unparalleled brutality. Simple farmers are the targets of assassination and kidnapping. Women and children are strangled in the night because their men are loyal to their Government." And the nation's security was imperiled. "Over this war, and all Asia, is another reality: the deepening shadow of Communist China. . . . The contest in Vietnam is part of a wider pattern of aggressive purpose. . . . There are great stakes in the balance." So that none might miss the point, Johnson drew a parallel to the mistakes of the 1930s:

> Let no one think for a moment that retreat from Vietnam would bring an end to conflict. The battle would be renewed in one country and then another. The central lesson of our time is that the appetite of aggression is never satisfied. To withdraw from one battlefield means only to prepare for the next. We must say in Southeast Asia, as we did in Europe, in the words of the Bible: "Hitherto shalt thou come, but no further."

While stressing the major themes of morality and national security, Johnson took up some minor ones as well. This was, he insisted, raw aggression rather than a civil war: "Of course, some of the people of South Vietnam are participating in this attack on their own government. But trained men and supplies, orders and arms, flow in a constant stream from North to South. This support is the heartbeat of the war." There was, he also maintained, a higher morality involved than might be obvious if one focused only on the horrors of battle: "We are there because we have a promise to keep. Since 1954 every American President has offered support to the people of South Vietnam. . . . Thus, over many years, we have made a national pledge to help South Vietnam defend its independence. And I intend to keep our promise." It was important, moreover, to "strengthen world order" by keeping in the world a force dedicated to freedom: "Around the globe, from Berlin to Thailand, are people whose well-being rests, in part, on the belief that they can count on us if they are attacked. To leave Vietnam to its fate would shake the confidence of all these people in the value of American commitment, the value of America's word." The recent escalation must not be seen as a change of purpose. "It is a change in what we believe that purpose requires." Finally, the president declared, he longed for peace and was ready at any time for "unconditional discussions"; he also proposed a massive foreign aid program for the hundred million wretched people of Southeast Asia.

If Johnson and his advisers thought that this reasonable and conciliatory expression of America's purposes would still the growing doubts about the war, they were quickly set straight. For a brief period White House mail indicated support for the policy. But ten days after Baltimore the SDS march on Washington took place, undeterred and right on schedule; teach-ins continued through the school year all across the country; and plans for new antiwar activities were being announced almost every week. The Johnson administration stepped up both its efforts to persuade and the warmth of its language. To counter the teach-ins, the State Department sent "truth squads" to the campuses, thereby suggesting that the campuses had been hearing something other than the truth. On April 23 Secretary of State Dean Rusk assailed "the gullibility" of the protesters and the "educated men . . . who are supposed to be helping our young to learn—especially to learn how to think." Washington officials agreed to a series of debates, culminating in a fifteen-hour "national teach-in" broadcast to dozens of colleges and universities on May 15 and a televised debate between Hans Morgenthau and McGeorge Bundy on June 21. Finally, Johnson attempted to demonstrate his good will by ordering a brief bombing pause in mid-May.

But neither the bombing nor the bombing pause, neither the introduction of the marines nor the expansion of their combat role brought the hoped for progress in the war. Instead, the Communists seemed more determined than ever, as if the bombing had somehow strengthened their will. They launched a new offensive in May 1965, inflicting dispiriting losses on the ARVN and leaving the South's military close to chaos. Meanwhile, Saigon was in yet another cabinet crisis and undergoing the fifth change of government since Diem's death. This deteriorating situation was the backdrop for the critical discussions that took place in Washington on July 21 and 22. With only George Ball putting forward the case for withdrawal, the president's advisers argued for immediate and dramatic escalation of the war. On July 28 Johnson went on television to announce that he was sending over another fifty thousand men and that more would follow. It was no longer possible to disguise the fact that Vietnam had become an American war.

Although the president wanted to "avoid undue concern and excitement in the Congress and in domestic public opinion," the July decisions effectively threw down the gauntlet. Opponents of the war saw the move as an open-ended commitment to an impossible and immoral crusade; proponents, some wishing for even more drastic action, were satisfied that the United States was at last going to stand up against the expansion of communism in Asia. As the summer of 1965 drew to a close, both sides were ready to take off the gloves. In the same August week that saw such massive antiwar demonstrations and the formation of the National Coordinating Committee to End the War in Vietnam, the Congress overwhelmingly passed a new law. From now on, any citizen who willfully destroyed a draft card would face the possibility of a $10,000 fine and five years in jail. The lines were drawn.

II.

More than two years later, at the end of 1967, *Harper's* magazine sent David Halberstam back to Vietnam. The former *New York Times* reporter, whose stories from the field had won the Pulitzer Prize in 1964, returned to see what difference had been made by the huge buildup of American power. He quickly noticed the outward signs of his countrymen's presence: the large number of Americans on the streets, the weaponry, the concrete, the TV, the barracks and bars and brothels, the car washes and the Vietnamese kids in Batman t-shirts. But it was not the transformation of Vietnam that most impressed Halberstam: "what finally struck me was how little had really changed here." Indeed, in the two and a half years since the fateful decision to make Vietnam into an American war, it did not seem as though the government's military and political objectives had advanced very far at all.

Despite increasing the number of military personnel (from 184,300 at the end of 1965 to 485,600 at the end of 1967), despite dropping ever more bombs on North Vietnam (from twenty-five thousand sorties and sixty-three thousand tons in 1965 to one hundred eighty thousand sorties and two hundred twenty-six thousand tons in 1967) and double that amount on the territory of the South Vietnamese ally, it was very hard to see much progress in the war. The Vietcong appeared as tough and elusive as ever, and the North Vietnamese, just as capable of infiltrating men and supplies south along the Ho Chi Minh trail. American field commanders might produce impressive body counts, but they could scarcely police the whole countryside, and gains proved ephemeral. "We can go into an area and improve the security," said an embassy official in November 1967. "But then pull the American boots out of the area and it would go Red in a week." South Vietnam's army was as inefficient, corrupt, and unreliable as Halberstam remembered; it was, he reported, "poorly led and barely motivated. Its officers represent a microcosm of existing privilege in Vietnam." Naturally, given the ARVN's uncertain dependability, the critical fighting was assigned to Americans. By the end of 1967 more than thirteen thousand of them had been killed. And although American troops were able to prevent an enemy victory, and although American officials continued to report progress and profess optimism, to many back home it looked a lot like a costly, unending stalemate.

Almost as frustrating as the record on the battlefield was the effort to construct a democratic South Vietnam. In spite of early pessimistic predictions, Premier Ky, who had taken over in May 1965, somehow managed to retain power. Hoping that a stable government had at last been found and anxious to signal his confidence in it, President Johnson arranged a meeting with Ky in Honolulu in February 1966. But Washington's hopes for democratic reforms were dashed less than a month later. A violent Buddhist uprising erupted in March and lasted through the entire spring of 1966, an uprising that revealed both considerable anti-American feeling and the fragile nature of Ky's command of his people's affection and loyalty. Finally, the pervasive corruption that had characterized so much of South Vietnamese society was worse than ever. Halberstam observed, during his return visit, that "each day in the Vietnamese government and the Vietnamese Army it is a little more likely that if a position is any good it must be bought"; he sadly concluded that "the sons are more corrupt than the fathers." This venality affected all aspects of the American effort. It filled the ARVN officer corps with incompetents, siphoned off millions of dollars of American supplies into the black market, winked at the growing narcotics traffic, and stole the necessities that American taxpayers thought they were sending to the wretched refugees they saw every night on television.

If there was any bright spot during the period from the end of 1965 to the close of 1967, it was the successful effort, under constant American prodding, to produce a democratic constitution for South Vietnam and to conduct elections under its provisions in September 1967. These elections resulted in a victory for the Thieu-Ky administration (Ky agreeing, under pressure, to accept second place and relinquish the presidency to the more dignified and steady Thieu). But it was hard for Americans to derive much confidence from the results. Even with the help of last minute fraud, Thieu and Ky got only about a third of the votes; the party advocating immediate negotiations with the Vietcong polled 17 percent. Thus even this determined exercise in democracy left many Americans unsure about the character of Saigon leadership or its ability to win the allegiance of its people, root out the corruption, and carry on the struggle against communism.

For Halberstam, as no doubt for many Americans, the new constitution and the elections did not make much difference. His return to Vietnam came two months after the Thieu-Ky victory; but his conclusions were not optimistic:

> I do not think we are winning, and the reasons seem to me to be so basic that while I would like to believe my friends that there is a last chance opening up again in Vietnam, it seems to me a frail hope indeed. I do not think we are winning in any true sense, nor do I see any signs we are about to win. That is why this is such a sad story to write,

for I share that special affection for the Vietnamese, and I would like to write that though the price is heavy, it is worth it. I do not think our Vietnamese can win their half of the war, nor do I think we can win it for them.

Thus the weakness of America's ally and the stolid resistance of the enemy combined, at the end of 1967, to spoil the predictions of an early and successful conclusion to the war. After more than two years of extraordinary American effort, the Communists seemed, at the very least, to be holding their own. Their stubbornness caused some surprise among those planning the war and more than a few expressions of grudging admiration on the part of those actually doing the fighting. For a great many ordinary Americans, however, there was growing impatience and a nagging suspicion—as the price mounted and the dead and wounded kept coming back home—that maybe the thing wasn't worth it.

To critics of the war it appeared that the enemy's stubborn resistance was drawing the United States into an insane and futile escalation and into acts of increasing and unconscionable brutality. The National Coordinating Committee to End the War, that umbrella organization founded in August 1965 to bring some unity to antiwar efforts, tried to show the growing discontent during the International Days of Protest on October 15 and 16. Demonstrations took place in cities throughout the world. In America they centered on both coasts with a big march from Berkeley to the Oakland Army Base and an even bigger one down Fifth Avenue in New York City. But instead of revealing a unified movement, the events exposed the unmistakable tensions that were to plague antiwar efforts for the next seven tumultuous years and destroy all hopes for solidarity among those trying to end the war. The central quarrel in the movement was still between those wishing to appear "respectable" in order to win to their cause the masses of uncommitted, everyday, middle-class Americans, and those who believed that middle-class Americans were the problem and that only dramatic, even outrageous, acts of defiance would awaken the country from its lethargy. These conflicts were acted out in interminable debates. Who should be permitted to participate, and who should be excluded? What slogans should be used, and what policies advocated? What tactics—from dignified petitions presented to persons in authority to bursting through police lines—were permissible? Two antiwar efforts at the very end of 1965 can be taken as symbolic of the two approaches.

The antidraft activities of the radicals seemed calculated to irritate middle America. Counseling young men on how to evade induction, picketing local draft boards, and pressuring colleges to keep students' records private so as not to endanger their deferments were examples of this sort of work. Above all, the public burning of draft cards in the face of the new law, as in the New York City ceremony on November 6, provoked hysterical anger both among bystanders on the sidewalk and across the entire nation. These gestures may have demonstrated graphically the outrage over American policy and the uncompromising rejection of this war on the part of many young people; they also—as others within the movement never tired of pointing out—enraged and alienated the very people needed in order to stop the killing in Vietnam. On the other hand, the November 27 march in Washington, D.C., organized by SANE, tried to win the respectable and decorous. *Time* magazine reported that the event was carried out by twenty-two thousand "older, quieter protesters," and *Newsweek* called it "remarkably peaceful." The organizers prepared a list of seventeen approved poster slogans and deputized three hundred monitors to insure good order. They chose, as sponsors and speakers, men and women of impeccable credentials: among others, Tony Randall, Arthur Miller, Coretta Scott King, Alexander Calder, Norman Thomas, Saul Bellow, Benjamin Spock, and Albert Sabin, inventor of the polio vaccine.

In the end, however, the SANE march revealed how difficult would be the dignified approach to large public demonstrations. First, the demonstrators could be ignored—President Johnson went to his Texas ranch, and the aide who met with the delegation, while perfectly polite, failed to give very satisfactory answers. In addition, not even SANE's strenuous efforts at dignity could prevent much of the media from ridiculing the whole enterprise. Finally, it simply proved impossible for organizers of the SANE march to maintain the tone they wanted. Radicals appeared in the crowd carrying some decidedly unauthorized slogans on their posters; some waved Vietcong flags; others chanted "Hey, hey, LBJ. How many kids did you kill today?" Reporters gave at least as much coverage to the rowdies as to the respectables. These disadvantages would continually haunt the decorous opponents of the war and practically foreclosed to them the benefits of large, open-air demonstrations against American policy.

During the years 1966 and 1967 the most effective moment for those who wished to oppose the war in moderate and socially acceptable terms, hoping to persuade average citizens to join them, came in early 1966, and it came in exactly the sort of closed forum most conducive to dignity, moderation, and expressions of patriotism: the United States Senate. The hearings before Senator William Fulbright's heavily antiwar Foreign Relations Committee—a result of the president's decision to resume bombing after a five-week pause and to do so despite the pleas of many congressmen and senators—were televised live by two of the major networks and commanded a huge audience of curious Americans. Testifying on behalf of administration policy were Secretary of State Rusk and General Maxwell Taylor. They made the usual arguments in favor of the war and were subjected to some sharp and testy questioning by the antiwar members of the committee.

Testifying against American policy were Lieutenant General James Gavin and George Kennan. General Gavin advocated an end to escalation and a strategy of holding defensible enclaves along the coast of South Vietnam, thereby denying the enemy a victory until a negotiated settlement could be reached. His position was promptly endorsed in a letter from General Matthew Ridgway. Kennan argued forcefully against the rationale of the Johnson policy, suggested that the country had no important interests in the area, and also warned of the perils of continued escalation. Gavin had been a professional soldier for thirty-five years, the commander of the army's Eighty-second Airborne Division when he was only thirty-seven, and President Kennedy's ambassador to France; Ridgway had commanded the U.N. forces in Korea and served as Supreme Allied Commander in Europe and chief of staff of the United States Army; Kennan was known to be one of the most thoughtful analysts of American foreign relations—in 1966 he was at the Princeton Institute for Advanced Study. Each of the three rejected precipitate, unilateral flight from Vietnam and favored liquidating the war with as much dignity and patriotism as was possible under the circumstances. Above all, none of them looked as though he was getting ready to set fire to his draft card. Their immense prestige and obvious authority lent a new respectability to criticism of the war and seemed to provide a clear, moderate, and honorable alternative to American policy. Key parts of the testimony (including the appearance of Secretary Rusk before the committee on January 28) were published by Random House so that even those who might have missed the broadcasts could familiarize themselves with the various positions.

If, during the years 1966 and 1967, the Fulbright hearings were the high point for the older, quieter protesters, "Stop the Draft Week," (October 16–22, 1967), which culminated in a spectacular march on the Pentagon, was the best example of the other sort of antiwar activity. The hectic week began with nationwide protests against the draft that included picketing and disrupting draft boards, urban guerrilla tactics, violent confrontations with the police, large numbers of draft card burnings and "turn-ins." Emboldened by a new organization called "The Resistance," urged on by women carrying signs that read "Girls say yes to men who say no," demonstrations erupted everywhere at once: Los Angeles, Chicago, Boston, Washington, Philadelphia, Cincinnati, San Francisco, Brooklyn, Ithaca, Madison, Portland. Hundreds were arrested in an orgy of hostility, tear gas, nightsticks, and profanity. The *New York Times* reporter at one protest felt obliged to mention that "a marijuana-like odor floated over the crowd." Middle-class America gasped in disbelief—which was, of course, at least part of the intent. Folks in the heartland may not have entirely made up their minds about the war, but they were pretty sure that this was no way to be behaving.

The march on the Pentagon, the center of America's war-making machinery, was chaos itself. There was no leadership ("that was what was so beautiful," remarked one protester). The successor group to the defunct National Coordinating Committee, calling itself the National Mobilization Committee to End the War in Vietnam, pretended to be in charge, but no one on earth could have harmonized the diverse purposes of the one hundred fifty peace groups represented on that sunny October Saturday of wild confusion. Participants ranged from ministers in business suits to long-haired hippies in bright-colored splendor, from celebrities like Robert Lowell, Benjamin Spock, and Norman Mailer to mothers with babies in their arms. Some wanted merely to petition their government peacefully against a policy they deemed unwise and immoral; others hoped to disrupt that government's business; still others, to provoke violence. After speeches at the Lincoln Memorial the tens of thousands headed for Virginia and the Pentagon.

When they arrived some charged the building and battled the soldiers and marshals; others heard speeches or sang folksongs; others attempted to persuade the soldiers to join them. Some listened to a rock band called the Fugs or staged outdoor dramas to illustrate the barbarities of the war. One sizable group, led by Abbie Hoffman, tried to levitate the Pentagon ten feet off the ground by the power of thought and, accompanied by Indian cymbals, finger-bells, chants, and prayers, performed an exorcism to cleanse the place of evil spirits. The *New York Times* shared the lurid details: "The surging disorderly crowd . . . shouted obscenities and taunted the forces on guard there. Some threw eggs and bottles as darkness fell, built bonfires and waved what they said were burning draft cards." Public relations got lost in the melee. James Reston noted that "many of the signs carried by a small number of the militants and many of the lines in the theatrical performances put on by the hippies are too obscene to print."

Naturally, there were no official statements issued by such a throng, but to whatever extent the various pronouncements purported to be official, they were pretentious and portentous. Some talked of the new transition from parades to confrontation; others suggested that the event marked the end of mere dissent and the beginning of resistance. By the end of the day there were clouds of tear gas in the air; the blood of protesters, some of them savagely beaten by the U.S. marshals, covered the Pentagon steps; and the local jails were full. All across the United States of America conservative editors had a field day.

Between the Fulbright hearings in February 1966 and "Stop the Draft Week" in October 1967, and occupying all shades of middle ground between staid dignity and extravagant hijinks, were hundreds of other antiwar activities. Some were brazenly outrageous, and their connection to Vietnam must have been a bit hard for most Americans to discern. In some cities, protesters snarled rush hour traffic. One group disrupted the wedding of President Johnson's daughter. Another interrupted Cardinal Spellman's high mass. A few activists broke into local draft boards and poured blood or spread feces on the records. Some carried on in ways that seemed positively calculated to discredit their purposes—like those who burned American flags or the young man who appeared at one demonstration dressed in a Batman costume with a face mask depicting Jesus Christ. A few traveled to Hanoi and held talks with officials there. Verbal indiscretions were sometimes enormous—unrestrained praise for the slain Cuban revolutionary, Che Guevara, for example, or the statement of SDS National Secretary Greg Calvert, in May 1967: "We are working to build a guerrilla force in an urban environment. We are actively organizing sedition."

But if some antiwar activities were bizarre, misdirected, and self-defeating, hundreds of others were clearly motivated by profound anguish over American policy in Southeast Asia. They were often undertaken at serious personal risk to participants: risk of imprisonment; risk of personal abuse, ridicule, and violence; risk of social and political ostracism; risk of being subjected to the devastating accusation by their friends and neighbors—sometimes unspoken, sometimes terribly unfair—that their high-sounding words merely covered an unworthy personal cowardice. Many chose to leave the country or perform "alternate service" rather than to participate in the war; a few soldiers—like "the Ft. Hood Three"—announced that they would not go to Vietnam. Hundreds of Americans refused to pay their taxes as a symbolic protest against the war. Hundreds more engaged in fasting, hunger strikes, and prayer vigils at the White House.

By the end of 1967 seven Americans had immolated themselves, in imitation of the Buddhist monks of South Vietnam. Some whose consciences led them into opposition were men and women of sober habits and high status: the priests, ministers, and rabbis who formed Clergy and Laymen Concerned About Vietnam; those who formed Business Executives Move for Peace in May 1967; actors, authors, doctors, attorneys; the fifty Rhodes Scholars who addressed a petition to the president in February 1967; the eight hundred Peace Corps workers who wrote him in March; the thousand divinity students who spoke out in April.

The most conservative of the war's opponents sought to oppose the war by the most traditional and approved method of all, the way that American citizens have always tried to render their opposition effective: political action. Sometimes this meant pressuring elected officials; sometimes it meant attempting to replace the prowar ones with others. By the end of 1967 neither the president, the vice president, nor leading members of the cabinet could expect to appear in public without encountering protesters carrying signs reminding them that many citizens disapproved. Thousands of petitions and letters poured into both the legislative and executive branches. In 1966 SANE announced a campaign to defeat particularly warlike congressmen. Some liberal Democrats formed a group called the National Conference for New Politics the same year. Both efforts failed badly, but in a Dearborn, Michigan, referendum, fourteen thousand voters (40 percent) voted for immediate withdrawal. Another organization, notable for the stature and respectability of its founders—Arthur Schlesinger, Jr., John Kenneth Galbraith, Victor Reuther of the United Auto Workers, and Norman Cousins, among others—was called Negotiations Now! Although its main purpose was to organize a huge petition urging a negotiated settlement, this group also offered to help promising antiwar candidates to get elected.

By the end of 1967, however, the main effort of dissident Democrats was to find an alternative to Lyndon Baines Johnson in 1968. Anyone who knew the first thing about politics knew that it was almost impossible for members of a party to elbow aside a sitting president. The attempt to do so was led by a young, experienced, and highly effective New York activist named Allard Lowenstein. After several possibilities had declined to make the challenge, Lowenstein found someone who was willing to give it a try. On the last day of November, eleven months before the election and nine before the Democratic convention was to open in Chicago, Eugene McCarthy announced his candidacy. He was mild mannered, affable, highly intelligent and thoughtful, witty, and properly presidential in appearance; he seemed almost as much a scholar or a poet as he did a savvy politician. He said he was disturbed by "the absence of any positive suggestion for a compromise or for a negotiated political settlement" and by the fact "that the Administration seems to have set no limit to the price it is willing to pay for a military victory."

Meanwhile, supporters of the war, in 1966 and 1967, were increasingly forced into more public expressions of their position in order to counter the efforts of opponents. Most of those who favored the war actively, or who acquiesced in it passively, did not feel much need to form organizations, march in the streets, or resort to politics. They were, after all, not challenging a national policy; they were supporting one. For them, simply declaring that they "stood by the president" or "backed up our fighting men" was often sufficient to locate them with respect to the Vietnam question, to make clear to their neighbors just where they stood on this thing. To justify their view, there was readily available to them a traditional rhetoric of honor and patriotism, of defending freedom and stopping communism. To voice one's support for the war in these terms must have been enough for most of the purposes of those who agreed with American policy. Some advocates of the war, on the other hand, believed that the president was not doing enough. They watched the situation with a greater or lesser degree of apprehension, lest the politicians bow to the demands of the protesters and not do what had to be done. These men and women were almost as merciless to Lyndon Johnson as the critics of the war, continually condemning him for having us "fight with one arm tied behind our back" or for not "fighting to win."

Supplementing private and quiet prowar sentiments were hundreds of small-scale, local gestures. Pennsylvanians sent thirty-five tons of cookies to Vietnam. Some New Jersey folks mailed one hundred fifty thousand greeting cards, and bags full of letters addressed to no GI in particular arrived there each week. The boys were remembered in ten thousand prayers emanating from ten thousand pulpits every Sunday morning. Private campaigns to send gifts, medicine, and clothing to South Vietnamese refugees sprang up all across the country. So did dozens of blood drives on campuses, in churches, at city halls and fire stations. A high school in New York raised money to send one soldier's wife to Hong Kong for a Christmas reunion; a Cincinnati labor union offered five hundred cases of beer, which the Defense Department politely declined. Some tried to organize countermarches or prowar rallies, but they were usually sparsely attended—in part, no doubt, because supporters of the war did not want to be associated with the same sort of behavior as the hippies. These activities were carried out by Young Republicans and Young

Democrats; by Lions, Moose, Elks and Masons; by the American Legion, the Jewish War Veterans, the VFW and the DAV; by church groups, women's clubs, PTAs, the Junior Chamber of Commerce, and the Boy Scouts; by garden clubs, labor unions, and 4-H groups; by local newspapers and television stations. They were motivated by sympathy for American soldiers and the people of Vietnam and by traditional patriotic feeling. But these little campaigns will be vastly misunderstood unless they are also seen as being expressions of approval of the war itself.

There were also some attempts to organize support of the war nationwide. The old pro-Diem group from the 1950s, the American Friends of Vietnam, continued into the 1960s but never had enough money to do very effective work. Another effort along this line was made by the Young Americans for Freedom and called the Student Ad Hoc Committee to Support the President's Policy in Vietnam. In late 1965 the experienced diplomat Arthur Dean formed the Committee for an Effective and Durable Peace in Asia, which could claim a number of prestigious members. The most influential group of this sort was started by the former senator from Illinois, the liberal Democrat, Paul H. Douglas. Begun in November 1967, it was called The Citizens Committee for Peace with Freedom in Viet Nam. Among its members were former presidents Truman and Eisenhower, ex-secretaries of state Acheson and Byrnes, former president of Harvard James Bryant Conant, and George Meany. Their first statement left no doubt about how they felt: "We want the aggressors to know that there is a solid, stubborn, dedicated, bipartisan majority of private citizens in America who approve our country's policy of patient, responsible, determined resistance."

If the antiwar movement was plagued by its most extreme and irresponsible elements, so were those who supported the war. The presence of representatives of the radical right was a continuing embarrassment to the more respectable proponents of the war. The American Nazi Party, for example, organized prowar rallies, agitated for more strenuous action against the Communists, and mounted its tiny counterdemonstrations at places where the antiwar forces were marching; party members somehow were able to combine appeals for the war with appeals to white supremacy. Other less restrained supporters of the war indulged their senses of humor by offering gasoline and matches to passing peace marchers. There was no shortage, on such occasions, of opportunities for unrestrained verbal abuse (emanating from both sides of the police barricades), and inevitably there were numerous instances of shoving, beatings, and small-scale street brawls.

Meanwhile, the Johnson administration, by now fully aware that it faced a public relations crisis, tried to contain the growing antiwar sentiment in the nation and the Congress. Lyndon Johnson was a man who enjoyed being loved. He resented even mild criticism and was stung and perplexed by the rising tide of invective against policies he regarded as necessary and moderate. When opposition to the war was announced by some old friend from Senate days or by some reporter or editor whom he had especially courted or by a man like Martin Luther King, Jr., who should have shown, in Johnson's view, more loyalty, the president was deeply hurt and angered. He countered as best he could. In the fall of 1965 a pamphlet and a movie narrated by Johnson himself (both called "Why Vietnam?") were widely distributed. In late 1965 he formed the Vietnam Information Group to manage public relations. The White House distributed other people's prowar advertisements, helped prowar senators with speeches, and worked to keep the Young Democrats in line. In late 1967 Johnson made a series of speeches, most of them at military bases—about the only place he could appear now without encountering protesters. He reiterated the moral and strategic necessity for the war, warned Hanoi not to mistake the protest for a sign of diminishing resolve, and emphasized the "progress" and "good news" coming from the commanders in Vietnam.

The most questionable aspect of the administration's work in the battle for public opinion was this incurable tendency to present the most optimistic and, in retrospect, self-deluding interpretations of American success and enemy failure. General Westmoreland and Ambassador Bunker were brought home in late 1967 to calm public opinion by spreading encouraging accounts of the progress being made. Critics of the war, both during the fighting and after it was over, accused the administration of being so desperate to report good news that it falsified figures and knowingly slanted information. There can be no doubt that the highly optimistic talk of late 1967 added to the shock of disbelief after the enemy launched its dramatic surprise offensive in early 1968.

There were other signs of slipping composure on the part of the president and those around him. First, they resorted to more frequent attacks on the media. Beginning with the famous CBS broadcast of August 5, 1965, where a marine was shown setting fire to a peasant's thatched hut with his cigarette lighter (after which the furious Johnson accused the network president of "trying to fuck me" and of having "shat on the American flag"), the administration grew more and more impatient with criticism. A second sign of the president's state of mind was the growing tendency to hint that the antiwar movement was taking its orders from the Communists. While never resorting to a full-scale red-baiting campaign, the president, his friend J. Edgar Hoover of the FBI, and others in the administration became ever more sure that the demonstrators were tools of the Communists or else their unwitting dupes, and numerous "security checks" were ordered on those who opposed the war. Finally, Johnson and the others charged, more frequently and with ever more emotion, that the protest encouraged North Vietnam to continue the war. Ho Chi Minh, they claimed, watched American opinion carefully and counted on his foe getting weary. To whatever extent opponents of the war gave him reason to hope, to that extent they were directly to blame for his unwillingness to negotiate. They were partly responsible, therefore, for increasing the number of American casualties. This argument, sincerely believed by many inside and outside the White House, was damaging to the peace movement and no doubt discouraged some from publicly criticizing the war.

How, then, did the debate over Vietnam stand at the end of 1967, with Halberstam and others so pessimistic and the president and others so optimistic? The president and his advisers saw themselves as mediating between an unreasonable, perhaps even a traitorous, antiwar movement on the one hand and the bellicose cries for more decisive action emanating from the far right, the Republicans, and the military on the other. Antiwar critics saw him irrevocably committed to the militarist solution and closed to the plain arguments of reason and morality. The American people as a whole were badly divided. By one poll, 45 percent were willing to say, in December 1967, that entering the war had been an error, but only around 10 percent advocated immediate withdrawal. Most Americans were getting tired of the whole thing. They were disturbed by the rising casualty figures, alarmed at the mounting cost, and troubled by the internal divisions being wrought by this war. For the time being, however, they were willing to trust presidential assurances about progress in the field, ready to believe the confident predictions of a reasonable end to this nightmare. The stunning events of 1968 were to upset the uneasy balance in public opinion, discredit the optimists, and turn the tide in favor of those who opposed the war.

III.

News of the Tet offensive hit America a little like one of those "earthquake bombs" being used in Vietnam to uproot forests and make landing fields. On the last day of January 1968, during the customary cease fire to celebrate the lunar new year, the Communists launched surprise attacks from one end of South Vietnam to the other. Within twenty-four hours they assaulted five of the country's six largest cities; they also hit thirty-six out of forty-four provincial capitals and more than a hundred other places, including key American army and air force installations. The most shocking news came, confusedly, out of Saigon itself. The enemy entered the capital in force and, in addition to some neighborhoods, struck the huge airport complex at Tan Son Nhut, President Thieu's palace, the government radio station, and the ARVN General Staff Headquarters. A small team of Vietcong sappers even blew its way onto the grounds of the American embassy and held out against the marines through the night. "The only thing that could have been more dramatic," remarked a Chicago professor on the day after the start of the offensive, "would have been if they had burst into [Ambassador Ellsworth] Bunker's private office and shot him as he sat at his desk signing letters." Senator McCarthy, campaigning in New Hampshire, told a crowd: "A few months ago we were told sixty-five percent of the population was secure. Now we know that even the American embassy is not secure."

The enemy paid a fearful price for the Tet offensive. Tens of thousands of North Vietnamese and Vietcong troops were killed in the effort, and the Vietcong political operation was badly damaged. Their hopes for a civilian uprising against the Thieu-Ky regime never materialized. With the exception of the occupation of Hue, which resulted in a bloody battle of three weeks and the destruction of the old city, their gains on the ground were short lived. American forces handled themselves superbly and, in most places, reversed enemy gains and "mopped up" the resistance within the week. With a few exceptions, even the ARVN fought doggedly and well. General Westmoreland, President Johnson, and other military and political officials issued calming and optimistic assessments of the situation.

But the full impact of Tet could not be measured by the confident reports of regained ground and devastating enemy body counts. The effect of the episode on American public opinion was titanic; indeed, the Tet offensive was probably the single most important event in reversing American support for the war. It seemed to substantiate the contentions of the war's opponents. Two of the most publicized stories of that traumatic week, for example, raised again the moral ambiguity of the whole effort. On the evening of February 2 twenty million Americans watching the Huntley-Brinkley Report on NBC saw General Nguyen Ngoc Loan, chief of the South Vietnamese police, draw his pistol, put it to the head of a terrified, captured Vietcong, hands tied behind his back, and pull the trigger. It was an act of such naked brutality, so at odds with civilized notions of justice and decency, that it served graphically to confirm the charges that America's allies in Vietnam were brutal men, morally indistinguishable from the brutal men on the other side. And then came the best known remark of that week, the comment, on February 7, of an American major at the village of Ben Tre in the Mekong Delta: "It became necessary to destroy the town in order to save it," he told Peter Arnett of the Associated Press. The village of thirty-five thousand had been attacked by twenty-five hundred enemy troops, and in order to kill them the bombers were called in. To opponents of the Vietnam war, the quote served as a summary of the entire policy; it seemed as though the United States was destroying the whole country in order to save it.

If the morality of the war was called into question by those two moments of Tet, its costs were also graphically illustrated to millions of people back home. The picture of the slain American boys on the embassy grounds (eleven hundred Americans died during the first two weeks of February); the haunted, wide-eyed faces of marines at Hue or in the Cholon District of Saigon, fighting house to house to retake lost ground; the sight of the American wounded, writhing in agony as they awaited evacuation to hospitals; the heart-breaking pictures of thousands of new, bewildered refugees; the estimate that the rural pacification program had been set back at least six months and that in many places it would mean starting over practically from scratch—all seemed to verify the claims of those in the antiwar movement who argued that the whole thing was simply not worth it. Finally, the contention of those opposed to the war that American leaders were inept or, even worse, that they were neither trustworthy nor honest seemed amply confirmed. How could they have been taken by surprise like this? How could the president and the generals and the others—if they were honest men—have given the country, only three or four months ago, such glowing reports of progress, such assuring predictions?

To military experts, therefore, Tet was a substantial, even a crushing, victory for America. To them (and to some scholars who have studied the matter closely), the media coverage was worse than an inaccurate overreaction; it was irresponsible sensationalism of the worst sort, and it severely undercut the ability of the United States to fulfill its responsibilities in Vietnam. To opponents of the war, on the other hand, the Tet offensive was persuasive proof of what they had been saying all along. It provided, moreover, an opportunity, however regrettable the circumstances, to convince the American people of the immorality and the futility of this war. The antiwar attack on the administration's Vietnam policy poured forth on every conceivable front.

Even before Tet, SDS had announced "Ten Days of Resistance" for April, and the year-old Student Mobilization Committee set out to organize a strike of one million high school and college students. Clergy and Laymen Concerned about Vietnam raised anew the moral issue by gathering in Washington in February to hold a prayer service at Arlington Cemetery and to issue its four-hundred-page book, *In the Name of America*, an inquiry into "the conduct of the war in Vietnam by the armed forces of the United States," raising questions about American behavior with respect to principles of law and morality. More pragmatically, the Business Executives Move for Vietnam Peace called for an end to the war simply because "when a policy hasn't proved productive after a reasonable trial it's sheer nonsense not to change it." Meanwhile the Congress was growing more restive. After new hearings that culminated in February, Fulbright and about half of his Foreign Affairs Committee concluded that the Gulf of Tonkin Resolution had been an overreaction that had been obtained through "misrepresentation." There were strident but futile calls, both for its repeal and for a full congressional investigation into our Vietnam policy. Most ominous of all, in the wake of Tet some who had been supportive or neutral in opinion began to express their doubts: Walter Cronkite of CBS, Frank McGee of ABC, the *Wall Street Journal*, and others. Even the president's so-called "Wise Men," that group of close, veteran advisers, developed serious second thoughts after Tet. Upon reassessing the situation at the end of March, one of them, Dean Acheson, concluded that "we must begin to take steps to disengage."

The meeting of "the Wise Men" was only one part of a major reassessment of the war by the Johnson administration. The enemy's impressive showing, General Westmoreland's well-publicized request for still another two hundred thousand men, and the recognition that public support for both the president and the policy was crumbling rapidly and doing so in an election year provided the cause and the backdrop for extensive discussions in February and March. These discussions—organized by Clark Clifford, who had just replaced Secretary of Defense Robert McNamara and begun his thorough review of all aspects of the war—were the most intense since the decision to Americanize the war in July 1965. They resulted in a number of decisions. The administration turned against the Westmoreland recommendation to expand the war and rejected his request for additional men. Westmoreland himself was brought home and replaced by General Creighton Abrams. The administration concluded, moreover, that much more of the fighting would have to be borne by the ARVN; there would be substantial material aid from America, but efforts would now have to be in the direction of a general de-escalation and the extrication of the country from the quagmire. These moves, writes historian George Herring, "represented a significant shift in American policy—a return, at least in part, to the principle that had governed its involvement before 1965 and adoption, at least in rudimentary fashion, of the concept of Vietnamization, which would be introduced with much fanfare by the Nixon administration a year later."

Rarely in American history has a president had a rougher time than Lyndon Johnson had in the first four months of 1968. Not all of it had to do with Vietnam. On January 23 the North Koreans captured the intelligence ship *Pueblo*, thus opening a long period of tension with yet another east Asian nation. During the first week of March, the National Advisory Commission on Civil Disorders, formed by the president the previous year to analyze the rash of race riots plaguing the nation's cities, issued its somber report. As if to give credibility to the commission's warnings about racial injustice and the creation of a biracial society, news of Martin Luther King, Jr's., assassination came on April 4, and rioting, burning, and looting exploded in 168 cities and towns across America, one of the worst instances occurring just three blocks from the White House. More than seventy thousand army and national guard troops were called to riot duty. Other problems faced the president: a serious "gold drain" to foreign nations, a suddenly alarming inflation rate, and bad publicity in connection with a rumored tax increase. But even with the problems assailing Johnson, the mounting political challenge against a sitting president, from within his own party, was still something quite extraordinary. On March 12 Senator McCarthy, capitalizing on the general discontent and with the enthusiastic help of thousands of antiwar college students who canvassed the state door-to-door, won 42 percent of the vote and twenty of twenty-four electors in the New Hampshire Democratic primary. It was taken as a stunning defeat for the president, and four days later things got even worse: the popular senator from New York, Robert Kennedy, announced that he too would seek the nomination on an antiwar program.

In a major speech to the nation on March 31, probably delivered primarily to quiet domestic antiwar protest, President Johnson took pains to appear as a man of peace and principle. He was ordering, he announced, a major reduction in the bombing of North Vietnam without demanding any reciprocal move by the enemy; he hoped that some gesture on its part would enable him to dispense with the bombing entirely. He was eager for peace talks at any time and in any place, he said, and if they should occur, America would be represented by

Averell Harriman. Then, thirty-five minutes into the speech, Johnson stunned all those viewers who were still watching on that Sunday night: "I shall not seek, and I will not accept, the nomination of my party for another term as your president." By withdrawing from the contest, he said, he hoped to emphasize the sincerity of his quest for peace. He could now make his decisions in the best interests of the country without worrying about the next primary or the views of political rivals. Predictably, some peace activists reacted to Johnson's announcement with unrestrained joy, others with sarcastic skepticism; but almost everyone realized that suddenly everything was changed.

There continued to be demonstrations, of course; after six years of trying to end the war, they proceeded out of a kind of habit. In early April a few antidraft rallies were held, but they were quickly eclipsed by the King assassination and the ensuing riots. The Student Mobilization's effort, the Ten Days of Resistance, occurred later in that month. There were numerous campus activities of various sorts—according to one accounting, more than two hundred in the first six months of 1968—but it is difficult to tell how many of these were concerned with Vietnam and how many with civil rights or with narrowly local matters. The most widely noticed protest of the season took place at Columbia University, where students led by SDS president Mark Rudd occupied some buildings until the police removed them forcibly after a week, but that dramatic episode had more to do with local issues than with the war. The plain fact was that after Johnson dropped out of the presidential race, attention turned almost entirely to politics, and seeing little prospect for a change in policy through the Republican party, antiwar activists directed their efforts to the Democrats. Increasingly they left the peace movement to organize rallies, man phones, and walk neighborhoods for Gene McCarthy or Bobby Kennedy. Not even Kennedy's assassination on June 5, the night of his victory in the California primary, changed the focus. All eyes were on the showdown, the Democratic National Convention scheduled for Chicago during the last week of August.

Americans had never seen a political convention like the one in Chicago in 1968. The city, under its tough mayor, Richard J. Daley (who, during the King riots in April, had ordered police to shoot-to-wound looters and shoot-to-kill arsonists), was an armed fortress. Chicago's twelve thousand police were put on twelve-hour shifts; six thousand soldiers at nearby Glenview Naval base were held in readiness; five thousand national guardsmen were deployed; and hundreds of plainclothes detectives, Secret Service men, sheriffs deputies, state police, and infiltrators were braced for the worst. There were no shortages of squad cars, tear gas and gas masks, night sticks, riot helmets, small arms, and shotguns. The Amphitheater, where the convention was to be held, was protected by a cyclone fence topped with barbed wire; elaborate procedures were devised to insure that only the authorized could get into the hall. For weeks before the event the most radical antiwar spokesmen had indulged in language that would have made anything less than maximum readiness irresponsible. The talk ranged from snarling traffic, disrupting the convention, and forcing confrontations with the authorities, all the way to preventing the convention from occurring, poisoning the city's water supply, setting fires in neighborhoods, and stirring up armed rioting in the huge black ghetto on the city's south side.

The actual debate over Vietnam took place, in Chicago, in two vastly differing settings. The convention itself faced the issue. As a concession to the minority of delegates supporting Eugene McCarthy or George McGovern (who had entered the race after Robert Kennedy's assassination and had inherited much of Kennedy's support), the convention permitted a full-scale, three-hour discussion of the war on national television. At issue were a Vietnam plank for the platform that had been dictated by the White House and a plank, critical of administration policy, drafted by followers of McCarthy and McGovern. After a dozen speeches repeating the usual arguments and making the usual appeals, and amid a boisterous, unruly, and rude assemblage of cheering and booing delegates on both sides, the majority plank, endorsed by Johnson's heir-apparent, Vice President Humphrey, prevailed by a vote of 1,568 to 1,041. The melee revealed, for all the nation to see, the deep divisions within the Democratic party over the war. Following the debate the Democrats chose Humphrey to be their standard bearer in the campaign ahead.

The second "debate" took place on the streets. It was wild, brutal, and inarticulate. Those who afterwards wanted to assess blame for the gross excesses could find plenty enough to go around. Along with those who came to Chicago to exercise their right to dissent and who wanted to work "within the system" as conscientious citizens of a free society, were some who came to cause trouble. Frustrated by years of futile efforts to stop the war, now, at last, refusing to worry about how their actions would be received by middle America, determined to force a confrontation, these few carried on their sport in the streets and parks of Chicago. They smoked dope and made love with equal abandon and equal openness; they burned American flags and waved Vietcong ones; they carried rude signs and held ill-organized, chaotic "actions" in various quarters of the city. They pelted the police with eggs and rocks, referred to them as "pigs" and "Fascists" and "cocksuckers," and cast aspersions about the sexual practices of their wives and mothers. They constituted a flowing, amorphous, combustible element. They monopolized media attention, provoking terror and hatred among those Americans who still believed in order, and they were able to quite overwhelm the more respectable, reasoned, and dignified opponents of the war. Meanwhile, the police were behaving no better. They committed countless acts of sadistic brutality, engaged in what a later investigation termed "a police riot," clubbed and gassed defenseless and innocent people—young and old, men and women, protesters, bystanders, journalists, tourists, and residents of Chicago who got caught in the middle. They charged crowds of dumbfounded onlookers, pushed people through the plate-glass windows of the Conrad Hilton Hotel, and aimed their nightsticks at heads and groins with unrestrained viciousness. They did these things in full view of the cameras, and when the reports and the pictures reached the delegates inside the Amphitheater, the outrage was hard to contain.

The campaign itself was a fitting climax to a year as harrowing as 1968. The Republicans chose the reborn Richard M. Nixon—defeated for the presidency in 1960, defeated for governor of California in 1962, and supposedly retired from politics—to attempt the impossible: bring the party back from its devastating defeat of 1964. Nixon and his running mate, Spiro Agnew, the governor of Maryland, emphasized unifying the American people after the orgies of civil disorder during the preceding four years. They would, they said, restore confidence in America and represent the concerns of the vast majority of silent Americans who were dismayed by what their country had become. Nixon was well positioned in the debate over Vietnam. The man who led the denunciation of Truman for having lost China and who stalked Alger Hiss to the bitter end had impeccable credentials as an uncompromising foe of communism. He took the position that Vietnam should not be a campaign issue because of the sensitive status of preliminary Paris peace talks. He advocated "an honorable peace," and there was a good deal of talk about his "secret plan" for bringing it about; but the details remained sketchy.

The contest was complicated by the presence of a third candidate, Governor George Wallace of Alabama, who also attempted to capitalize on the general discontent with social disorder and the policies of Democratic liberals and intellectuals. He once threatened to run over any demonstrator stupid enough to lie down in front of *his* car and offered to throw the intellectuals and their briefcases into the Potomac after he was elected president. By demanding "law and order" and attacking "the welfare state," Wallace was able to appeal subtly to a latent racism that he found equally present among southern rural folks and northern blue-collar workers. His position on Vietnam was not much different from that of his running mate, former General Curtis LeMay, who suggested bombing North Vietnam "back to the stone age" and once remarked that America suffered from "a phobia about nuclear weapons."

As always, the Vietnam issue was hardest for the Democrats. They left Chicago with a shattered party and with very bitter feelings toward one another. Some antiwar Democrats blamed Humphrey, as much as Mayor Daley, for the violence and brutality in the streets. Not even Humphrey's record as a consistent champion and innovator of liberal causes could save him from the Vietnam quandary. He had to walk the impossible line between supporting the Johnson policies and winning the allegiance of the war's critics. He trailed badly in the polls from the beginning. During the campaign he edged cautiously away from the president by advocating a complete bombing halt, and McCarthy begrudged him a tardy and lukewarm endorsement. Not even Johnson's announcing a complete bombing halt a week before the election could close the gap, although it helped, and some observers thought that Humphrey might have pulled out a victory had the campaign lasted another week or ten days.

As it was, Nixon was elected with 43.4 percent of the vote, the smallest share of any winner since 1912; Humphrey got 42.7 percent; and Wallace, the rest. The Democrats took both houses of the Congress. The war in Vietnam was now the responsibility of a Republican president, and it remained to be seen if he could bring it to an end. And how soon.

IV.

1968 had affected the debate over Vietnam in important ways. At the end of 1967, as we have seen, around 45 percent of the American people thought the war had been a mistake and around 10 percent favored immediate withdrawal. At the end of 1968 almost 60 percent thought the war was mistaken and almost 20 percent favored getting out immediately. Some of that shift had come, no doubt, because events confirmed the contentions of antiwar critics: the increasing brutality during and after Tet emphasized the moral questions; the calls to pour ever more men and money into that little country provoked fresh consideration about the real importance of Vietnam to the national security; and the sight of Americans fighting each other on the streets of Chicago and in other cities lent substance to the argument that this war was dangerously dividing the country. But if some moved against the war because they were persuaded by arguments, it is likely that more did so because they were just weary of it, frustrated by it, angry at how long it was apparently going to take. These inchoate feelings were also fed by the events of 1968.

In addition, the presidential campaign encouraged two trends that held enormous importance for the future of the national discussion over the Vietnam war. First, many people, including many among the young, were convinced that "working within the system" had been given a fair trial and that it had failed. They had labored, night and day, to change the policy through grass-roots politics and the electoral process, and what had happened? Two heroes of the attempt had been gunned down by assassins; the election was fought between two proponents of the war (three if you counted Wallace), and the most militant "cold warrior" had won. If this war was to be brought to an end, some now reasoned, it would have to be done by radical action taken outside of traditional politics. And second, some Democrats who had harbored misgivings about the war, but who were restrained from open opposition by loyalty to their party, were now free to dissent. They had kept quiet out of deference to Johnson and Humphrey, or perhaps out of fear. But now look who was in the White House. Over the years, thousands of Democrats had nursed an enthusiastic, even an irrational, animosity toward Richard Milhous Nixon, and, should the chance for effective opposition arise, it was unlikely that they would be giving him the benefit of the doubt. Both of these developments promised to intensify an already intense debate.

It was soon clear that President Nixon had no secret plan. Insofar as he and his chief adviser for foreign affairs, Henry Kissinger, possessed any approach to ending the war, it consisted of a set of principles that they summarized with the phrase "peace with honor." The administration was committed to getting out of Vietnam as quickly as was practicable, but to doing it with dignity, without seeming to flee, and without appearing to abandon either the dream of a stable and independent South Vietnam or the administration of President Thieu. Implementing these principles involved Nixon in a two-front battle: he had to accomplish certain things in Vietnam, and he had to accomplish certain things at home. The first task required that he quickly strengthen the Saigon government's military and political effectiveness so that it could take over more of the war as American forces were being withdrawn and then be able to defend the country once the United States was gone. This policy of "Vietnamization," was essentially the one that the Johnson administration had come to during the post-Tet reassessment in the spring of 1968. But, at the same time that Americans were withdrawing anyway, Nixon and Kissinger had to convince North Vietnam that there were good reasons for them to negotiate seriously. This would require a very deft combination of force and concession. At home, Nixon, who was as certain as Johnson that antiwar protest only made the enemy more intractable, had to contain that protest long enough to get the enemy to be reasonable and the troops headed home.

On the first front, the battlefield, Nixon and Kissinger set out to do nothing less than to reform the South Vietnamese. The ARVN was increased in size, and measures were taken to raise its morale; massive quantities of military equipment were transferred to it in 1969 and 1970: more than a million M-16 rifles and enough machine guns, howitzers, ships, aircraft, and helicopters to make South Vietnam, at least on paper, one of the five or six most powerful armed nations on earth. At the same time, enormous energy was poured into the effort to win the loyalties of the citizenry. Security forces at the village level were increased, extensive construction and agricultural projects were begun, efforts to get the Vietcong to defect were stepped up, and land reform projects were started in early 1970. In order to persuade Hanoi to negotiate, Nixon and Kissinger sent private messages indicating America's desire for meaningful talks. And so that there would be no mistaking its determination to see the business through, the administration ordered a massive bombing campaign (an average of more than thirty tons of bombs each day for fifteen months) on North Vietnamese sanctuaries in the neutral country of Cambodia—something that Lyndon Johnson had refused to do. The bombing of Cambodia was kept secret from the American people for fear of fueling antiwar protest at what would appear to be a widening of the war. The results of these steps were mixed. On the one hand, there was clear progress in rural pacification; a large number of Vietcong defected; and the ARVN showed signs of improvement. On the other hand, there was still widespread civilian and military corruption, a persistent unwillingness to engage the enemy in battle, and no noticeable increase in loyalty to the Thieu government. The North Vietnamese, moreover, showed little disposition to negotiate on the Nixon-Kissinger terms.

Managing protest at home also proved difficult for the new administration. On this second front, however, Nixon was aided by a combination of good luck and carefully chosen policies, and, initially at least, he enjoyed some success. He was facing a peace movement that had been badly demoralized and discredited by the Chicago debacle: in the view of many Americans, antiwar activity was largely the work of ill-kempt troublemakers who burned American flags and abused policemen. The opening of peace talks in Paris, five days after the inauguration, quieted anxiety by encouraging the (false) hope that the war was about to end. A strategic decision made in Hanoi to lower temporarily the level of fighting had the effects of reducing the number of American casualties, the amount of media coverage of the war, and the sense of urgency about working for its conclusion. Finally, there is in American politics an underlying civility that allows new presidents some time to fix problems and that restrains, for a little while, partisan criticism. Nixon and Kissinger were well aware of these advantages, and they set about to press them if they could.

Nixon's approach to containing public opinion resembled his approach to getting North Vietnam to negotiate, a combination of conciliatory gestures and tough policies. In May 1969 he announced a comprehensive peace plan that envisioned the eventual removal of all Americans from Vietnam. In June he told the nation that the number of American forces in Vietnam would be reduced by twenty-five thousand, and in September and December he lowered the total by another eighty-five thousand. For the first time in nearly two years the troop level dipped below the half-million mark. The decrease in draft calls and the decision, at the end of 1969, to use the lottery system to fill military needs relaxed the anxiety of thousands of young men and may have reduced their tendency to protest the war. Nixon also proved adept at balancing his public statements between those that yearned for peace and those that sharply criticized people who would surrender to the Communists or disgrace the honor of the nation. He also increased enormously Johnson's initiatives aimed at direct intimidation of activists. Under the new administration surveillance, wiretapping, spying, infiltration, and the use of provocateurs became standard ways of combating critics of the war. Numerous federal agencies—including the CIA, whose charter prohibited domestic spying—were engaged in this sort of work. No one at an antiwar meeting could ever be sure that the person in the next chair was not an FBI spy, sent either to report on the meeting or, in some well-documented cases, even to propose outrageous and illegal actions leading to embarrassment of the participants or to their arrest. There were many instances of "dirty tricks," including break-ins, thinly veiled threats against protesters, or harassment by continually investigating antiwar critics by the lengthy questioning of their friends, relatives, neighbors, or employers.

For the first six months of 1969 these actions against the antiwar movement must have seemed to many like overkill of the worst sort. The peace movement was in such disarray that in March the *New York Times*'s Pentagon reporter was able to report that "public pressure over the war has almost disappeared." Beset by weariness and wariness, by hopes that peace was at hand, and by fears of intimidation, opposition to the war in Vietnam appeared to be token, scattered, and ineffectual. There were campus demonstrations (perhaps three hundred across the country during the spring semester), but they were generally about things unrelated to the war (university policies, civil rights, the environment) or only tangentially related (the place of ROTC in higher education, secret research in war technology, the presence of CIA recruiters in the student union). Off the campus, those actively opposing the war still tried, but their efforts—as in the case of the sparsely attended "counter-inauguration" held in Washington while Nixon was taking his oath of office at the capitol or the Easter protests during the first week in April—fizzled humiliatingly.

And yet, somehow, by the middle of 1969 active antiwar sentiment was showing distinct signs of revival. The task of the critics was to take the movement out of the hands of the ever more irresponsible radicals—those whom Harvard's president, Nathan Pusey, said "played at being revolutionaries"—and restore it to those who had some credibility with the American people. One step in that direction was the appearance in Washington in late April of more than two hundred fifty student body presidents and campus editors. They were from the best colleges and universities in the country; they took pains to look respectable and to speak respectfully; and, insisting that they accurately represented thousands of their fellow students, they gathered to make their views clear. They declared, to wide publicity, that they could not "participate in a war which we believe to be immoral and unjust. . . . We will not serve in the military as long as the war in Vietnam continues." If that dramatic gathering, eight months after Chicago, effectively announced the rebirth of a serious antiwar movement, two highly successful events of the fall of 1969 must have convinced the Nixon administration that the honeymoon period was over, that progress toward peace was widely perceived as being inadequate, and that it was about to confront the same hostility to American policy in Vietnam as had helped to bring down Lyndon Johnson.

On October 15 Vietnam Moratorium Day was observed all across the country. There has been a long tradition of American citizens protesting the acts of their government, but there had never been anything as large or as emotional as this. *Time* magazine, no friend of demonstrators, summed up the day:

M-day 1969 was a peaceful protest without precedent in American history because of who the participants were and how they went about it. It was a calm, measured and heavily middle-class statement of weariness with the war that brought the generations together in a kind of sedate

Woodstock Festival of peace. If the young were the M-day vanguard, many in the ranks wore the housewife's apron and the businessman's necktie, and many who clambered to enlist were political leaders.

Time's Chicago bureau chief wrote that "so many of these folks—far from being professional liberals or agitators or youths simply trying to avoid the draft—were pure, straight middle-class adults who had simply decided, in their own pure, straight middle-class way, that it was time for the U.S. to get the hell out of the war in Viet Nam." Church bells tolled in hundreds of cities and towns; candlelight marches, like the massive one that moved quietly past the White House, occurred in dozens of places; men and women slowly read out the names of American boys killed in action. Mayor Lindsay of New York City ordered the flags flown at half-mast; the Pittsburgh city council endorsed the purpose of the day; and dozens of senators and representatives participated in one way or another. Coretta King, Helen Hayes (the actress), President Kingman Brewster of Yale, Bill Moyers (Johnson's former press secretary), and Arthur Goldberg (Johnson's former U.N. ambassador), joined by hundreds of other notables, spoke out against the continuation of the war. The day was characterized by dignity, obvious sincerity, and an almost complete absence of violence and disorder. Over the whole outpouring, coast to coast, endlessly repeated and yet somehow hauntingly powerful, echoed the solemn notes of Beatle John Lennon's antiwar chant: "All we are saying . . . is give peace a chance."

One month later, the antiwar movement produced a second highly successful demonstration, this one the work of the New Mobilization Committee to End the War. The protest started with a "March against Death" that began on Thursday evening, November 13. Gathering near Arlington National Cemetery, the marchers—each one carrying a sign with the name of an American killed in Vietnam—passed over Memorial Bridge and headed the four miles to the White House. There each marcher spoke out the name. Some wept; some barely whispered; some shouted defiantly. At the rate of around a thousand each hour they came: all through a freezing Thursday night, all through the daylight hours on Friday, all through Friday night and into Saturday morning. It was a powerful demonstration of what the war had cost and a highly emotional one. Some of the marchers were the widows, the brothers, or sisters of those whose names they spoke. The March against Death was preliminary to a huge rally at the Washington Monument on Saturday the fifteenth. Probably half a million Americans came to object to the war, more than had ever before gathered in one place to register a protest (perhaps double the number who had come to the huge civil rights march there in 1963). Another two hundred thousand gathered in San Francisco at the same time. The speeches were dull; the whole affair was confused and riven by internal tensions; and an ugly incident—a few radicals attacked the Justice Department and were dispersed by police and a flood of tear gas that hung over the capital—marred the day. But the prevailing impression was dignified, somber, and effective, a compelling demonstration of deepening discontent with the war.

Then a rather surprising thing happened. Nationally, the moderate peace movement seemed almost to commit suicide. The causes were many: some of the war's opponents gravitated to other causes such as civil rights or the environment; others went to work locally, involving themselves in the effort to elect peace candidates in the upcoming off-year elections of 1970; still others were just plain tired. Nixon's Vietnamization made it harder to arouse everyday Americans to oppose the war. And the bitter divisions within the movement, the factional in-fighting, the constant clashes with radicals and revolutionaries, provoked many to quit in disgust and frustration. As Nancy Zaroulis and Gerald Sullivan, two chroniclers of the antiwar movement, put it, "The internal strain on the antiwar movement—the strain of carrying on for years its home-front struggle—was beginning to show as well. Tempers were short; patience was thin; lives were disrupted and sometimes destroyed; careers neglected, sleep lost, recreation time lost, friends and families lost—and for what? some people said."

If there were many causes for the eclipse of the dignified peace movement after the successes of the fall of 1969, there was one principal effect. Attention swung to the militants, whose increasingly extreme actions hypnotized the media and appalled the American people. There were sensational raids on draft boards and the destruction of records; there was a rash of arsonist attacks on campus buildings, federal installations, banking institutions, and corporate headquarters. Bombings became commonplace, one of the specialties of the Weathermen, a small splinter group of the now defunct SDS committed to the most extreme and violent of acts; in March 1970 a "bomb factory" in New York City exploded killing three of them. There was a good deal of solemn talk about "bringing the war home" to the streets of America, of kidnapping public officials or their families, of underground cells committed to the overthrow of the government.

On the lighter side was the trial of the so-called Chicago Eight, mesmerizing the nation from September 1969 to February 1970. Eight men, including David Dellinger, Abbie Hoffman, Rennie Davis,

Jerry Rubin, Tom Hayden, and a Black Panther named Bobby Seale, were tried in connection with the disturbances at the Chicago Democratic Convention a year earlier. The courtroom became a circus. The defendants interrupted the proceedings, shouted profanity, ridiculed the judge, and often had to rush from the courtroom to the airport, at the end of the day, in order to fulfill speaking engagements before throngs of cheering students on campuses from coast to coast. Judge Julius Hoffman, testy, aged, and arbitrary, issued more than one hundred twenty-five contempt citations against the defendants and their lawyers and, at one point, ordered that Seale (who kept calling him a Fascist pig) be tied in his chair and gagged during the proceedings. Ultimately the accused were found innocent on appeal, but the trial—like the raids on draft boards and the bombs in the streets—left many feeling that this was a much different country from the one they had grown up in and that the war in Vietnam was to blame.

Not even the stunning My Lai revelations seemed capable of producing more than a momentary flurry of outrage. Slowly, in the late fall of 1969, the horrifying story began to emerge. It seemed that in the aftermath of Tet, back on March 16, 1968, a platoon leader named William Calley, Jr., led his twenty-five men into the small hamlet, marched a number of Vietnamese (variously estimated from one hundred fifty to five hundred and including many women, children, and old people) into a ditch, and ordered them gunned down without mercy. The incident was concealed by the army for a whole year, until a former infantryman distributed a letter detailing the massacre. An army inquiry led to formal charges and a long court martial of more than a dozen men. Beginning in mid-November 1969 with the syndicated stories of Seymour Hersh, a flood of exposure rehearsed the details of both the incident and the cover-up. In the end, everyone was acquitted except Calley, who was sentenced to life in prison in March 1971, a sentence later reduced to ten years. For critics of the war, of course, the My Lai massacre was additional confirmation, if any was needed, of the immorality and brutality of the war. Supporters of our policy tended to sympathize with the men who were fighting in an ugly war where it was impossible to tell friend from foe and where the pressures of combat were unbearable to the breaking point. But the discussion of My Lai centered on the subordinate question of whether or not Lieutenant Calley was merely a scapegoat for officers higher up the chain of command, for a morally bankrupt policy, even, in some versions, for an entire nation guilty of unspeakable crimes and unwilling to admit its delinquency.

Thus President Nixon, by a deft combination of policies, was able to outflank domestic critics of the war. Vietnamization reduced draft calls and casualty figures. His carefully chosen and effective rhetoric alternately abused opponents of the war as an unpatriotic and noisy minority (as opposed to a patriotic silent majority) and portrayed himself as ready to take any reasonable step toward peace. Meanwhile, the suicidal tendencies and sheer fatigue of the antiwar movement contributed to his success by rendering organized opposition relatively impotent. In early April of 1970 Gallup found that 48 percent of those polled approved of the way the president was handling Vietnam and 41 percent disapproved. On April 19 the Vietnam Moratorium Committee, no longer able to produce large-scale, peaceful demonstrations, disbanded itself; the next day President Nixon announced the withdrawal of another one hundred fifty thousand troops over the next year. By appearing to channel the war into paths that led toward eventual peace, in short, Nixon seemed able to quiet the critics.

The movement for peace in Vietnam was awakened from its slumber by the president himself. What he and Kissinger had *not* been able to do was to convince Hanoi to make concessions in a negotiated settlement. Nixon decided upon a bold move. Without consulting either Congress or important officials in his own administration, he sent American troops across the border into neutral Cambodia and renewed the bombing of North Vietnam. The purpose of the "incursion" into Cambodia, he told the nation in a tough, emotional speech on April 30, was to strike at North Vietnamese "sanctuaries," including a "nerve center" of enemy operations—although he had been told by responsible military and intelligence advisers that no such nerve center existed. In addition to his stated reasons, Nixon probably hoped to win time for Vietnamization, to send a signal to Hanoi about being willing to go the distance (especially since he had announced that one hundred fifty thousand man withdrawal only ten days before), and to demonstrate his grit to various opponents at home who might suspect that he was getting soft.

All hell broke loose. Within hours of the speech dozens of campus demonstrations took place, and hundreds more were planned. Then, on May 4 four students at Kent State University were shot to death by Ohio National Guardsmen as they protested against the war. The combination of the Cambodian incursion and the Kent State killings (as well as an incident unrelated to the war where two black students were killed by police at Jackson State College in Mississippi) caused an explosion of fury on campuses from coast to coast. Nixon added fuel to the fire by calling the protesters "bums"; and Vice President Agnew outdid himself: American colleges, he said in a speech at Ft. Lauderdale, had become "circus tents or psychiatric centers for overprivileged, under-disciplined, irresponsible children of the well-to-do blasé permissivists." Egged on by intemperate officials who could not understand the depth of their anger, helped along by the spring weather that invited them to spontaneous outdoor protests, the college students of America bellowed their answer to what both *Time* and *Newsweek* labeled "Nixon's gamble."

The president and his advisers had expected some expressions of anger as a result of the Cambodian incursion, but nothing like this. They wanted to believe that the outcry was caused more by the Kent State killings than by the invasion of Cambodia. But there can be little doubt that the outburst came because an unpopular war, that seemed to be winding down, was suddenly and dangerously expanded. Historian Melvin Small summarized the furor: "Between May 4 and May 8, campuses experienced an average of 100 demonstrations a day, 350 campus strikes were called with varying degrees of success, 536 colleges shut down, and 73 colleges reported significant violence in their protests. On the weekend of May 9–10, from 75 to 100,000 people gathered to protest in Washington. By May 12, over 150 colleges were on strike. . . . Ultimately, over 450 colleges closed down for at least some of the period in May and the National Guard had to be called out at least twenty-four times." Spirited antiwar demonstrations erupted even on staid and conservative campuses that had never witnessed disturbances before.

Although the protest against the Cambodian incursion centered on the nation's campuses, it was not confined there. A handful of former Peace Corps members staged a sit-in in the Peace Corps building and flew the Vietcong flag; two hundred fifty employees of the State Department signed a statement; a thousand New York City lawyers appeared in Washington to lobby the Congress; businessmen and Asian scholars and some labor leaders spoke out in one way or another; and new organizations sprang up, both nationally and locally, aiming to influence the fall elections or to gather names for petitions. In the wake of Cambodia, even Congress seemed prepared to mount a significant opposition. Angered, perhaps in equal measure, by the expansion of the fighting and by the failure of the Nixon administration to consult it, the Senate voted to repeal the Gulf of Tonkin Resolution on June 26 (the House agreeing on December 31). The Senate also debated two other antiwar measures. The Cooper-Church amendment ended funding for the Cambodian operation after July 1, the date the president said the incursion would end; it passed in the Senate but died in a joint House-Senate committee. The McGovern-Hatfield amendment would have ended funding for the war in December 1971 unless there was a proper declaration of war; it was defeated in the Senate by a vote of 55–39.

V.

After the angry reaction to Cambodia and Kent State in the late spring of 1970, the war and the movement that arose to oppose it both sputtered into final and inglorious declines. Neither death was a steady downhill march, and neither was particularly quick. Both those who favored and those who opposed the Vietnam war were facing nagging problems by the end of 1970.

Proponents of U.S. policy had finally to come to terms with the intransigence of the North Vietnamese, their stubborn refusal to be coerced into a settlement on the Nixon-Kissinger terms. Instead of being intimidated into concessions by the Cambodian incursion, the enemy resolutely refused even to continue the secret peace discussions until American troops were withdrawn from Cambodia. At the same time, they took advantage of the decreasing American strength on the field and sharply increased their infiltration of men and Russian-made weapons into the South. And if the Cambodian gamble had revealed the bankruptcy of a policy of force, it also pointed out starkly the obvious war-weariness of the American people. If the flare-up of angry protest revealed nothing else, it showed that Americans had come to expect the steady reduction of the commitment, the steady return of their fighting men, the steady winding down, not escalating up, of the war in Vietnam. Indeed, the pollster Lou Harris observed that "a literal race was on between successive Nixon announcements of further troop withdrawals and a growing public appetite for faster and faster removal of troops from Vietnam." The percentage of Americans who thought withdrawals were too slow, Harris reported, went from 26 percent in late 1969 to 34 percent in 1970, to 45 percent in May 1971, to 53 percent by November of that year. At the start of 1971 better than six out of every ten Americans favored a total withdrawal of our men by the end of the year.

Nixon moved to meet this domestic unrest with his usual mix of conciliation and toughness. A month before the congressional elections of 1970 he proposed a cease fire (rejected by Hanoi) and announced the removal of forty thousand more troops before Christmas. By the end of 1970 the number of American military personnel in Vietnam was down to three hundred thirty-four thousand. By the end of 1971 the total was down to one hundred fifty-six thousand; by the end of 1972, only twenty-four thousand. At the same time, Nixon lashed out at his critics, toured the country for pro-administration candidates in the fall of 1970, and increased his reliance on spying, intimidation, and the infiltration of peace groups. The president began showing signs of personal instability as well. Some aides later reported that a debilitating and unhealthy mentality of "us versus them" began to pervade the White House. An "enemies list" was drawn up, and, obsessed with "leaks" to the media, Nixon formed a "plumbers" group in 1971 to "plug" them by whatever means were necessary.

In Vietnam itself, the Nixon administration was still faced with the impossible task of wringing concessions from the enemy while obligingly reducing troop strength. The president authorized an attack into Laos in February 1971—this time avoiding a domestic outcry by having the South Vietnamese do the ground fighting. When, despite very heavy American air support, the ARVN was badly mauled in the operation, the effect was to throw into question the efficacy of Vietnamization. In the end, American reliance was placed on bombing. Heavy raids, causing massive destruction and many casualties, were conducted in Laos and Cambodia and throughout North Vietnam up to the outskirts of Hanoi and Haiphong. There was little evidence, however, that this tactic was effective in either military or diplomatic terms.

Meanwhile the peace movement was confronting its own difficulties. Buoyed by the steady growth in antiwar sentiment as the conflict dragged on, the antiwar activists were able to claim a few victories between the spring of 1970 and the end of the war. Some of the growth in antiwar sentiment, of course, had little to do with organized antiwar activities. The continuing publicity attending the court martial of Lt. Calley in connection with the My Lai massacre, culminating in a guilty verdict on March 29, 1971, focused renewed attention on the barbarity of the war. Ten weeks later the *New York Times* began publishing *The Pentagon Papers*, the secret study of Vietnam policy-making that had been begun in 1967 by Secretary of Defense McNamara. The documents, which revealed a train of shoddy decisions based on political considerations and a string of misleading public statements by officials in the Johnson administration, had been classified Top Secret. Daniel Ellsberg, a former marine and supporter of the war, was one of the bright young men working for McNamara. After turning against the war, he began photocopying the papers and finally gave them to the *Times*. Perhaps as damning in the eyes of the public as the content of the papers was the unseemly way that the Nixon administration scrambled to prevent their publication. By the time the Supreme Court decided that they could be printed, many Americans who might never actually read through the thousands of pages were perfectly certain that they must contain some pretty damaging information.

In addition to gains in peace sentiment caused by war-weariness, the Calley trial, and the publication of *The Pentagon Papers*, antiwar activists could also count a few achievements of their own. Foremost among them was the recruitment into the effort of a sizable number of former combat soldiers. The Vietnam Veterans against the War had been founded in 1967; by 1971 the organization numbered several thousand and its members were, not surprisingly, accorded a certain credibility denied to protesters who had never fought. In February 1971 they held the so-called "Winter Soldier" hearings in Detroit. Outraged by the persistent assertion that the My Lai incident had been nothing more than an unfortunate aberration, veterans testified for three days about the atrocities they had witnessed, even committed themselves, while serving in Vietnam. They spoke of "taking no prisoners," of torture, of willful destruction of civilian habitats by saturation bombing, of chemical warfare, of every manner of brutal and unconscionable act. The hearings, published in 1972, were the latest in a series of such disclosures starting with the Stockholm hearings organized by the British philosopher Bertrand Russell in 1967, and including the study by Clergy and Laymen Concerned about Vietnam, published in 1968. The veterans' most spectacular antiwar testimony, however, was Operation Dewey Canyon III, a week of antiwar demonstrations in Washington, D.C., in mid-April 1971. Led by mothers of boys killed in action and by men in wheelchairs or on crutches, the fatigue-clad veterans collared congressmen, held a prayer service at Arlington National Cemetery, and camped on the mall. On April 23 around a thousand of them marched to the Capitol and flung the medals they had won in Vietnam over a barricade and onto the steps of the building.

On the next day, April 24, a huge march marked one of the final high points of the antiwar movement. Hundreds of thousands of people came to ask Congress to end the long nightmare; one hundred thousand more gathered simultaneously in San Francisco. The Washington march was marked both by wide diversity among the participants and, unlike the one in San Francisco, by unusual dignity and decorum (the protesters made it a point to collect their own garbage and dispose of it neatly). On the next day, however, some extremists occupied buildings, snarled traffic by deserting their cars on the thruway, smeared themselves with blood, and painted the peace symbol on the floor of the capital building. The real fireworks came during the next week, however, when Rennie Davis's "Mayday Tribe" descended on the Capitol with the express intention of bringing government business to a halt. They ran wildly through the streets, stopped traffic, engaged in pitched battles with the police and the National Guard, threw rocks and bottles, shouted at government employees, and went limp on the sidewalk when they were arrested. Before it was over twelve thousand were in custody. They did not pick up their trash.

Despite the growth of antiwar sentiment and the ability to still stage an occasional effective demonstration, the antiwar movement was, by now, more notable for its weakness than for its strength. The activists were faced by the two problems that had plagued them for so long. The internal petty bickering over tactics, goals, and demands continued unabated. And the policy of Vietnamization had persuaded so many Americans that the war was ending that, despite continued growth of dissatisfaction in the polls, fewer and fewer were ready to engage in organized protests. To the activists, dropping bombs and supporting the ARVN was just as reprehensible morally as having Americans doing the fighting themselves; Vietnamization, they argued, merely changed the color of the corpses. Other Americans, however, did not seem to feel that way. Once the bodies stopped coming home and the casualty figures dropped and the draft calls lowered month by month, they seemed content to let the war wind down in its own way—wishing, maybe, that it could be done faster; ready, maybe, to say that it had all been a terrible mistake; but not upset enough to take to the streets. Thus neither the Laos invasion in February, nor the publication of *The Pentagon Papers* in June, was able to provoke particularly strenuous, large-scale protest; the ambitious peace campaigns announced for the autumn fizzled because so few came. When the administration ordered a sharp increase in bombing at Christmas, the antiwar response was feeble; a dozen members of the Vietnam Veterans occupied the Statue of Liberty for three weeks, but otherwise the response was hard to detect. As Zaroulis and Sullivan put it, "Nixon's Vietnamization plan, a failure in Vietnam, was succeeding in the United States."

The deadlock between a paralyzed Nixon administration and a faltering peace movement was broken by the North Vietnamese. In March 1972, as the American presidential campaign was busily gearing up, they launched a massive attack on the South, sending one hundred twenty thousand well-equipped regular troops across the demilitarized zone and over the Cambodian border. The invasion, apparently catching intelligence officials by surprise, made quick gains against Thieu's forces (there were only ninety-five thousand Americans left in Vietnam at this point, less than ten thousand of them combat troops). Given his own political situation, Nixon could neither reintroduce American fighting men to stem the tide nor permit South Vietnam to fall to the Communists. The only recourse seemed to be more bombing, and in April he ordered a massive air campaign against the North that included strikes against the cities of Hanoi and Haiphong. In May he announced a naval blockade that included the mining of Haiphong harbor and intense bombing of both the North and enemy concentrations in the South. In June alone the military dropped more than one hundred thousand tons of bombs. After terrible slaughter among the Vietnamese on both sides, the war settled back into a temporary stalemate.

The antiwar response to these developments was scattered, weak, and violent. There were numerous campus demonstrations and other actions, but nothing like the explosion of fury following the Cambodian incursion two years before. This time activities were generally small and often resulted in the occupation of some building, confrontation with the police, and numerous arrests. Participants usually numbered in the hundreds rather than the thousands. Whatever impression was made on the general public was made by small groups of protesters—seizing this building, blocking that highway, vandalizing or torching some government or university installation, trying to scale the wall around the United Nations building. Meanwhile, Peace Action Day, scheduled for April 22, was poorly attended and so was a nationwide moratorium two weeks later. Everything from bad weather to college students getting ready for final exams was blamed, but two principal factors caused the decline of the organized peace movement in the summer of 1972. The first was the continuing, steady pace of withdrawal, which convinced many Americans that there was no need; and the second was politics—the presidential election was approaching, and much of the energy required to mount successful demonstrations was siphoned off into one, last, desperate attempt to end the war by "working through the system."

The presidential race of 1972 was essentially an anticlimax. The Democrats chose one of their chief antiwar senators, George McGovern of South Dakota. He was scholarly, unmagnetic, and a mediocre public speaker. He was also honest, thoughtful, and decent, "the most decent man in the Senate," Robert Kennedy had once remarked. He was the heir to the Kennedy wing of the party, and he gained the nomination by holding that body of support while his rivals, Hubert Humphrey and Edmund Muskie, battled over the center. He was also aided by new quota rules adopted by the Democrats, rules that replaced hard-headed party veterans with neophyte representatives of women and minorities. Insofar as the campaign against Nixon turned on domestic issues, McGovern seemed to represent that part of

American politics that wanted rights for gays, permissive abortion legislation, the legalization of marijuana, more civil rights laws, and the diversion of funds from the Pentagon budget into programs of social welfare and aid to the poor. The fact that he was the son of a minister and a highly decorated bomber pilot in World War II never seemed enough to distance him, in the minds of many voters, from the suspect politics of the counterculture. He was also badly damaged by an unfortunate fiasco involving the dumping of his running mate (after vowing not to do so), thereby appearing to be indecisive and incompetent. The slowly emerging story of the June 17 break-in at the Watergate office of the Democratic National Committee, a break-in by shadowy men who seemed to have some connection to the White House and the Committee to Re-elect the President, was still too vague to have any effect on the election.

Insofar as the campaign turned on the issue of peace, McGovern was hopelessly outflanked by Richard Nixon. Wasn't the president, after all, withdrawing from Vietnam as fast as good sense and considerations of honor permitted? He had been respectfully received by America's enemies in China during his path-breaking visit there in February and had been toasted by the enemies in Moscow in May. Surely, the Republicans claimed, those who wanted peace without "crawling" to North Vietnam for it (as McGovern said he would do if it proved necessary) should stick with the incumbent. And just in case the peace issue was not quite wrapped up, Henry Kissinger paused from his intense talks with the North Vietnamese to announce on October 31, a week before the election, that "peace is at hand." A combination of regular Republicans and conservative Democrats handed McGovern—and the peace activists who had, as usual, labored so hard to win an election—one of the worst defeats in the history of American politics. He carried Massachusetts and the District of Columbia and lost everything else—521 to 17 in the electoral college.

Just as Nixon had no "secret plan" for bringing the war to an end back in 1968, so too was peace not "at hand" in October of 1972. This time the tentative agreement crafted by Kissinger and North Vietnam's Le Duc Tho foundered on the intransigence of President Thieu, who had no interest in a final settlement that would leave him on his own. He refused to be sold down the river just so that Americans could wrap up their Vietnam problem before election day. The talks, like the fighting itself, went wearily on through mid-December when they were broken off in frustration. Starting on December 18 and lasting through the rest of the year, the United States embarked upon the most intense and unrestrained bombing campaign of the entire war, the so-called "Christmas bombings" of 1972—brutal saturation attacks by B-52s that, in two weeks, hit Vietnam with more tonnage than had been dropped in the entire three-year period from 1969 to 1971. Paul Kattenburg called the Christmas bombings "one last spasm of violence." *The New Republic*, in a front page editorial, called it "madness" and begged for "a resurgence of sanity and conscience." Anthony Lewis, in the *New York Times*, described those who ordered the bombing as "men without humanity. They talk about football while arranging to impose on little countries that thwart them the punishment of mass death." Why had no one in the administration, he asked, broken with "a policy that many must know history will judge a crime against humanity."

Protest against the murderous bombing of December 1972 was weak and ineffective. Here and there a dozen or fifty or two hundred gathered for one sort of demonstration or another, but no nationwide activity took place and none was announced for the coming spring. Zaroulis and Sullivan quote a veteran of the movement: "By that time it was just one blow after another after another and you just get numb. . . . You don't feel any particular surge of rage because it's spent. It was a kind of quiet dull horror—what are these people capable of? What next?" Europe's reaction to the bombing, on the other hand, was furious: the Swedish Premier and the leader of the British Labour party condemned it in extreme terms; there were large marches against American policy in London, Rome, Berlin, and Amsterdam; some European seamen's unions voted to boycott American ships.

On January 8 talks resumed between Kissinger and Le Duc Tho. The Nixon administration claimed that the strenuous bombing had caused Hanoi to see the futility of continuing the war; critics claimed that the North had never been the obstacle and that peace was delayed by the administration's stubborn commitment to the Thieu regime and a lingering hope of improving the final terms by a show of military strength. In any case, the final agreement was very close to the terms agreed upon back in October. In his second inaugural address on January 20, with thousands observing a quiet protest a few blocks away, President Nixon confidently asserted that "we stand on the threshold of a new era of peace." A week later an agreement was signed in Paris and a ceasefire was instituted. By the end of March the last combat troops were withdrawn from South Vietnam. The peace settlement of 1973, wrote Frank Snepp, the CIA's chief strategy analyst in Vietnam, was "a cop out of sorts, an American one. The only thing it definitely guaranteed was an American withdrawal. . . . The rest of the issues that had sparked the war and kept it alive were essentially unresolved—and unresolvable." Kissinger had successfully resisted the Communist demand that Thieu be ousted, but as Snepp noted, "what had happened in the process was a deferral of the very question that had kept the two sides fighting for so long: the problem of who would rule postwar South Vietnam."

The rest of the story is easily told. Thieu was determined not only to hold power, but to increase the territory he ruled. Numerous violations of the cease-fire occurred on both sides. The peace talks between Vietnamese factions that had been envisioned by the 1973 agreement inevitably broke down, each party blaming the others; scattered fighting resumed. When the Communists began their final offensive on March 9, 1975, they rolled over a dispirited, demoralized, and panic-stricken ARVN with a speed that surprised even them. By the last week of April they controlled practically the whole nation; Thieu resigned his office on April 21 and fled the country. Both the Congress and President Gerald Ford, who had replaced Richard Nixon after the latter had been forced to resign in the aftermath of the Watergate scandal, refused to intervene this time.

The people of the United States had one more harrowing picture to endure: the wild, unseemly, inglorious evacuation of the last of the embassy staff, other remaining American citizens, and whichever Vietnamese could fight, beg, or cajole their way into one of the helicopters on the roof of the embassy. On the night of April 29, with enemy tanks rapidly closing in, the eyewitness Snepp recalled, "the roof of the Embassy was a vision out of a nightmare." The collapse had come so fast that there were not enough helicopters. In the end, there was a blind, relentless scramble to get out. Guards had to club down, beat with rifle butts and fists, the screaming, wailing Vietnamese who charged the barbed wire to get onto the ladder leading to the landing. They had worked for the American government in dozens of capacities or for the Thieu regime; many of them had been promised a way out should it ever come to that; but now there was no room, and they had to be beaten back, left to the uncertain mercies of the advancing foe. At 5 AM on the morning of the thirtieth, Ambassador Graham Martin boarded one of the last of the helicopters and lifted off. The last to go were the marine embassy guards, fighting a desperate rearguard action, spraying mace at the Vietnamese trying to get through. And then the final helicopter was gone. Eight hours later the first Communist tanks rolled into Saigon.

CONCLUSION

I.

In November 1962, *Field and Stream*, "America's number one sportsman's magazine," published an article entitled "Vietnam: A Lesson for Gun Bigots." It was written from the combat scene by Richard Starnes, and its message was simple and direct. "No Minute Men with cherished rifles stood ready to defend this tormented land. And so the Communists, adept in hit-and-run warfare, cowed a peaceful but pitifully unarmed population." The peasants' inexperience in handling firearms, according to Starnes, was permitting the Vietcong to succeed. The author could not help but compare the ineptitude of the Vietnamese with the skill of his two sons back in New York, "both good hands with rifle, shotgun, and pistol, even though the older one isn't in his middle teens yet." About two-thirds of his article was devoted to lamenting this deficiency in the peasants. But then Starnes smoothly shifted attention to the United States: "I do know that it would take a lot more than one armed terrorist to extort food and logistical support out of the tiniest American farm hamlet," he wrote. That remark provided the transition to a discussion of Starnes's fear "that the United States is determined to fritter away the built-in protection that goes with a gun-wise public." He concluded with a denunciation of gun-control proposals in America.

When Richard Starnes wrote his article there were fewer than ten thousand American military personnel in Vietnam. John Kennedy was in the White House and Ngo Dinh Diem, in uneasy control in Saigon, was busy resisting American pressures for reform. Few, if any, could have foreseen the agony that was destined to attend the American career in Vietnam. But Starnes's article is worth noticing for two reasons. First, it was among the very earliest of the attempts to draw "lessons" from the Vietnam experience, attempts that were to become a major preoccupation as the war proceeded and a minor industry in the years after the American withdrawal. And second, Starnes's article illustrates an important tendency among those who derived those lessons. The quest for the meaning of the Vietnam war, the endeavor to draw instruction from the long presence there, has always been deeply affected by the political views, the social agendas, the personal prejudices of those doing the instructing. Starnes happened to be a strong proponent of the right to bear arms and the author of many articles on the subject. Others, with different views, different values, and different experiences, saw in the travail of Vietnam substantiation for their own opinions about the world.

As might have been predicted, a good part of the search for lessons involved military matters. Endless discussions ensued about what had gone wrong and how to prevent similar mistakes in the future. Some of the issues addressed in these troubled post-mortems were highly technical and largely the province of experts. Were the men whom America sent over properly trained and prepared for the special kind of war they were asked to fight? Had the strategists placed too much confidence in a program of aerial bombardment that might have been ill suited to the terrain of Vietnam? Were those costly "search and destroy" operations the best tactic, or should the military have concentrated more on counterinsurgency or on an enclave strategy or on searching out mainline North Vietnamese units? Could more have been done to make the ARVN a reliable fighting force? Why had efforts to win the allegiance of the peasants in the countryside not enjoyed more success? Had the decision to increase the pressure gradually, to slowly squeeze the North Vietnamese harder and harder in the hope of bringing them to see reason, been wise; or would it have been better to have unleashed the full fury of our massive, overwhelming force from the very start? Above all, perhaps, had the country assigned to its military men tasks in nation-building, in economic development, in political reform, and in diplomacy that were beyond the capacity of any military organization to perform?

It would undoubtedly be expecting too much of human nature to suppose that, after the war was over, civilian and military experts debating the military lessons of Vietnam would not, on the whole, take positions that vindicated their wartime views. By and large, those who had advocated bombing then were reluctant to say now that it had all been a terrible mistake, and those who had favored "search and destroy" or particular programs of rural pacification or a policy of gradualism continued to insist that they had, in fact, given good advice at the time. The causes of the failure in Vietnam, they have tended to argue, would have to be located somewhere else. On the other hand, those who had been on the losing side of the wartime decisions about the choice of tactics, were now in the enviable position of being able quietly to hint that had their advice only been taken, things just might have come out differently.

To whatever extent it required some expertise to engage these questions and others like them, most Americans were at a distinct disadvantage in the search for the military lessons of the Vietnam war. Nevertheless, thousands of nonexperts were not without their own opinions, and many seemed eager to offer them. Here too, detecting the lessons of the Vietnam experience often seemed to depend upon personal experiences, general views, and previous opinions about the propriety and wisdom of the war itself. As is often the case where technical knowledge falls short, moreover, the comments of nonexperts sometimes came forward in the form of some fairly bold generalizations. It is a curious characteristic of many human beings that what they may lack in knowledge they compensate for in self-confidence.

Those who had opposed the war tended to draw its military lessons in terms of America's overextension and the nasty habits the nation had acquired since 1945. The Vietnam experience, they argued, should teach Americans about the limits of their power, about their inability to police the whole world effectively, and about what had become an excessive reliance upon force even in situations where political, economic, and diplomatic solutions were far more preferable and likely to work. The main lesson the country should have learned is the necessity to temper its sometimes arrogant and automatic reliance upon its power, to recognize that even its unprecedented strength must sometimes bow before the dogged and plucky determination of people fighting for a moral cause in which they deeply believe. It is not hard to see in this formulation of Vietnam's lesson one lingering legacy from the old, post-1935 ideology: the desire on the part of these Americans to be able to subscribe to policies that emphasized ethical principle and approved themselves to conscience, the abiding faith in the potency of morality as a factor in any successful resort to force.

Those who had supported the war, of course, tended to draw a rather different lesson from the experience. They increasingly took the position that, in fact, the war could have been won. The failure to win, they thought, was due in part to an excessive sentimentalism of American leaders and their unwillingness to go all the way to victory. In its most extreme version, those making this argument sometimes regretted the hesitancy to use nuclear weapons or to employ saturation bombing of North Vietnam's cities. Their most common complaint about the conduct of the war, however, was about political interference. If Vietnam should have taught the nation anything, many of them argued, it was to let the military alone. Instead, the politicians refused to loosen their grip; they prohibited certain tactics, exempted certain targets, reversed the requests of commanders in the field for men and materiel, ordered bombing halts in response to domestic pressure, and in other ways impeded the efficient and resolute completion of the military task. For these Americans, the chief lesson of the Vietnam war was simple: don't get in a war unless you intend to win, and if you intend to win, trust the military men who are trained to know how to achieve victory. It is not hard to see in *this* response the profound faith that many Americans had developed, since World War II, in the invincibility of the American fighting man. Nor is it hard to see reflected in this lesson another of the continuing legacies of the traditional ideology of American foreign policy: that the country had legitimate interests in the world and that it would sometimes be necessary to pursue them with great energy and determination.

Discussions about the meaning of the Vietnam experience for the future of American foreign policy were also characterized by differences of opinion and also shaped, to some extent, by previous views regarding the war. It is, however, always easier to speculate about the future than it is to assess blame for the past—probably because no one's immediate reputation is quite so seriously exposed and there is no possibility, in the process of looking ahead, of anyone saying "I told you so!" Thus searching the Vietnam experience for lessons about the future conduct of international relations was often a more rational, civilized, and useful enterprise. Another reason for the difference in tone in this aspect of the quest for wisdom, after Vietnam, was the fact that both the antiwar and the prowar advocates were required to do a little backtracking.

To some extent, antiwar spokesmen had availed themselves of arguments that verged close to traditional isolationism. What was going on in Vietnam, they repeated again and again during the war, was none of America's business, not worth a single American life. The United States, they insisted, had enough unfinished work to do at home without roaming the far reaches of the Third World in search of causes to champion. In addition to arguments that sounded isolationist, some segments of the antiwar movement had resorted to ones that were classically pacifist, particularly those contentions that deplored the use of violence and the inevitable brutality of war. Of course some antiwar spokesmen were, in fact, isolationists or pacifists;

most, however, were not. These might have employed such arguments knowing that they connected to deep-seated emotional predispositions in many Americans. But they were also sensitive to the charge that they represented reactionary isolationism or starry-eyed idealism. Now that the war was over, many of these antiwar veterans took pains to insist that they never favored an ostrich-like approach to foreign policy, nor did they deny the need for force under certain circumstances. In short, they were required to argue that whatever the lesson of Vietnam was, for the future of American foreign policy, it was *not* (as might have been suggested during the war) either a retreat from the world or a simple faith in nonviolence.

At the same time that the antiwar side was modifying some of its most extreme positions, the prowar side found itself engaged in a similar exercise. During the war, after all, its advocates had placed heavy stress on the frightening picture of falling domino-nations that would be more or less inevitably absorbed into the Communist sphere should South Vietnam fail to survive as a free nation. They also emphasized the heavy blow to America's prestige, its reputation for credibility, for reliability, for loyalty to allies that would necessarily follow any appearance of defeat in Indochina. Now that the war had ended in what seemed very like the appearance of defeat, it was clearly necessary to back away from those somber wartime predictions. Washington officials, who had until recently managed the war, were now required to assure the American people and their allies that the United States was still strong, resolute, and reliable, that its position in the world had not changed, that its word could still be trusted—in other words, they were forced to assert that Vietnam had not really mattered all that much. Whatever the lesson of Vietnam was, for the future of American foreign policy, it was *not* (as might have been suggested during the war) the inevitability of further Communist domino gains or the necessary loss of America's prestige or reputation for reliability.

As many members on one side of the debate over Vietnam fled from any imputation of either isolationism or pacifism, and as many on the other fled from any imputation of defeatism, something that might have seemed like a rough, but exceedingly vague, consensus emerged. Almost everybody agreed that the United States had an important role to play in the world, but almost everybody also agreed that the country must be much more careful than it had been in Vietnam in deciding how and when to exercise its power. In the future, decisions to intervene or to remain aloof would have to be based upon rigorous analyses of local conditions, of prospects for success, of the viability of those to whose aid America was coming, of the likelihood of being able to persuade Americans of the propriety or the necessity of the venture, of a half-dozen other factors that had not been sufficiently considered when it was decided to enter the conflict in Vietnam. Similarly, in the future the United States would have to give much more careful thought to the methods it employed in cases where intervention seemed warranted and much more careful thought to the extent of such commitments. No doubt these areas of agreement between former proponents and former opponents of the war, this consensus on the lessons that the Vietnam experience had to impart for the future, were heartening signs of the process of healing. But the terms of agreement were so unclear, the precise application of these general principles so open to varying interpretation and subject to lasting differences of temperament that, in actuality, the consensus was more apparent than real. The debate that erupted in the 1980s over possible American intervention in Central America revealed how far Americans were from a genuine meeting of minds.

Those who had been on opposite sides of the debate could agree on at least one additional point. One certain effect of Vietnam would probably be to make the nation's political leadership more hesitant about embarking on other such interventions any time in the near future. Vietnam had been such a chastening, bruising, embittering episode—both on the battlefields of Indochina and in the arena of domestic politics—that politicians would probably be very reluctant to get involved that way again. This generally agreed upon prediction, however, could scarcely camouflage the momentous difference that lurked below the surface. To many former proponents of the Vietnam war this expectation of a new political timidity was both regrettable and dangerous. American leaders, they believed, had to be able to act decisively and efficiently if the country's voice was to be heard and respected in the world. To whatever extent the Vietnam experience prevented bold presidential initiatives whenever they appeared, even remotely, to lead in the direction of a lengthy military commitment, to precisely that extent the future conduct of effective foreign relations had been damaged by the war. Even the mere perception of a reluctance to act might tempt potential adversaries into perilous undertakings. To most opponents of the late war, of course, the prediction that from now on presidents would have to be a lot more careful about committing the nation to untenable situations was comforting; if true, they believed, it marked perhaps the greatest triumph of the antiwar movement. These arguments were repeated vigorously in the debate over the War Powers Act of November 1973. By that law, eventually passed over Richard Nixon's veto, the ability of the president to commit American troops overseas for long periods was theoretically restricted.

There were also wide-ranging and inconclusive speculations about what the war had revealed about the American spirit, the national psyche. As might be expected, opinions on so subjective a matter ranged over the whole gamut of possible answers. For some of the war's supporters, particularly for some of those who recalled World War II, the pusillanimous response to the war in Vietnam revealed a deep sickness in the American population, and a few indulged in bleak predictions about the decline of national glory in the face of hedonism, irresolution, cowardice, and the eclipse of patriotism. The speculations over this question by those who had opposed the war usually took one of two paths. For some the lesson of Vietnam was that Americans had become so numbed to brutality, so accustomed to horror, that they could tolerate any crime provided only that it was committed far away from their own shores and preferably upon people who were not white. Others took quite the opposite view. The fact that so many Americans, however reluctantly or tardily, were roused to oppose this immoral war, they said, showed that there still existed within the people of the country an instinct for decency and fair play; the resistance to an evil and unwise policy proved that what was best in the American spirit was still alive and well.

On May 6, 1975, one week after the last marines had scrambled off the roof of the American embassy in Saigon, President Gerald Ford held a news conference. Helen Thomas of the United Press International asked him if he thought a congressional inquiry into the war would help Americans learn some lessons from the past. The president insisted that such an inquiry would be "divisive, not helpful" and that the country should now concentrate on the future. "I think the lessons of the past in Vietnam have already been learned—learned by Presidents, learned by Congress, learned by the American people." We may give President Ford credit for one correct and for one incorrect answer. That a congressional inquiry would have been divisive, would have filled the air with recriminations and opened old wounds, is very hard to doubt. But the view that the lessons of Vietnam had been so quickly assimilated seems like wishful thinking. Not only was there no real evidence of Americans having learned a list of Vietnam lessons, there was not even a sign of agreement on what lessons belonged on that list. The postwar search for lessons, absorbing and varied and widespread as it was, must, in the end, be regarded as nothing more than a continuation of the debate over Vietnam.

II.

There is no reason to be particularly surprised, of course, that acrimony and division should have continued after the war itself was over. In his book, *Americans Interpret Their Civil War* (1954), historian Thomas J. Pressly studies the ways in which that earlier conflict got discussed and judged. For a full generation, Pressly notes, commentators on the Civil War were partisans: "Most of them had experienced the coming of war and the passions of wartime at first hand." Most of them had so much invested in one view or another of the war that their postwar observations were little more than spirited repetitions and vindications of earlier positions. "So long as the emotions of wartime retained their hold, so long as Civil War issues were burning questions bitterly contested in the arena of day-to-day politics, interpretations of the war's causes were dominated by the effort to locate the blame for the struggle upon the enemy." In the case of Vietnam, it was also natural that the powerful emotions that were aroused and engaged by the wartime debate should continue to ferment for awhile. There have been, in this case too—as the quest for Vietnam's lessons reveals—numerous postwar analyses that seem intent on fixing the blame, and on fixing it in terms reminiscent of the discussions that took place in America while the war raged.

The noteworthy phenomenon, however, is not that wartime passions should persist after the war's conclusion. The noteworthy phenomenon is the extent to which both sides in the debate have been able to find some common ground, to take the first, tentative steps toward binding up the wounds. No doubt the leading governmental officials and military officers, on the one hand, and the leading antiwar activists, on the other, will continue to produce vociferously self-justifying memoirs. But it would be most surprising if professional historians did not avoid the partisanship of their post-Civil War predecessors—indeed, there are already impressive signs, among historians and other writers, of a desire to understand the war and its accompanying travail without vindicating their former opinions or finding a set of villains. The reason for this probably has much to do with changed ideas about the professional historian's role and responsibility. Even more significant than this development among professional historians, however, is what seems to be a parallel development among the general public.

In May 1887, twenty-two years after Appomattox, President Grover Cleveland ordered that all captured Confederate battle flags be returned to southern states; the clamor throughout the North was deafening—the commander of the Grand Army of the Republic prayed, "May God palsy the hand that wrote the order." Without denying that there are considerable numbers of everyday Americans who still cling, with undiminished vehemence, to the fevered slogans uttered during the heat of the wartime debate over Vietnam, it seems clear that rhetoric has softened substantially on both sides. In part, of course, this is because the stakes in Vietnam were not nearly as high as in the Civil War, but also, in part, the moderated tone is the product of a certain mellowing of positions. The harshest charges have, on the whole, been dropped. Nowadays, one seldom hears former opponents of the war assailing its advocates as racist murderers of small children. Nor does one often encounter former advocates of the war who continue to charge that the protesters were nothing but craven cowards and Communist traitors who took their orders from the Kremlin.

Today, perhaps the noun most commonly linked to "Vietnam" is "tragedy," and "tragic" is perhaps the most commonly used adjective. It would be a mistake to believe that this generally mild terminology indicates an evaporation of all of the causes for animosity that so divided Americans during the war. The shapes of the old contentions can still be detected beneath the blanket of the generally agreed-upon new language. Thus, upon probing it might emerge that for many of the war's former opponents Vietnam was tragic because so much blood was spilled for so useless and immoral an enterprise; while for many former proponents, Vietnam was a tragedy because the nation got itself involved in a shooting war it was unprepared to pursue with the necessary vigor and patriotism, unwilling to see through to a proper conclusion. And yet, despite the shadowy outlines of old arguments lurking below the surface, most Americans would count it a gain that the discourse has somehow become more civilized, more tempered, less bellicose.

No factor has been more important in enabling the two sides to draw closer together than the growth of widespread sympathy for the Vietnam veterans. For a period immediately after the war's conclusion, returning vets received a rather chilly reception back in the United States. As they themselves often pointed out, there were no welcoming parades, scant special attention was accorded to them, and few admiring tales of their heroism were being circulated in the general population. Indeed, there were numerous instances of returning soldiers being abused and taunted in restaurants or on the streets, pelted with eggs as they boarded busses and headed for home. Several factors combined to produce this unfriendly atmosphere. For years, opponents of the war had criticized the unspeakable atrocities committed against helpless Vietnamese peasants. This picture of bru-

tal American troops was reinforced, not only by such spectacular episodes as the My Lai revelations of 1969–70 or the "Winter Soldier"
hearings of early 1971, but by dozens and dozens of horrifying tales
told by returning vets, many of whom were enthusiastic supporters of
the war.

Even supporters of the war, although probably in greater sympathy with the veterans than many antiwar activists, also had reasons to
be cool toward them. The many accounts of the demoralization of the
military in Vietnam—tales of alcoholism and prostitution, of serious
drug abuse and "fragging," of slovenly dress, shocking language, the
refusal to obey orders—certainly contributed to a picture of the Vietnam combat soldier that made him seem a good deal less appealing
than the more gentlemanly and respectable returned veterans of
World War II. In addition, the very visible part that some veterans
took in antiwar demonstrations near the end of the war and the fact
that these men claimed to speak for thousands of bitter comrades also
cost veterans in general some sympathy among those civilians who
thought that the war was necessary and noble. If these things were
not enough, Vietnam veterans had other liabilities to contend with. It
could not be plausibly claimed for them, as for the vets of earlier
generations, that they returned home having vanquished the foe and
having vindicated the nation's purposes. Moreover, the battlefield was
so far away and the direct threat to America seemed so remote to most
Americans that it was hard to portray these men as engaged in defending the nation against fearful dangers. Finally, a picture of the
returned veteran emerged in popular accounts, movies, and television dramas that was far from complimentary: he was often portrayed
as deeply disturbed, emotionally unbalanced, unable to adjust sucess-
fully to a peaceful world, subject to hallucinations or bad dreams, and
filled with a rage that could explode at any moment into uncontrol-
lable hysteria or acts of breathtaking violence. Most of all, one suspects, ignoring the Vietnam vet was just one part of the more general
phenomenon of ignoring the nation's entire, shattering, unhappy
Vietnam experience in all of its aspects—a phenomenon that hints at
a need to suppress, a deep wish to forget.

Before very long, however, the reputation of the Vietnam veteran
began to undergo considerable change. Veterans themselves played a
large part in this reevaluation. They did so, in the first instance, by
organizing to meet the needs that were being ignored by the larger
society. Often in small groups that later grew into national organizations, veterans set up storefront centers to provide counseling, em-
ployment agencies, information about drugs, or just the opportunity
to talk over wartime and postwar experiences with others who shared

them. These activities started to enlist the support of various professionals and to attract respectful attention across the country. It became clear, first, that the vast majority of the vets had made relatively smooth and quite satisfactory adjustments to civilian life and, second, that those who had not done so deserved proper medical and psychological help and sympathy from other Americans. Scientific studies of post-combat stress indicated that intense reactions to such situations were much more normal than had previously been believed. The crusade, on the part of veterans who had been exposed to Agent Orange and other poisonous chemicals in Vietnam and who complained about serious disabilities and health problems in themselves and their children, to bring their plight before the government and the public also gained considerable national attention and sympathy.

Within the last fifteen years, moreover, a series of widely read books and popular films have reopened the combat experience of the Vietnam veteran to new scrutiny. Many of the books, fiction and nonfiction, were written by veterans or by other Vietnam eyewitnesses, and they are characterized by a deep yearning to "tell what it was like," to confront other Americans with the raw truth of what these men saw and knew and did there, and of what happened to them and inside them when they returned home from the jungles. Among the most read and discussed books of the late 1970s and 1980s that touch upon the veteran's experiences have been Michael Herr, *Dispatches* (1977), Philip Caputo, *A Rumor of War* (1978), Gustav Hasford, *The Short-Timers* (1979), Tim O'Brien, *Going After Cacciato* (1978) and his *If I Die in a Combat Zone* (1979), Mark Baker, *Nam* (1981), Al Santoli, *Everything We Had* (1981), Terry Wallace, *Bloods* (1984), Bobbie Ann Mason, *In Country* (1985), and Larry Heinemann, *Paco's Story* (1987). These novels, journalists' accounts, personal memoirs, oral histories—and many others like them—have vividly described the ordeal of the veteran to a considerable American audience.

The films were particularly effective in shaping attitudes toward the veterans because of the huge numbers of Americans who were exposed to them. Among the most popular were *The Boys in Company C* (1978), *Coming Home* (1978), *Go Tell the Spartans* (1978), *The Deer Hunter* (1978), *Apocalypse Now* (1979), *First Blood* (1982), *Uncommon Valor* (1983), *Missing in Action* (1984), *Rambo* (1985), *Platoon* (1986), *The Hanoi Hilton* (1987), *Gardens of Stone* (1987), *Full Metal Jacket* (1987), and *Hamburger Hill* (1987). It might be possible to locate these films on a spectrum running from those that applauded to those that condemned American purposes and policies in Vietnam, but to do so would be to miss the point, their strongest impact on public opinion. In fact, these films, in general, are relatively silent on American objec-

tives and ideals—in this they are rather different from the films of
World War II. The Vietnam films are about the men who fought
there, the way they were trained, the surrealistic horrors they encoun-
tered, the life they found upon their return. They emphasize the
stunning ugliness of the war, the terrors to which young men were
subjected, the traditional virtues of courage, self-sacrifice, and com-
radeship, and the shabby treatment of these brave men by the society
that sent them to fight. The cumulative effect of these books and films
has probably been to enlarge the society's admiration and esteem for
these veterans, to accord to them a measure of honor and respect that
had been withheld before. By April 1985 *Newsweek* could summarize
the transformation: "America's Vietnam veterans, once viewed with a
mixture of indifference and outright hostility by their countrymen,
are now widely regarded as national heroes."

Honoring the vets provided a way for the two sides in the wartime
debate to temper their fiercest contentions and, thereby, to begin to
smooth the way toward healing the national wound. But in order to
do so, both the opponents and the advocates of the war had to modify
subtly their most extreme and irritating arguments. For the war's opponents, this has meant softening the charges of atrocity. While holding to the view that the war was immoral and unnecessary, the critics
began to see the eighteen year olds who fought there less as perpetrators of evil and more as victims of a callous and misguided policy. In
short, the animosity that was once, in part, directed against common
soldiers has gradually become focused against politicians, technical
planners, and the Pentagon. For the war's supporters, the adjustment
has been even more substantial. While insisting on the valor of the
warriors, fewer and fewer, as time passes, now justify the war. The
anger they felt against all who opposed the war now tends to be concentrated on those who abused and villified the fighting men. By the
spring of 1985, ten years after the last chopper lifted off the roof of
the American embassy in Saigon, a considerable majority of Americans were ready to say that the war had been "a mistake"—by *Newsweek's* poll, 64 percent; by one conducted by the *New York Times*, 73
percent. Thus there has begun to emerge an outline for a national
reconciliation to which most Americans, in time, will be able to subscribe: the war was a tragic mistake, but the men who fought there
were brave and deserving of honor and respect.

If the new way in which most Americans were willing to regard the
Vietnam veterans had a tangible symbol, it was the National Vietnam
Veterans' Memorial in Washington, D.C. The memorial, conceived by
a small group of veterans and built entirely with private contributions,
was dedicated in November 1982. It stands near the Lincoln Memo-

rial and has, significantly, become one of the most frequently visited historic sites in the capital. Designed by Maya Ying Lin, a young architectural student from Yale (who was nine years old when the Tet offensive occurred), the memorial consists of two wings of black granite, rising out of the earth and sinking back into it. On the reflecting panels are carved the names of the nearly sixty thousand who died. The original concept was so plain, so unadorned, so stark, that as an aesthetic compromise a statue depicting three soldiers was placed nearby. From the start, the project's advocates, knowing that the war itself was still a divisive issue, concentrated on the limited purpose of honoring the brave Americans who fell there. By the early 1980s both sides in the debate were willing to begin the process of national reconciliation in this way (the committee sponsoring the memorial included both General Westmoreland and Senator McGovern).

Probably no one could have predicted the emotional impact that the wall of names would have on those who came to see it. Men—some dressed in battle fatigues, some in wheelchairs or on crutches, some carrying their children in their arms, many with tears streaming down their faces—come to find the names of fallen comrades. Parents come to touch a son's name, and widows, the names of their husbands. People leave little mementos—a flower, a combat decoration, a photograph—near the name of some loved one. Even those who had known none of those thousands of dead men, even those who fought against the war, are deeply moved, shaken, and filled with sadness at what the war cost.

III.

There are two principal ways to describe any single thing that belongs to a larger class—trees, rocks, buildings, men and women. One can concentrate on the subject's uniqueness, on those features that distinguish, that set apart this one from the others, or one can concentrate on the similarities, the traits that the particular example shares with the whole class. Each man, for example, has certain things about him that make him like all other men and certain things about him that make him unique. And if a group of students was asked to write essays about, say, Abraham Lincoln, some would discuss those traits—his wisdom, his compassion, his sensitivity—that tended to set him apart from other men of his generation, while others might emphasize how his attitudes—about the Union, freedom, race, women, democracy, and a dozen other things—were typical of his time and place. We may agree that a fully rounded picture of Lincoln must partake of both of these aspects.

The same is true about wars and about the discussions that attend them. It is possible to approach particular instances here too as if they were most remarkable for their uniqueness, and it is possible to approach them as if they were most notable for what they had in common with similar episodes in the history of a nation or of the world. It is difficult to escape the conclusion that almost all of the consideration of the Vietnam experience has concentrated on its uniqueness. Americans have chosen to talk and think about the Vietnam war and the debate that surrounded it as if these were almost entirely unlike earlier wars, earlier debates. In a way this is only natural; the first considerations of any new thing usually concentrate on its special features. But, as in the case of essays on Lincoln that consider only the ways he was different from everyone else, inevitable distortions occur.

It seems safe to predict that as Americans move further away from the era of the Vietnam war, as they get more distance, more perspective on those years, they will be better able to round out the picture. Even the two points where strong cases can be made for the uniqueness of the war—the ferocity of the weaponry and the intimacy of the media's coverage of the fighting—will probably diminish in importance. (As a general rule, the ferociousness of weapons has increased from war to war in modern history, each successive war seeming to represent, in its turn, the ultimate in human perversity, and as a general rule, the intimacy of the reportage to those back home increases as fast as advances in technology permit.) In the end, it may be that the war's unusual length may come to be regarded as its most critical special feature. And just as the war itself may seem less and less distinctive as time passes, so too may the debate among Americans over its propriety seem less separable from earlier such debates. It may well be that historians of the future will wish to note the ways in which the discussion was like earlier ones in the nation's history, that they will want to make connections and mark continuities.

When this is done, some valuable and clarifying insights should emerge. Three connections with the past may prove especially worthy of notice. First, the debate over Vietnam should serve as another illustration of how wars are justified (or how they fail to be justified) among men and women. It turns out that, quite unconsciously, we fall inevitably into the patterns of discourse outlined by the old philosophers of "the just war," requiring, as they did, that our wars be necessary to our defense and palatable to our consciences. If there is any lesson for future statesmen in the Vietnam debate, as in earlier ones, it is that leaders ought to be confident that they can persuade their fellow citizens on both scores before they engage them in warfare. Second, the debate over Vietnam should serve as another illustration of Tocqueville's general point about democratic wars. The American people—whether to their credit or their shame—have not been particularly easy to persuade about the necessity of engaging in armed hostility. The resistance to the official justifications of the war in Vietnam will look a lot more like this country's experience during the Mexican War or the War of 1812 than it may today. Finally, the debate over Vietnam should remind us of what Socrates pointed out to Euthyphro twenty-four centuries ago. The differences between us that cannot be resolved, that "make us angry and set us at enmity with one another" are not usually disputes about facts. Nor are they very often quarrels between a group of good people and a group of evil ones. As the debate over Vietnam illustrates, our most serious differences arise from differing visions of what *is* good and what evil, from divergent definitions of the honorable and the dishonorable.

Bibliographical Essay

So many books and articles have been written about the Vietnam war and about the domestic debate that surrounded it that merely listing them would require half a dozen additional volumes the size of this one. Much of that writing was produced during the war and constitutes raw material for any study of the national discussion of our Vietnam policy, but there have also been thousands of postwar efforts to describe and explain aspects of this country's experience in Vietnam. Some of those works were written by those who fought—views of the war from the highest ranking generals to the lowliest combat grunts. Writing about Vietnam has also appeared in the form of official government reports, novels and poetry, self-justifying memoirs by men and women on all sides of the policy, leading political figures, and journalists. A flood of literature by historians, political and social scientists, scholars, critics and commentators, and by many others has also inundated the reading public. There is little sign that the outpouring of literature on Vietnam is going to slow. Therefore, the claims made for an essay like this one must be suitably modest and tentative. I have included titles here on the basis of two criteria. First, I mention those contributions to the literature that I have particularly relied upon and been helped and informed by; I do this both to acknowledge gratefully my own indebtedness and to call attention to the merits of these works so that others can profit from them as I have. Second, I mention those works that I think readers might find interesting and useful in case they may wish—as I very much hope—to probe more deeply some of the issues I may have touched upon inadequately.

General Works

There are numerous bibliographical guides to writing about Vietnam. In a class by itself is Richard Dean Burns and Milton Leitenberg, *The Wars in Vietnam, Cambodia, and Laos, 1945–1982: A Bibliographic Guide* (1984). It lists 6,200 items, is usefully arranged by subject, and contains helpful chronologies and an index of authors. Burns and Leitenberg list no fewer than fifty other bibliographical aids, all of them, of course, published before 1984. Also extremely valuable, both for its organization and its concise comments, is Louis A. Peake, *The United States in the Vietnam War, 1954–1975* (1986), which directs readers to 1,550 items. John H. M. Chen, *Vietnam: A Comprehensive Bibliography* (1973), which lists 2,300 items in strict alphabetical order, and Christopher L. Sugnet and John T. Hickey, *Vietnam War Bibliography* (1983), another alphabetical listing, are not as valuable as either Burns and Leitenberg or Peake, but are also worth consulting. The best bibliography on Vietnamese society, apart from the war, is Michael Cotter, *Vietnam: A Guide to Reference Sources* (1977). Most of the books listed below also contain bibliographies, some of them quite good. Serious students of the topic will be repaid by spending some time with Ronald H. Spector, *Researching the Vietnam Experience* (1984).

Those exploring the Vietnam war should bear in mind the following reference books. Both Danny J. Whitfield, *Historical and Cultural Dictionary of Vietnam* (1976), and William J. Duiker, *Historical Dictionary of Vietnam* (1989), contain short entries for hundreds of individuals, locations, and terms; the latter has the advantage of an excellent recent bibliography. Both Harry G. Summers, Jr., *Vietnam War Almanac* (1985), and James S. Olsen, ed., *Dictionary of the Vietnam War* (1988), are most valuable for their entries on all aspects of American involvement in the war; both of them, moreover, offer additional reading suggestions for almost every entry. The Summers and the Olsen books contain chronologies of American involvement, but perhaps the most ambitious work in this category is Lawrence M. Connell, *Vietnam Chronology: 1940–1973* (1974), a 152-page listing of events in chronological order. Briefer, more manageable, and generally adequate chronologies, however, can be found as parts of many works on the war.

Of the one-volume surveys of the Vietnam war, none has yet surpassed the balanced, concise, and authoritative George C. Herring, *America's Longest War: The United States and Vietnam, 1950–1975* (1986 edition); if a reader has only enough time to read a single book, it should probably be this one. Stanley Karnow, *Vietnam: A History* (1983), is another fine survey; it is more than twice as long as Herring's book and is characterized by engaging writing, the firsthand knowledge of an experienced reporter, and admirable fairness. Paul M. Kattenburg, *The Vietnam Trauma in American Foreign Policy, 1945–1975* (1980), is less a "history" of our involvement than it is an extremely thoughtful analysis by a leading expert on Southeast Asia; Kattenburg tackles difficult questions with an unusual balance of detailed knowledge and reasoned judgment. In a similar vein are two provocative studies of bureaucratic decision-making, Leslie H. Gelb, with Richard K. Betts, *The Irony of Vietnam: The System Worked* (1979), a work undertaken by the Brookings Institution, and Patrick Lloyd Hatcher, *The Suicide of an Elite: American Interventionists and Vietnam* (1990), an interesting analysis of how high-level policy-makers erred. The most impressive scholarly defense of our presence in Vietnam, while offering some criticism of our policy, is Guenter Lewy, *America in Vietnam* (1978). On the other side is the thorough critique by Gabriel Kolko, *Anatomy of a War: Vietnam, the United States, and the Modern Historical Experience* (1985). George McT. Kahin and John W. Lewis, *The United States in Vietnam* (1966, 1969), is a very early attempt that holds up remarkably well. An imaginative and highly intelligent attempt to relate our Vietnam policies to deep cultural and intellectual propensities is Loren Baritz, *Backfire: A History of How American Culture Led Us into Vietnam and Made Us Fight the Way We Did* (1985). All of these surveys are more helpful on the military, political, and diplomatic aspects of the war than they are on the activities of the antiwar movement.

The fundamental collection of primary documents is, of course, *The Pentagon Papers*. There are several versions of this vast body of materials, gathered secretly at the behest of Secretary of Defense McNamara in 1967–68 and leaked to the press by Daniel Ellsberg in 1971. A twelve-volume edition was issued by the House Committee on the Armed Services (1971); a four-volume version, the so-called Senator Gravel edition, was also published in 1971, to which was added, in 1972, a fifth volume of critical essays on the papers by fifteen authorities. The *New York Times* edition (1971), edited by Neil Sheehan, et al., contains eight hundred pages of summaries and documents. Users should begin by reading George McT. Kahin, "The Pentagon Papers: A Critical Evaluation," *American Political Science Review* 69 (1975): 675–84. Other useful collections of documents include Gareth Porter, ed., *Vietnam: The Definitive Documentation of Human Decisions*, 2 vols. (1979); Marvin E. Gettleman, ed., *Vietnam: History, Documents, and Opinions on a Major World Crisis* (1965, 1970); Marcus G. Raskin and Bernard B. Fall, eds., *The Vietnam Reader* (1965); Steven Cohen, ed., *Vietnam: Anthology and Guide to a Television*

History (1983), prepared in connection with the PBS series on the Vietnam war; William A. Williams, ed., *America in Vietnam: A Documentary History* (1985), and Jeffrey P. Kimball, *To Reason Why: The Debate about the Causes of U.S. Involvement in the Vietnam War* (1990). The photographic record of this episode in American history is extremely rich. Readers can sample the best of it in Joel D. Meyerson, *Images of a Lengthy War* (1985), a volume in the Center of Military History series on the U.S. Army in Vietnam. Stunning photographs can also be found in profusion in *The Vietnam Experience*, a multivolume series published by the Boston Publishing Co.

Preface

On the evolution of "just war" doctrine, there have been many superb scholarly studies. For the pre-Vietnam background, excellent places to start are Frederick H. Russell, *The Just War in the Middle Ages* (1975); Roland Bainton, *Christian Attitudes toward War and Peace* (1960); Paul Ramsey, *War and the Christian Conscience* (1961); Robert L. Phillips, *War and Justice* (1984); or two works by James Turner Johnson, *Ideology, Reason, and the Limitation of War: Religious and Secular Concepts, 1200–1740* and *Just War Tradition and the Restraint of War: A Moral and Historical Inquiry* (1981). Michael Walzer's challenging and provocative book, *Just and Unjust Wars: A Moral Argument with Historical Illustrations* (1977), is a general discussion of morality and war, in which one can see the influence of the Vietnam experience. For works dealing specifically with the Vietnam conflict and the doctrines of "the just war," see the suggestions below, for chapter four.

Alexis de Tocqueville's views on war and the American democracy may be found in the chapter of *Democracy in America* entitled "Why Democratic Nations Naturally Desire Peace, and Democratic Armies, War." For a brief overview of American resistance to previous wars, see Russell F. Weigley, "Dissent in Wars," in Alexander DeConde, ed., *Encyclopedia of American Foreign Policy: Studies of the Principal Movements and Ideas*, 1: 253–67 (1978). Another survey of the subject is Arthur Ekirch, *The Civilian and the Military: A History of the American Antimilitarist Tradition* (1972 edition). The early opponents of war and militarism are covered exhaustively in Peter Brock, *Pacifism in the United States: From the Colonial Era to the First World War* (1968). For the Revolution, see Robert McCluer Calhoon, *The Loyalists in Revolutionary America, 1760–1781* (1973); for the war of 1812, see either James M. Banner, Jr., *To the Hartford Convention: The Federalists and the Origins of Party Politics in Massachusetts, 1789–1815* (1970), or the essay by Samuel Eliot Morison in Morison, Frederick Merk, and Frank Freidel, *Dis-*

sent in Three American Wars (1970); for the Mexican War, see Merk's essay in the same volume; for the Civil War, see Georgia Lee Tatum, *Disloyalty in the Confederacy* (1972), and Joel Sibley, *A Respectable Minority: The Democratic Party in the Civil War Era* (1977); for the Spanish-American war and its aftermath, the essay by Frank Freidel in *Dissent in Three American Wars*, cited above, David B. Schirmer, *Republic or Empire: American Resistance to the Philippine War* (1977), David S. Patterson, *Toward a Warless World: The Travail of the American Peace Movement, 1887–1914* (1976), or C. Roland Marchand, *The American Peace Movement and Social Reform, 1898–1918* (1972); for World War I, still valuable is H. C. Peterson and Gilbert C. Fite, *Opponents of War, 1917* (1957).

Chapter 1. The Consensus

Perhaps the most efficient way to obtain a broad overview of American foreign relations leading to World War II is to read the relevant chapters in one of the diplomatic history textbooks; excellent texts have been written by Thomas A. Bailey (1980 edition); Nelson M. Blake and Oscar T. Barck, Jr. (1960); Wayne S. Cole (1974); Alexander DeConde (1978); Robert H. Ferrell (1975); Walter LaFeber (1989); Richard W. Leopold (1962); Thomas G. Paterson, Garry J. Clifford, and Kenneth J. Hagan (1988 edition); Howard Jones (1988 edition); Julius W. Pratt, Vincent P. De Santis, and Joseph M. Siracusa (1980 edition); and Daniel M. Smith (1972).

There has been a great deal written about the international troubles of the 1930s and the great debate between isolationists and interventionists. An excellent guide to this material is Justus D. Doenecke, *Anti-Intervention: A Bibliographical Introduction to Isolationism and Pacifism from World War I to the Early Cold War* (1987). Some older studies that have stood the test of time are Selig Adler, *The Isolationist Impulse: Its Twentieth Century Reaction* (1957), Dorthy Borg, *The United States and the Far Eastern Crisis of 1933–1938* (1964), Wayne S. Cole, *America First: The Battle against Intervention* (1953), Robert A. Divine, *The Illusion of Neutrality* (1962), Herbert Feis, *The Road to Pearl Harbor* (1950), Robert H. Ferrell, *American Diplomacy in the Great Depression* (1957), Manfred Jonas, *Isolationism in America, 1935–1941* (1966), William Langer and S. Everett Gleason, *The Challenge to Isolation, 1937–1940* (1952), and John E. Wiltz, *From Isolation to War, 1931–1941* (1968). Among the best of the newer works on the pre-World War II discussion is Mark L. Chadwin, *The Warhawks: American Interventionists before Pearl Harbor* (1970 edition), Wayne S. Cole, *Roosevelt and the Isolationists, 1932–45* (1983), Robert Dallek, *Franklin D. Roosevelt and American*

Foreign Policy, 1932–1945 (1979), and Robert A. Divine, *The Reluctant Belligerent: American Entry into World War II* (1979 edition). For Roosevelt's "Quarantine Speech" of 1937, see Dorothy Borg, "Notes on Roosevelt's 'Quarantine' Speech," *Political Science Quarterly* 72 (1957): 405–33, and Travis B. Jacobs, "Roosevelt's 'Quarantine Speech,'" *Historian* 24 (1962): 483–502.

Those wishing to do research on virtually any aspect of the Cold War will be greatly helped by two splendid bibliographies: Richard Dean Burns, ed., *Guide to American Foreign Relations since 1700* (1983), chs. 24–31, and J. L. Black, *Origins, Evolution, and Nature of the Cold War* (1986). The origin of the Cold War has been a virtual battleground for historians. For discussions of the historiography, see either J. Samuel Walker, "Historians and Cold War Origins: The New Consensus," in Gerald K. Haines and J. Samuel Walker, eds., *American Foreign Relations: A Historiographic Review* (1981): 207–36, or John Lewis Gaddis, "The Emerging Post-Revisionist Synthesis on the Origins of the Cold War," *Diplomatic History* 7 (1983): 171–90, and the four responses to Gaddis's article. Two reliable introductions are Thomas G. Paterson, *On Every Front: The Making of the Cold War* (1979), and John Lewis Gaddis, *The United States and the Origins of the Cold War, 1941–1947* (1972)—both have fine bibliographies. For balanced general surveys of the Cold War, see Stephen E. Ambrose, *Rise to Globalism: American Foreign Policy Since 1938* (1985 edition); Walter LaFeber, *America, Russia, and the Cold War, 1945–1984* (1985 edition); or John W. Spanier, *American Foreign Policy since World War II* (1983 edition). On the Marshall Plan, the best study is Michael J. Hogan, *The Marshall Plan: America, Britain, and the Reconstruction of Western Europe* (1987); but see also John Gimbel, *The Origins of the Marshall Plan* (1976), Harold L. Hitchens, "Influences on the Congressional Decision to Pass the Marshall Plan," *Western Political Quarterly* 21 (1968): 51–68, Michael Wala, "Selling the Marshall Plan at Home: The Committee for the Marshall Plan to Aid European Recovery," *Diplomatic History* 10 (1986): 247–65, and Alan G. Raucher, *Paul G. Hoffman: Architect of Foreign Aid* (1986). On Korea, see Burton I. Kaufman, *The Korean War* (1986), David Rees, *Korea: The Limited War* (1964), Charles M. Dobbs, *The Unwanted Symbol: American Foreign Policy, the Cold War, and Korea, 1945–1950* (1981), and Rosemary Foot, *The Wrong War* (1985).

On the growth of the power of the executive branch of the government in foreign policy formulation, see the fine overview, David M. Pletcher, "Presidential Power in Foreign Affairs," in DeConde, ed., *Encyclopedia of American Foreign Policy*, 3: 805–26. Arthur M. Schlesinger, Jr.'s *The Imperial Presidency* (1973) is an engaging historical account of the expansion of executive authority. For the post-World War II period, see Edgar E. Robinson, ed., *Powers of the President in Foreign Affairs, 1945–1965* (1966), Thomas F. Eagleton, *War and Presidential Power: A Chronicle of Congressional Surrender* (1974), and John Lehman, *The Executive, Congress, and Foreign Policy: Studies of the Nixon Administration* (1974).

Chapter 2. The Contest

The early history of Vietnam is explored in three pioneering works, in English, by Joseph Buttinger: *The Smaller Dragon: A Political History of Vietnam* (1958), *Vietnam: A Dragon Embattled*, 2 vols. (1967), and *Vietnam: A Political History* (1968). Readers desiring a briefer overview of Vietnamese history are directed to either Chester A. Bain, *Vietnam: The Roots of Conflict* (1967), or Hal Dareff, *The Story of Vietnam* (1966), a book aimed at younger readers. The coming of French rule over Vietnam is very well covered in John F. Cady, *The Roots of French Imperialism in Eastern Asia* (1954). Vietnamese opposition to the French, through 1954, has been recounted in some exceptionally fine monographs. The early period is examined in two books by David G. Marr, *Vietnamese Anticolonialism, 1885–1925* (1971) and *Vietnamese Tradition on Trial, 1920–1945* (1981), and in the shorter, but careful and scholarly, William J. Duiker, *The Rise of Nationalism in Vietnam, 1900–1941* (1976); from that point the story is picked up in Ellen J. Hammer, *The Struggle for Indochina, 1940–1955* (1966 edition). Very thoughtful and perceptive observations are made in John T. McAlister, Jr., and Paul Mus, *The Vietnamese and Their Revolution* (1970). For exciting accounts of the battle of Dienbienphu, see Bernard Fall, *Hell in a Very Small Place: The Siege of Dien Bien Phu* (1966) or Jules Roy, *The Battle of Dien Bien Phu* (1965); the winner's view is Vo Guyen Giap, *Dien Bien Phu* (1962). On the Geneva settlement of 1954, the definitive work is Robert F. Randle, *Geneva 1954: The Settlement of the Indochinese War* (1969); but an adequate briefer book is James Cable, *The Geneva Conference of 1954 on Indochina* (1986). Well-written biographies of Ho Chi Minh are Jean Lacouture, *Ho Chi Minh: A Political Biography* (1968), and David Halberstam, *Ho* (1971).

The best overviews of American involvement with the Vietnam problem before 1954 are Lloyd Gardner, *Approaching Vietnam: From World War II through Dienbienphu* (1988), and George McT. Kahin, *Intervention: How America Became Involved in Vietnam* (1986). The earliest part of the story is told in E. R. Drachman, *United States Policy toward Vietnam, 1940–1945* (1970), Walter LaFeber, "Roosevelt, Churchill and Indochina, 1942–1945," *American Historical Review* 80

(1975): 1277–95; two articles by Gary R. Hess, "Franklin D. Roosevelt and Indochina," *Journal of American History* 59 (1972): 353–68, and "The First American Commitment in Indochina: The Acceptance of the Bao Dai Solution, 1950," *Diplomatic History* 2 (1978): 331–50. For Truman's part, see George C. Herring, "The Truman Administration and the Restoration of French Sovereignty in Indochina," *Diplomatic History* 1 (1977): 97–117, and Mark N. Katz, "The Origins of the Vietnam War, 1945–1948," *Review of Politics* 42 (1980): 131–51. Russell D. Buhite's *Soviet-American Relations in Asia, 1945–1954* (1981) places the story of early Vietnam policy within its Cold War Asian context. For developments during the Eisenhower administration, see George C. Herring and Richard H. Immerman, "Eisenhower, Dulles, and Dienbienphu: 'The Day We Didn't Go to War' Revisited," *Journal of American History* 71 (1984): 343–68; Herbert S. Parmet, *Eisenhower and the American Crusades* (1972), chs. 30–31; Townsend Hoopes, *The Devil and John Foster Dulles* (1973), chs. 15–16, and, for the context, Robert A. Divine, *Eisenhower and the Cold War* (1981), especially ch. 2. The beginning phases of American military activities in Vietnam are expertly told in Ronald H. Spector, *Advice and Support: The Early Years of the U.S. Army in Vietnam, 1941–1960* (1985).

For the next steps in American involvement, a good place to begin is William J. Rust, et al., *Kennedy in Vietnam* (1985). The inner circle of Kennedy-Johnson policy planners is dissected in David Halberstam's long, prolix, and brilliant *The Best and the Brightest* (1972), a minor classic; the same author's *The Making of a Quagmire* (1965) contains an early firsthand account of how the United States was drawn into Vietnam during the Kennedy years. The context of JFK's Vietnam policy can be found in Theodore Sorensen, *Kennedy* (1965), Arthur Schlesinger, Jr., *A Thousand Days: John F. Kennedy in the White House* (1965), Roger Hilsman, *To Move a Nation: The Politics of Foreign Policy in the Administration of John F. Kennedy* (1967), or Richard J. Walton, *Cold War and Counterrevolution: The Foreign Policy of John F. Kennedy* (1972). Ellen J. Hammer, *A Death in November: America in Vietnam, 1963* (1987), tells the story of the removal of Diem. Neil Sheehan's remarkable study, *A Bright Shining Lie: John Paul Vann and America in Vietnam* (1988), examines the American advisory role through the life of a single, fascinating individual.

Lyndon Johnson's own version of his Vietnam policy can be found in his *The Vantage Point: Perspectives of the Presidency 1963–1969* (1971). For an important civilian policy-maker's perspective, see Walt W. Rostow, *The Diffusion of Power: An Essay in Recent History* (1972), and for two key military officials', Maxwell Taylor, *Swords and Plow-*

shares (1972), and William C. Westmoreland, *A Soldier Reports* (1976). Highly sympathetic to Johnson is Eric F. Goldman, *The Tragedy of Lyndon Johnson* (1969). A controversial but provocative psychological biography is Doris Kearns, *Lyndon Johnson and the American Dream* (1976). A revealing study of the Johnson cabinet and advisory staff is Henry F. Graff, *The Tuesday Cabinet: Deliberation and Decision on Peace and War under Lyndon B. Johnson* (1970). Perhaps the most systematic account is Herbert Y. Schandler, *Lyndon Johnson and Vietnam: The Unmaking of a President* (1977). The Tonkin Gulf incident has been exhaustively examined in Joseph C. Goulden, *Truth Is the First Casualty: The Gulf of Tonkin Affair—Illusion and Reality* (1969), Anthony Austin, *The President's War: The Story of the Tonkin Gulf Resolution and How the Nation was Trapped in Vietnam* (1971), and John Galloway, *The Gulf of Tonkin Resolution* (1970). The momentous decision to escalate the war, culminating in the decisions during the summer of 1965 is thoroughly covered in Larry Berman's important study, *Planning a Tragedy: The Americanization of the War in Vietnam* (1982). For the view of a dissenting insider, see George W. Ball, *The Past Has Another Pattern: Memoirs* (1982), chs. 24–27.

Both official and unofficial justifications of the war in Vietnam can be found in many of the works listed above. For two compilations, see the Gravel edition of *The Pentagon Papers*, which contains in each of the first four volumes an exhaustive section of official explanations of our policy, and F. M. Kail, *What Washington Said; Administration Rhetoric and the Vietnam War: 1949–1969* (1973). On the "domino theory," see Ross Gregory's judicious article by that title in DeConde, ed., *Encyclopedia of American Foreign Policy*, 1: 275–80.

Chapter 3. The Contentions

Those interested in the history of the American peace movement should start with the venerable survey by Merle Curti, *Peace or War: The American Struggle, 1636–1936* (1936), or with a fine, modern counterpart, Charles DeBenedetti, *The Peace Reform in American History* (1980). For the period immediately before the Vietnam war, see Lawrence S. Wittner, *Rebels against War: The American Peace Movement, 1941–1960* (1969), or Maurice Isserman, *If I Had a Hammer . . . : The Death of the Old Left and the Birth of the New Left* (1987). A sampling of pacifist opinion in the pre-Vietnam period can be found in Walter Millis et al., *A World without War* (1961).

Virtually all aspects of the legal arguments surrounding the Vietnam policy may be explored in a magnificent four-volume collection, Richard A. Falk, ed., *The Vietnam War and International Law* (1968–

76). Despite Falk's own strong antiwar position, these excellent volumes, nearly four thousand pages, present arguments on all sides of the legal issues that entered into the debate over Vietnam. A helpful short summary, generally supportive of American policy, is Roger H. Hull and John C. Novogrod, *Law and Vietnam* (1968) but the fullest defense of the prowar legal position is John Norton Moore, *Law and the Indo-China War* (1972). The other side is put forward in two articles by Falk, "International Law and the United States Role in the Viet Nam War," *Yale Law Journal* 75 (1966): 1122, and "International Law and the United States Role in Viet Nam: A Response to Professor Moore," *ibid.* 76 (1967): 1095. On the constitutionality of the war see Edward Keynes, *Undeclared War: Twilight Zone of Constitutional Power* (1982), or Leon Friedman and Burt Neuborne, *Unquestioning Obedience to the President: The ACLU Case against the Illegal War in Vietnam* (1972).

The role of the media in portraying the Vietnam war is thoughtfully explored in Daniel C. Hallin, *The "Uncensored War": The Media and Vietnam* (1986), and in Michael J. Arlen, *Living Room War: Writings about Television* (1982), a collection of his earlier essays. For an exhaustive study, see Francis D. Faulkner, "Bao Chi: The American News Media in Vietnam 1960–1975," a Ph.D. dissertation from the University of Massachusetts (1981). William M. Hammond, *Public Affairs: The Military and the Media, 1962–1968* (1988), one of the volumes in the Vietnam series done by the Center of Military History of the U.S. Army, is thorough, valuable, and filled with interesting information. A fascinating study, with a helpful bibliography on the subject, is Kathleen J. Turner, *Lyndon Johnson's Dual War: Vietnam and the Press* (1985). Other work on the journalistic coverage of the war is listed under chapter four, below.

The conduct of the war by the American military has been studied and analyzed exhaustively. A place to start is the widely discussed book by Colonel Harry G. Summers, *On Strategy: A Critical Analysis of the Vietnam War* (1982), which focuses on the failures of American strategic thinking. Douglas Kinnard, *The War Managers* (1977), reports the revealing results of a poll of the generals who commanded in Vietnam and who were invited by Kinnard, himself a former brigadier general, to reflect (anonymously) on their experiences. Each branch of the service has produced, or is in the process of producing, an offical multivolume history of its own role in Vietnam (for individual titles, see Burns and Leitenberg, *The Wars in Vietnam, Cambodia, and Laos*, pp. 147–50). In general, these volumes are of high quality and most of them contain excellent bibliographies to help those who wish to explore further. For useful brief overviews, see Andrew F.

Krepinevich, Jr., *The Army and Vietnam* (1986); J. Robert Moskin, *The U.S. Marine Corps Story* (1977), ch. 15; and Richard L. Schreadley, "The Naval War in Vietnam, 1950–1970," *U.S. Naval Institute Proceedings* 97 (1971): 182–209. For a survey of the weapons used in Vietnam and pictures of them, see Edgar C. Doleman, Jr., *The Vietnam Experience: The Tools of War* (1984).

The story of American air power in Vietnam is told in Raphael Littauer and Norman Uphoff, eds., *The Air War in Indochina* (1972), Carl Berger, ed., *The United States Air Force in Southeast Asia, 1961–1973: An Illustrated Account* (1973), and Peter B. Mersky and Norman Polmar, *The Naval Air War in Vietnam, 1965–1975* (1981). Those who want to do research in the subject should start by consulting Myron J. Smith, Jr., *Air War Southeast Asia, 1961–1973: An Annotated Bibliography* (1979). For some discussions of cluster bombs and other antipersonnel weapons, see Michael Krepon, "Weapons Potentially Inhuman: The Case of Cluster Bombs," in Falk, ed., *The Vietnam War and International Law*, 4: 266–74, numerous articles by experts or eyewitnesses in either John Duffett, ed., *Against the Crime of Silence: Proceedings of the International War Crimes Tribunal* (1970 edition), Ken Coates, Peter Limqueco, and Peter Weiss, eds., *Prevent the Crime of Silence: Reports from the International War Crimes Tribunal Founded by Bertrand Russell* (1971), or Eric Prokosch, "Anti-Personnel Weapons," *International Social Science Journal* 28 (1976): 341–58. On napalm, see either J. C. Dreyfus, "Napalm and Its Effects on Human Beings," in Coates et al., eds., *Prevent the Crime of Silence*, 191–98, or Peter Reich and Victor W. Sidel, "Napalm," *New England Journal of Medicine* 277 (July 13, 1967): 87ff. On the harm to the landscape and topography of Vietnam caused by American bombing, see Arthur H. Westing and E. W. Pfeiffer, "The Cratering of Indochina," *Scientific American* 226 (May 1972): 20–29. For the use of herbicides and defoliants, a good introduction is J. B. Neilands et al., *Harvest of Death: Chemical Warfare in Vietnam and Cambodia* (1972). Serious research on the topic should begin with Arthur H. Westing, *Herbicides as Weapons: A Bibliography* (1972); similarly, research on Agent Orange will be very much expedited by Caroline D. Harnly, *Agent Orange and Vietnam: An Annotated Bibliography* (1988), which lists and comments upon almost 2,400 items on that subject.

Graphic and harrowing charges of war crimes and atrocities committed by Americans in Vietnam were widely circulated. In addition to the books by Duffett and Coates et al., cited above, see any of the collections of such stories published during the war: Clergy and Laymen Concerned about Vietnam, *In the Name of America: The Conduct of the War in Vietnam by the Armed Forces of the United States* (1968), Richard

A. Falk, Gabriel Kolko, and Robert Jay Lifton, eds., *Crimes of War* (1971), Erwin Knoll and Judith N. McFadden, eds., *War Crimes and the American Conscience* (1970), *The Winter Soldier Investigation: An Inquiry into American War Crimes* (1972), prepared by the Vietnam Veterans against the War, and Mark Lane, *Conversations with Americans* (1970). The applicability of the Nuremberg precedent is debated in Telford Taylor, *Nuremberg and Vietnam: An American Tragedy* (1970), Joseph W. Bishop, Jr., "The Question of War Crimes," *Commentary* 54 (December 1972): 85–92; James Reston, Jr., "Is Nuremberg Coming Back to Haunt Us?" *Saturday Review* 53 (July 18, 1970): 14–17, 61, Guenter Lewy, "The Punishment of War Crimes: Have We Learned the Lessons of Vietnam?" *Parameters* 9 (December 1979): 44–45; and in many articles in the Falk volumes, *The Vietnam War and International Law*, cited above. For studies of the My Lai massacre of 1968, see the suggestions listed under chapter five, below.

Frances FitzGerald's much celebrated classic, *Fire in the Lake: The Vietnamese and the Americans in Vietnam* (1972), is a wonderfully sensitive examination of the cultural clash resulting from the intrusion of American ways upon a rural, peasant society. Especially provocative on the imposition of our technological might and the resulting dislocation of traditional Vietnamese society are Loren Baritz, *Backfire*, cited above, and a fascinating study, James William Gibson, *The Perfect War: Technowar in Vietnam* (1986). Kim McQuaid also has some perceptive things to say about technological warfare in *The Anxious Years: America in the Vietnam-Watergate Era* (1989).

The demoralization of our armed forces in Vietnam was a matter of such high concern here at home that much was written about it. For general surveys of the problem, see Richard Boyle, *The Flower of the Dragon: The Breakdown of the U.S. Army in Vietnam* (1972), Cecil B. Curry's book, published under the name "Cincinnatus," *Self-Destruction: The Distintegration and Decay of the United States Army during the Vietnam Era* (1981), Peter G. Bourne, *Men, Stress, and Vietnam* (1970), Seymour Hersh, "The Decline and Near Fall of the U.S. Army," *Saturday Review* 55 (November 18, 1972): 58–65, or Wendell S. Merick, "Sagging Morale in Vietnam: Eyewitness Report on Drugs, Race Problems and Boredom," *U.S. News and World Report* 70 (January 25, 1971): 30–33. For revealing discussions of the problem of drug abuse, the hearings before the Senate Committee on Armed Forces, *Drug Abuse in the Military* (1972), Alfred W. McCoy, *The Politics of Heroin in Southeast Asia* (1972), or Larry H. Ingraham, "'The Nam' and 'The World': Heroin Use by U.S. Army Enlisted Men Serving in Vietnam," *Psychiatry* 37 (1974): 114–28. On the murder and attempted murder of officers, see Eugene Linden, "The Demoralization of an Army: Fragging and Other Withdrawal Symptoms," *Saturday Review* 55 (January 8, 1972): 12ff. On tensions between whites and blacks serving in Vietnam, see Byron G. Fiman, Jonathan F. Borus, and M. Duncan Stanton, "Black-White and American Vietnamese Relations among Soldiers in Vietnam," *Journal of Social Issues* 31 (1975): 39–48, and Zalin Grant, "Whites against Blacks in Vietnam," *New Republic* 160 (January 18, 1969): 15–16.

For the so-called "realist" critique of American policy in Vietnam, see Hans J. Morgenthau, *Vietnam and the United States* (1965), a collection of early essays, or the remarks in his *A New Foreign Policy for the United States* (1969). See also George F. Kennan's testimony before the Fulbright committee in *The Vietnam Hearings* (1966), or the summary of his views on the subject in David Mayers, *George Kennan and the Dilemmas of U.S. Foreign Policy* (1988), 276–84.

Chapter 4. The Conflicts

For no other war in our history has "public opinion" been so assiduously measured, carefully analyzed, or widely discussed. The most easily accessible raw material for tracing popular opinion with regard to Vietnam is the third volume of *The Gallup Poll: Public Opinion, 1935–1971* (1972). Pollster Louis Harris reviews the data from his own surveys in his *The Anguish of Change* (1973), chs. 4 and 5. Two especially helpful early analyses are John E. Mueller, *War, Presidents, and Public Opinion* (1973), which is particularly valuable for its comparisons to the public's response to the Korean war, and Milton J. Rosenberg, Sidney Verba, and Philip E. Converse, *Vietnam and the Silent Majority: The Dove's Guide* (1970), an excellent survey of American opinion about the war by three distinguished students of democratic politics. See also Seymour Martin Lipset, "Doves, Hawks, and Polls," *Encounter* 27 (October 1966): 38–45, Lester Markel, "Public Opinion and the War In Vietnam," *New York Times Magazine* (August 8, 1965): 9, and William L. Lunch and Peter W. Sperlich, "American Public Opinion and the War in Vietnam," *Western Political Quarterly* 32 (1979): 21–44.

The story of the GOP and the Vietnam question is admirably summarized in Terry Dietz, *Republicans and Vietnam, 1961–1968* (1986). For the division within Democratic party ranks caused by the issue, readers should consult, in addition to Lyndon Johnson's *Vantage Point* and David Halberstam's *Best and Brightest*, some of the following works: either Lee Riley Powell, *J. William Fulbright and America's Lost Crusade: Fulbright's Opposition to the Vietnam War* (1984), or William Berman, *William Fulbright and the Vietnam War: The Dissent of a Political*

Realist (1988), Edward P. Harley, *Congress and the Fall of South Vietnam and Cambodia* (1982), Walter A. Zelman, *Senate Dissent and the Vietnam War, 1964–1968* (1971), Clark Clifford, "A Viet Nam Appraisal: The Personal History of One Man's View and How It Evolved," *Foreign Affairs* 47 (1969): 601–22, Warren I. Cohen, *Dean Rusk* (1980); David Halberstam, "McCarthy and the Divided Left," *Harper's* 238 (March 1968): 32–44, Arthur Herzog, *McCarthy for President* (1969), Arthur M. Schlesinger, Jr., "Vietnam and the 1968 Elections," *New Leader*, 50 (November 6, 1967): 5–12, Theodore White, *The Making of the President, 1972* (1973), and George S. McGovern, *An American Journey: The Presidential Campaign Speeches of George McGovern* (1974). A marvelous study of the influence of certain insiders is Walter Isaacson and Evan Thomas, *The Wise Men: Six Friends and the World They Made* (1986)—see especially chs. 21–24.

The Ph.D. dissertation by Robert R. Tomes, "American Intellectuals and the Vietnam War, 1954–1973" (1987), is a splendid analysis of the topic. For the intellectuals of the left, see Sandy Vogelgesang, *The Long Dark Night of the Soul: The American Intellectual Left and the Vietnam War* (1974), Noam Chomsky, *American Power and the New Mandarins: Historical and Political Essays* (1967), and Philip Nobile, *Intellectual Skywriting: Literary Politics and the New York Review of Books* (1974). For an understanding of the intellectuals of the right, the place to begin is George Nash, *The Conservative Intellectual Movement in America since 1945* (1976); also informative is John B. Judis, *William F. Buckley, Jr.: Patron Saint of the Conservatives* (1988). A highly articulate conservative explains his own intellectual migration in Norman Podhoretz, *Breaking Ranks: A Political Memoir* (1979), and his mature reflections on the war in *Why We Were in Vietnam* (1982). Finally, see the perceptive chapter, "The War, the Liberals, and the Overthrow of LBJ," in Allen J. Matusow, *The Unravelling of America: A History of Liberalism in the 1960s* (1984).

Phillip Knightley's *The First Casualty: From the Crimea to Vietnam: The War Correspondent as Hero, Propagandist, and Myth Maker* (1975) is an engrossing survey of combat journalism; Vietnam is considered in ch. 16. For first hand accounts of the hardships of covering the war, see Daniel Lang, "A Reporter at Large: Home Again," *New Yorker* 47 (September 4, 1971): 35ff., David Halberstam, "Getting the Story in Vietnam," *Commentary* 39 (January 1968): 30–34, Peter Braestrup, "Covering the Vietnam War," *Nieman Reports* 23 (December 1969): 8–13, or Stanley Karnow, "The Newsman's War in Vietnam," *Nieman Reports* 17 (December 1963): 3–8. The various views of how well or how poorly the war was being reported can be sampled in Noam Chomsky, "Reporting Indochina: The News Media and the Legitimation of Lies," *Social Policy* 4 (September 1973): 4–19, Robert B. Rigg, "How Not to Report a War," *Military Review* 49 (June 1969): 14–24, Ralph W. Blanchard, "The Newsman in Vietnam: Responsible or Irresponsible?" *Naval War College Review* 20 (June 1968): 14–42, Clayton Fritchey, "Are We Being Told the Truth about Vietnam?" *Harper's* 234 (March 1967): 121–22, or DeWayne B. Johnson, "Vietnam: Report Card on the Press Corps at War," *Journalism Quarterly* 46 (Spring 1969): 9–19. Walter Lippmann's movement into opposition is traced in Ronald Steel, *Walter Lippmann and the American Century* (1980), ch. 43.

The positions of various religious denominations regarding the war have been explored in several scholarly articles: see Jerold M. Starr, "Religious Preference, Religiosity, and Opposition to War," *Sociological Analysis* 36 (1975): 323–34, Harold E. Quinley, "The Protestant Clergy and the War in Vietnam," *Public Opinion Quarterly* 34 (Spring 1970): 43–52, Richard J. Neuhaus, "The War, the Churches, and Civil Religion," *Annals of the American Academy of Political and Social Science* 387 (1970): 128–40, Clarence E. Tygart, "Social Movement Participation: Clergy and the Anti-Vietnam War Movement," *Sociological Analysis* 34 (1973): 202–11, and James H. Smylie, "American Religious Bodies, Just War, and Vietnam," *Journal of Church and State* 11 (1969): 383–408. For American Jews, see the helpful discussion in Balfour Brickner, "Vietnam and the Jewish Community," *Christian Century* 87 (1970): 531–34.

The difficulty with the Vietnam issue experienced by American Catholics is considered in two articles by antiwar Catholic Gordon C. Zahn: "The Great Catholic Upheaval," *Saturday Review* 54 (September 11, 1971): 25–27ff, and "The Scandal of Silence," *Commonweal* 95 (October 22, 1971): 79–85. The range of Catholic opinion can be seen by comparing the dozens of editorials on the war in *Commonweal* with those in *America*. On the Berrigan brothers, see the sympathetic collection of tributes in William Van Etten Casey and Philip Nobile, eds., *The Berrigans* (1971) or Daniel Berrigan's play, *The Trial of the Catonsville Nine* (1970). For another strenuous Catholic critic of the war, see Robert F. Drinan, *Vietnam and Armageddon: Peace, War, and the Christian Conscience* (1970).

Religious criticism of the war on moral grounds can be sampled in Robert McAfee Brown, Abraham J. Heschel, and Michael Novak, *Vietnam: Crisis of Conscience* (1967), or Michael P. Hamilton, ed., *The Vietnam War: Christian Perspectives* (1967). To explore the various views of the war in Vietnam with respect to the "just war" tradition, see Paul T. Menzel, ed., *Moral Argument and the War in Vietnam: A Collection of Essays* (1971), William V. O'Brien, *The Conduct of Just and Limited War*

(1981), especially ch. 11, Paul Ramsey, *The Just War: Force and Political Responsibity* (1968), especially chs. 18–24, Peter Steinfels, "Just War Theory: A Question," *Commonweal* 99 (1974): 478, Roger L. Shinn, "Our Cause is Not Just," *Christian Century* 89 (1972), 1099–102, Marvin Bordelon, "The Bishops and Just War," *America* 126 (1972): 17–19, or portions of Michael Walzer's *Just and Unjust Wars*, cited above.

Scholarly attempts to assess the climate of opinion at the nation's institutions of higher education include E. M. Schreiber, "Opposition to the Vietnam War among American University Students and Faculty," *British Journal of Sociology* 24 (1973): 288–302, Alexander W. Astin, "New Evidence on Campus Unrest, 1969–70," *Educational Record* 52 (Winter 1971): 41–46, David J. Armor et al., "Professors' Attitudes toward the Vietnam War," *Public Opinion Quarterly* 31 (1967): 159–75, Everett Carll Ladd, Jr., "American University Teachers and Opposition to the Vietnam War," *Minerva* 8 (1970): 546–47, and Howard Schuman and Edward O. Laumann, "Do Most Professors *Support* the War?" *Transaction* 5 (November 1967): 32–35. An interesting theoretical framework is provided in Louis Feuer, *The Conflict of Generations: The Character and Significance of Student Movements* (1969). For literature dealing directly with campus protest against the war, see the listings for chapter five, below.

The data showing the opposition to the war on the part of both women and blacks can be found in the works by Mueller, Rosenberg et al., and Lunch and Sperlich, mentioned above. Both Sara Evans, *Personal Politics: The Roots of Women's Liberation in the Civil Rights Movement and the New Left* (1979), and Leslie Cagan, "Women and the Anti-Draft Movement," *Radical America* 14 (May 1980): 9–11, emphasize the subordination women experienced in the antiwar movement. Phyllis Schlafly's views can be found in Carol Felsenthal, *The Sweetheart of the Silent Majority: The Biography of Phyllis Schlafly* (1981). Brief but informative surveys of black participation in the war can be found in Jack D. Foner, *Blacks and the Military in American History: A New Perspective* (1974), ch. 9, or Martin Binkin et al., *Blacks and the Military* (1982), 32–38. Official figures are in the Department of Defense summary, *Negro Participation in the Armed Forces and in Southeast Asia* (1971). Problems of the black soldier are examined in a special issue of *Ebony* (August 1968). Fascinating firsthand accounts are found in Wallace Terry, ed., *Bloods: An Oral History of the Vietnam War by Black Veterans* (1984). A good, wide-ranging collection is Clyde Taylor, ed., *Vietnam and Black America: An Anthology of Protest and Resistance* (1973). Dr. King's work against the war is well covered in Stephen B. Oates, *Let the Trumpet Sound: The Life of Martin Luther King,*

Jr. (1982), chs. 7 and 9. The position of Meany and the AFL can be found in Joseph C. Goulden, *Meany* (1972). An illuminating study of rank-and-file labor opinion is James D. Wright, "The Working Class, Authoritarianism, and the War in Vietnam," *Social Problems* 20 (1972): 133–50. For antiwar feeling in the rank-and-file, see Harlan Hahn, "Dove Sentiments among Blue Collar Workers," *Dissent* 17 (1970): 202–5, and Al Richmond, "Workers against the War," *Ramparts* 9 (September 1970): 28–32. Division of opinion among leading celebrities is noted in "Activism—Hollywood Style," *Newsweek* 70 (August 28, 1967): 74–75, "Political Techniques: A Cast of Thousands," *Newsweek* 71 (April 8, 1968): 43–44, "The Pulchritude-Intellect Input: Notable Names for Bobby and Gene," *Time* 91 (May 31, 1968): 11–12, and "That's Show Biz," *Newsweek* 79 (May 1, 1972).

There is a growing literature devoted to describing and analyzing the cultural climate of the 1960s, a climate that touched the debate over Vietnam in so many important ways. One good place to start is William L. O'Neill, *Coming Apart: An Informal History of America in the 1960s* (1971). An excellent collection of articles is Gerald Howard, ed., *The Sixties* (1982), which contains a good chronology of the decade and a useful bibliography. Morris Dickstein, *Gates of Eden: American Culture in the Sixties* (1977), is an engaging book particularly strong on the literary aspects of the period. For radical politics of the decade, see James Miller, *Democracy Is in the Streets: From Port Huron to the Siege of Chicago* (1987), Irwin Unger, *The Movement: A History of the American New Left, 1959–1972* (1974), Wini Breines, *Community and Organization in the New Left: The Great Refusal* (1982), the superb study by Kirkpatrick Sale, *SDS* (1973), and the engaging essay, Joseph R. Conlin, *The Troubles: A Jaundiced Glance Back at the Movement of the 1960s* (1982). The psychedelic culture is marvelously described in Tom Wolfe, *The Electric Kool-Aid Acid Test* (1969). No doubt the best way to feel the mood of the 1960s is to read some of the most widely acclaimed "classics" of the decade: Betty Friedan, *The Feminine Mystique* (1963), Theodore Roszak, *The Making of a Counter-Culture: Reflections on the Technocratic Society and Its Youthful Opposition* (1969), Philip Slater, *The Pursuit of Loneliness: American Culture at the Breaking Point* (1970), or Charles Reich, *The Greening of America* (1970).

Chapter Five. The Confrontation

A thorough and sympathetic chronological account of the antiwar movement is Nancy Zaroulis and Gerald Sullivan, *Who Spoke Up? American Protest against the War in Vietnam, 1963–1975* (1984). Two early attempts to cover the story, somewhat less satisfactory because of their broader and less focused approaches, are Alexander Kendrick, *The Wound Within: America in the Vietnam Years, 1945–1974* (1974), and Thomas Powers, *The War at Home: Vietnam and the American People, 1964–1968* (1973). The protest is described and accompanied by dramatic photographs in Clark Dougan and Samuel Lipsman, *The Vietnam Experience: A Nation Divided* (1984). Two books by leading participants in the antiwar movement have unusual merit: Fred Halstead, *Out Now! A Participant's Account of the American Movement against the Vietnam War* (1978), and Todd Gitlin, *The Sixties: Years of Hope, Days of Rage* (1987). A balanced and judicious effort to discover how much the antiwar movement really mattered in the formation of policy is Melvin Small, *Johnson, Nixon, and the Doves* (1988).

The antiwar movement produced a vast body of literature. A useful bibliography is contained in Sandy Vogelgesang's *Long Dark Night of the Soul*, cited above. Readers who want to immerse themselves in the arguments and tone of the antiwar agitation are advised to page through any of the leading magazines that took stands against the Vietnam war: *The New York Review of Books, The New Republic, The Nation, Ramparts, Dissent, The Partisan Review, Liberation, The Monthly Review, I. F. Stone's Weekly, The National Guardian*, and others would serve this function. There were, in addition, hundreds of so-called "underground" newspapers published in the United States during the Vietnam war. They were generally small circulation, irregularly published, locally distributed, and of widely varying quality. A survey and perceptive discussion of the phenomenon, accompanied by a listing of about 450 such papers, can be found in Robert J. Glessing, *The Underground Press in America* (1970). Another listing is the table of contents for the Bell & Howell Micro Photo Division's *Underground Newspaper Microfilm Collection, 1963–1975* (n.d.), an alphabetical listing running more than 230 pages.

G. Louis Heath, ed., *Mutiny Does Not Happen Lightly: The Literature of the American Resistance to the Vietnam War* (1976), is a compilation of 118 "flyers, leaflets, letters, reports, manuals and documents" by those opposed to the war. A much smaller collection of statements, these by some leading antiwar activists, is *We Accuse* (1965), published in connection with the first "Vietnam Day" protest at Berkeley. It is possible here to give only a few examples of antiwar literature that was circulated during the conflict and that may have helped to define the issues and shape public opinion. The titles that follow were effective and rather widely read, and although they are written from varying antiwar points of view, they impart some of the spirit of skepticism about American policy as well as of the opposition and resistance to the war:

American Friends Service Committee, *Peace in Vietnam: A New Approach in Southeast Asia* (1966), Richard N. Goodwin, *Triumph or Tragedy: Reflections on Vietnam* (1966), Franz Schurmann, Peter Dale Scott, and Reginald Zelnik, *The Politics of Escalation in Vietnam: A Citizens' White Paper* (1966), Arthur M. Schlesinger, Jr., *The Bitter Heritage: Vietnam and American Democracy, 1941–1966* (1966), *Ramparts* Magazine, *Vietnam Primer* (1966), Howard Zinn, *Vietnam: The Logic of Withdrawal* (1967), John Kenneth Galbraith, *How to Get Out of Vietnam* (1967), Benjamin Spock and Mitchell Zimmerman, *Dr. Spock on Vietnam* (1968), Noam Chomsky, *At War with Asia: Essays in Indochina* (1970), Ralph Stavins, Richard J. Barnet, and Marcus G. Raskin, *Washington Plans an Aggressive War* (1971), or Mary McCarthy, *The Seventeenth Degree* (1974), a collection of earlier pieces.

One branch of antiwar literature that captured considerable attention was the sympathetic treatment of the antidraft movement and of individual draft resisters. For examples, see Norma Sue Woodstone, *Up against the War: A Personal Introduction to U.S. Soldiers and Civilians Fighting Against the War in Vietnam* (1970), Michael Ferber and Staughton Lynd, *The Resistance* (1971), or Alice Lynd, ed., *We Won't Go: Personal Accounts of War Objectors* (1968). Another important kind of writing against the war was by western eye-witness visitors to North Vietnam, who graphically described the devastation caused by American military might and the courageous determination of the enemy to pursue the battle to the end. Some especially moving examples are Harrison E. Salisbury, *Behind the Lines—Hanoi* (1967), Staughton Lynd and Thomas Hayden, *The Other Side* (1966), Noam Chomsky, "North Vietnam," in his *At War with Asia*, mentioned above, John Gerassi, *North Vietnam: A Documentary* (1968), James Cameron, *Here Is Your Enemy* (1966), Wilfred G. Burchett, *Vietnam North* (1966), or Mary McCarthy, *Hanoi* (1968).

On the protest against the war centered on American college campuses, see Louis Menashe and Ronald Radosh, eds., *Teach-Ins, USA: Reports, Opinions, Documents* (1967), Seymour Martin Lipset, *Rebellion in the University* (1971), Joan Scott Wallach, "The Teach-In: A National Movement or the End of an Affair?" *Studies on the Left* 5 (Summer 1965): 82–87, Daniel Bell and Irving Kristol, eds., *Confrontation: The Student Rebellion and Universities* (1968), Janet Harris, *Students in Revolt* (1970), or Steven Kelman, *Push Comes to Shove: The Escalation of Student Protest* (1970).

Particular episodes in the war and particular moments in the protest have called forth a number of worthy contributions. The march on the Pentagon (October 1967) is unforgettably described by one of its most famous, articulate, and controversial participants in Norman

Mailer, *Armies of the Night: History as a Novel, The Novel as History*
(1968); see also the thoughtful reflections on the episode in Bruce
Jackson, "The Battle of the Pentagon," *Atlantic Monthly* 221 (January
1968): 35–42. On the Tet offensive of early 1968, see the graphic and
detailed account, Don Oberdorfer, *Tet!* (1971); Peter Braestrup com-
pares the reality of the offensive with the media coverage in an impressive two-volume work, *Big Story: How the American Press and Television Reported and Interpreted the Crisis of Tet 1968 in Vietnam and
Washington* (1977). For the battle at Hue, told from the point of view
of the common fighting man, see Michael Herr's magnificent book,
Dispatches (1978). For the traumatic events in Chicago through the
eyes of outraged observers and protesters, see Norman Mailer, *Miami
and the Siege of Chicago* (1971), Walter Schneir, ed., *Telling It Like It
Was: The Chicago Riots* (1969), or John Schultz, *No One Was Killed*
(1969); a very good scholarly account is David Farber, *Chicago '68*
(1988). The campaign as a whole is very well covered in either Theodore White, *The Making of the President, 1968* (1969), or Lewis Chester,
Godfrey Hodgson, and Bruce Page, *An American Melodrama: The
Presidential Campaign of 1968* (1969).

   Reading on the My Lai massacre should start with two books by
Seymour Hersh, *My Lai 4* (1970) and *Cover-Up: The Army's Secret In-
vestigation of the Massacre at My Lai 4* (1972). Another fine overview is
Richard Hammer, *One Morning in the War: The Tragedy at Son My*
(1970). Deeper study of the incident should move to either the U.S.
Army's investigation, *Report of the Department of the Army Review of the
Preliminary Investigations Into the My Lai Incident* (1974), or that of the
House Committee on Armed Services, *Investigation of the My Lai Inci-
dent* (1970). For Lt. Calley's side, see either his own book, *Lieutenant
Calley: His Own Story* (1971), written with John Sack, or Martin Ger-
shen, *Destroy or Die: The True Story of Mylai* (1971). Also revealing is
Mary McCarthy's *Medina* (1972). The legality of President Nixon's
Cambodian "gamble" of spring 1970 is debated in a symposium in
The American Journal of International Law 65 (January 1971): 1–83, in
The Boston University Law Review 50 (Spring 1970): 1–188, and in *The
New York Law Review* 45 (1970): 625–78. The staff of the Fulbright
committee produced *Cambodia: May 1970* (1970), and the State De-
partment's view is John R. Stevenson, "United States Military Action
in Cambodia: Questions of International Law," *Department of State
Bulletin* 62 (June 22, 1970): 765–70. A standard, if critical, work is
William Shawcross, *Sideshow: Kissinger, Nixon, and the Destruction of
Cambodia* (1979). On the Kent State incident, see either James A.
Michener, *Kent State* (1972), or I. F. Stone, *Killings at Kent State: How
Murder Went Unpunished* (1971).

By the end of the war, much of the debate surfaced and was reflected in a series of dramatic courtroom battles. A good overview of the most important of these is John F. and Rosemary S. Bannan, *Law, Morality and Vietnam: The Peace Militants and the Courts* (1974). By far the best account of the Chicago conspiracy trial is Jason Epstein, *The Great Conspiracy Trial: An Essay on Law, Liberty, and the Constitution* (1970), but see the critique by Alexander Bickel, "Judging the Chicago Trial," *Commentary* 51 (January 1971): 31–40. Excerpts from the trial record accompanied by satirical drawings of Jules Feiffer are found in Feiffer's *Pictures at a Prosecution* (1970). One of the defendants had his say in Tom Hayden, *Trial* (1970). Other trials are covered in Jessica Mitford, *The Trial of Dr. Spock* (1969), William O'Rourke, *The Harrisburg 7 and the New Catholic Left* (1973), Sanford J. Unger, "The Pentagon Papers Trial," *Atlantic Monthly* 230 (November 1972): 22–34, and, in a somewhat different category, Richard Hammer, *The Court-Martial of Lieutenant Calley* (1971). Daniel Berrigan's *The Trial of the Catonsville Nine* (1970) is a play based on that celebrated case.

The closing episodes of the war are described in a fine account by a war correspondent, Arnold I. Isaacs, *Without Honor: Defeat in Vietnam and Cambodia* (1983), which also can boast a superb bibliography on the subject. Frank Snepp's *Decent Interval: An Insider's Account of Saigon's Indecent End* (1978) is the story told by a CIA eyewitness. Wilfred Burchett gives the view of a foreign sympathizer with the North Vietnamese in *Grasshoppers and Elephants: Why Viet Nam Fell; The Viet Cong Account of the Last 55 Days* (1977), while Anthony T. Bouscaren, ed., *All Quiet on the Eastern Front: The Death of South Vietnam* (1977) is a collection of the views of some leading American conservatives. For the winner's perspective, see either Van Tien Dung, *Our Great Spring Victory: An Account of the Liberation of South Vietnam* (1977), or Vo Nguyen Giap, *How We Won the War* (1976).

Conclusion

The search for the lessons and legacies of our Vietnam experience is a topic that is worthy of a book in itself. Nor would there be any shortage of raw materials for such a study. Two good places to begin are two edited collections of opinions on various aspects of the experience: Anthony Lake, ed., *The Vietnam Legacy: The War, American Society, and the Future of American Foreign Policy* (1976), and William S. Thompson and D. D. Frizzell, eds., *The Lessons of Vietnam* (1977). Another broad gathering of opinions is Harrison Salisbury, ed., *Vietnam Reconsidered: Lessons from a War* (1984). One of the memorable books from the Vietnam era will be Gloria Emerson, *Winners and Losers: Battles, Retreats, Gains, Losses, and Ruins from a Long War* (1976). Bill McCloud's *What Should We Tell Our Children about Vietnam* (1989) is a fascinating collection of brief reflections by many of the leading participants. Robert W. Gregg and Charles W. Kegley, Jr., eds., *After Vietnam: The Future of American Foreign Policy* (1971), gathers together some intelligent speculation on how Vietnam will affect our relations with various parts of the world. See also, George W. Ball, "Have We Learned or Only Failed," *New York Times Magazine* (April 1, 1973): 12ff, Walter Goldstein, "The Lessons of the Vietnamese War," *Bulletin of Atomic Scientists* 26 (February 1970): 41–45, Stanley Hoffman, "Vietnam Reappraised," *International Security* 6 (Summer 1981): 3–26, Sol W. Sanders and William Henderson, "The Consequences of 'Vietnam,'" *Orbis* 21 (Spring 1977): 61–76, or the four articles by critics of the war in a symposium entitled "The Vietnam War: Who Will Control the Past," *Ramparts* 13 (August-September, 1975): 29–40.

Richard Severo and Lewis Milford, *The Wages of War: When American Soldiers Came Home—from Valley Forge to Vietnam* (1989) is a readable and informative survey of the experience of the veterans of American wars, emphasizing the similarities in the way they were treated. One of the earliest books on the returning Vietnam vet is still one of the most engrossing, Robert Jay Lifton, *Home from the War: Vietnam Veterans: Neither Victims Nor Executioners* (1973). A serious attempt by social scientists to measure the behavior of veterans is Arthur Egendorf et al., *Legacies of Vietnam: Comparative Adjustment of Veterans and Their Peers* (1981), a study mandated by the Congress. Also worthy contributions are Egendorf's *Healing from the War: Trauma and Transformation after Vietnam* (1985) and the unforgettable book by Myra MacPherson, *The Long Time Passing: Vietnam and the Haunted Generation* (1984). A survey of grievances of the vet is David E. Bonior, Steven M. Champlin, and Timothy S. Kolly, *The Vietnam Veteran: A History of Neglect* (1984). A moving account of how the memorial was built, together with photographs and an alphabetical listing (235 three-columned pages of small print) of the names of the war dead, is Jan C. Scruggs and Joel L. Swerdlow, *To Heal a Nation: The Vietnam Veterans Memorial* (1985); Scruggs was the moving force behind the project.

The trouble with listings of Vietnam fiction is that the lists are constantly rendered obsolete by new additions. John Newman, with Ann Hilfinger, eds., *Vietnam War Literature: An Annotated Bibliography of Imaginative Works about American Fighting in Vietnam* (1988 edition), lists more than seven hundred novels, short stories, poems, and plays (everything from serious literature to items like Joe Sakai's *Sex Slaves of the Viet Cong* [n.d.]). For some highly intelligent discussions of Vietnam fiction, see Gordon O. Taylor, "American Personal Narrative of the War in Vietnam," *American Literature* 52 (1980): 294–308, Philip D. Beidler, *American Literature and the Experience of Vietnam* (1982), or Thomas R. Myers, *Walking Point: American Narratives of Vietnam* (1988), which has a useful, short bibliography. The winter 1988 issue of *Genre*, "The Vietnam War and Postmodern Memory," is devoted to this topic and contains several stimulating articles. On the Vietnam film, see Gilbert Adair, *Hollywood's Vietnam: From the Green Berets to Full Metal Jacket* (1989), Albert Auster and Leonard Quart, *How the War Was Remembered: Hollywood and Vietnam* (1988), and three fine articles by Leo Cawley, Andrew Sarris, and J. Hoberman in the *Village Voice*, September 8, 1987.

Index

Designed by Glen Burris

Set in Baskerville text and Franklin Gothic display by G & S Typesetters, Inc.

Printed on 50-lb Glatfelter Natural and bound in Holliston Roxite cloth

by Edwards Brothers, Inc.